Traveling The Path Back To The ROAD IN THE SKY

A Strange Saga Of Saucers, Space Brothers & Secret Agents

by George Hunt Williamson
aka Brother Philip

With Nick Redfern
Special Commentary By Brad Steiger
And An Introduction By Tim Beckley

Traveling The Path Back To The
ROAD IN THE SKY

**From The Original Source Material By George Hunt Williamson
With Additional Material by Timothy Green Beckley;
Nick Redfern, and Brad Steiger**

This edition Copyright © 2012 by Timothy Green Beckley

All rights reserved. No part of these manuscripts may be copied or reproduced by any mechanical or digital methods and no exerpts or quotes may be used in any other book or manuscript without permission in writing by the Publisher, Timothy Green Beckley, except by a reviewer who may quote brief passages in a review. If you are the legitimate copyright holder of any material inadvertently used in this book, please send a notice to this effect and the offending material will be removed from all future printings. The material utilized herein is reproduced for educational purposes and every effort has been made to verify that the material has been properly credited and is available in the public domain.

**ISBN 13: 9781606111338
ISBN 10: 1606111337**

Published by Timothy Green Beckley
Box 753 · New Brunswick, NJ 08903
Printed in the United States of America

Staff Members
Timothy G. Beckley, Publisher
Carol Ann Rodriguez, Assistant to the Publisher
Sean Casteel, Associate Editor
Tim R. Swartz, Editorial Consultant
William Kern, Layout, Typesetting and Art Consultant

Sign Up On The Web For Our Free Weekly Newsletter
and Mail Order Version of Conspiracy Journal
www.ConspiracyJournal.com

**Order Hot Line: 1-732-602-3407
PayPal: MrUFO8@hotmail.com**

TRAVELING THE PATH BACK TO THE ROAD IN THE SKY

CONTENTS

Return To The Road In The Sky—1

George Hunt Williamson And The FBI—3

And So It Was Not Meant To Be—27

Road In The Sky—29

Return To The Road In The Sky

By Timothy Green Beckley

There can be no doubt but that George Hunt Williamson – aka Brother Philip – was one of the movers and shakers of the early UFO contact movement, recruiting a sizeable fandom that followed his exploits be they in attendance at one of his frequent lectures or via printed venue.

Almost everyone knows that Williamson was there when George Adamski says he first met the fair-haired, Aryan-appearing Space Brother known as Orthon. From a "safe distance" George Williamson reportedly saw a landed bell shaped flying saucer out of which stepped the extraterrestrial who pointed to the heavens to indicate his outer-worldy origins. Under the synonym of Brother Philip, he had explored the highlands of Peru and dense jungles of South and Central America digging into the many legends of visitors from the sky throughout humankinds's early development. He wrote several books on his studies of "ancient astronauts" (he didn't invent the term so you wont find references to the space visitors of antiquity by this name), the Road in the Sky being among his most popular literary achievements. We are hereby presenting the complete text of this almost impossible to find New Age mindstone – of course in a greatly expanded adaptation with newly presented information from the mighty pens of Nick Redfern and Brad Steiger.

Perhaps because of his public persona as a spokesperson for the then virgin West Coast New Age community, or because of political radicalism, or his association with two mysterious men who had disappeared because of their UFO ties, Williamson was kept under close scrutiny for over a decade by the FBI.

As Redfern found out while working on his book, **The Contactees**: "The Contactee movement of the 1950s attracted a great deal of attention, and not all of it from UFO researchers and flying saucer enthusiasts. For years,

TRAVELING THE PATH BACK TO THE ROAD IN THE SKY

the FBI kept a close and secret watch on the friends of the Space Brothers, including George Adamski, Daniel Fry, George Van Tassel, and Truman Bethurum. The Bureau also opened a dossier on George Hunt Williamson, a fascinating character who was present at one of George Adamski's most famous encounters. Williamson also claimed to have contacted the Space Brothers by nothing less than a Ouija Board." Nick Redfern recently obtained Williamson's FBI file and digs deep into its contents, which includes tales of crashed UFOs, Hangar 18, alien encounters, a missing aircraft, and an intriguing puzzle of the archaeological kind. You won't find out what he discovered anywhere else but in the pages of this updated presentation on Rick and the gang who popularized the possibility of outer space visitors both modern and historically.

Williamson's entanglement with the "powers that be" must have caused him to realize that in America if you try to buck the status quo or change the system you can easily be slandered and identified as a dangerous dissident, whether it be a communist, a fascist, or a Neo Nazi. George was labeled with all these distinctive anti-American, political leanings. Some of it was definite "guilt by association," other acquisitions were most likely "pot shots," in an attempt to ruffle his feathers.

As for me, I never met Williamson nor did I have the opportunity to invite him to speak at one of my numerous flying saucer gatherings held in sunny San Diego, Palm Springs or Phoenix. By the time of my conclaves he had passed from this mortal coil, but apparently he would have had something vital to say because he did try desperately to set up a meeting with world rewound researcher/author Brad Steiger, which Brother Brad laments over in these pages for the first time.

If this "tribute" hits your solar plexus like a cannon blast we have reprinted and expanded on several of Williamson's other titles. If any of you reading this knew Rick or corresponded with him and would like to share any information pro or con please do e-mail me or send me a note.

New York City, 2012
Mrufo8@hotmail.com
www.ConspiracyJournal.com
Or find me on Face Book

TRAVELING THE PATH BACK TO THE ROAD IN THE SKY

George Hunt Williamson and the FBI:
A Strange Saga of Saucers, Space Brothers, and Secret Agents
By Nick Redfern

The Coming of the Space Brothers

Since the early-1950s, countless people, all across the world, have claimed face-to-face contact with eerily human-like aliens from far-off planets. The aliens in question are usually seen dressed in tight-fitting, one-piece-outfits, while sporting heads of lush, long and flowing blond hair. Not only that: our cosmic visitors assure those of us who they deem worthy of contact that they are deeply concerned by our warlike ways. They wish us to disarm our nuclear arsenals, live in peace and harmony with one another and elevate ourselves to whole new spiritual levels. The aliens in question have become known as the Space Brothers; while those whose lives have been touched and forever changed by their encounters with such alleged extraterrestrial entities are an elite body of people known as the Contactees.

Allegedly preferring face-to-face encounters with everyday members of society, the Space Brothers arranged their clandestine meetings at such out-of-the-way locations as blisteringly hot deserts, dense forests, stark mountain-peaks, and even within isolated diners situated on long stretches of dusty, sand-and-wind-blasted highway. And California was a particularly favorite haunt and haven of the Space Brothers, too.

It was against this background of high-strangeness on the West Coast that a controversial and enigmatic character named George Hunt Williamson became a major player on the flying saucer scene and even attracted the secret attention of none other than J. Edgar Hoover's Federal Bureau of Investigation, the FBI. Since the story is a complex and conspiratorial one,

TRAVELING THE PATH BACK TO THE ROAD IN THE SKY

there's no better place to start than at the beginning...

Activity of the I AM Kind

Back in the 1930s, a man named Guy Warren Ballard, along with his wife, Edna, created what became known as the I AM Activity. Born in Iowa, and someone who served with the U.S. military during the First World War and later worked as a mining engineer, Ballard told a story that was as fascinating as it was undeniably controversial. As someone whose life and belief systems were steeped in both occult teachings and theosophy, Ballard claimed that while hiking on Mount Shasta, California in 1930 he encountered one Count of Saint Germain.

An 18th Century alchemist who, it was claimed by many, had uncovered the secrets of nothing less than literal immortality, the count was variously described as being the so-called Wandering Jew that taunted Jesus Christ on the way to the Crucifixion; the son of Francis II Rakoczi, a prince of Transylvania; or the illegitimate child of the widow of Charles II of Spain, Maria Anna of Pfalz-Neuburg. Or: maybe all of them! That, at the very time of his most fortunate encounter, Ballard was on the mountain looking for what was described as an esoteric brotherhood – possibly, it was rumored, an offshoot of the very same brotherhood that guarded the Tibetan *Book of Dzyan* as described by the legendary Helen Blavatsky - only made matters even weirder.

During this experience on Mount Shasta the enigmatic count reeled off to Ballard countless data on the future, positive role the United States would play in ushering in a new era for the people of Earth, as well as his personal knowledge of so-called Ascended Masters. The latter, the I AM Activity came to solidly accept, were once human people of both historical renown and major influence, including Jesus Christ and Maitreya.

After their physical deaths, Ballard told his followers – which, by the dawning of the 1940s, were in excess of a highly impressive *one million* – that the Ascended Masters existed in supernatural form, but would impart words of deep wisdom to certain people on Earth who had significant roles to play in the Earth's future, including, of course, Guy and Edna Ballard. And that Ballard claimed loudly to have been the re-embodiment of no less than George Washington only added further fuel to the controversial fire that forever seemed to surround him.

TRAVELING THE PATH BACK TO THE ROAD IN THE SKY

There was, needless to say, a great deal of debate concerning the I AM Activity and the Ballard family. Many within the local media of the day considered the whole thing to be nothing more than one big scam designed to ensure the pair a great deal of money from gullible souls willing to donate their hard earned wages and savings to the curious cause.

In 1942, three years after Guy Ballard's death, Edna and their son, Donald, were charged with no less than eighteen counts of mail fraud, as a result of the unproved data contained in a variety of their books and pamphlets relative to Ascended Masters, Lemuria, Mount Shasta, and much more of an interconnected nature. And although the pair was convicted on each count, in what ultimately turned out to be a landmark case when it came to what could or could not be said, or published, in the name of religion without offering any form of evidence in support of such claims, the convictions were finally, and somewhat dramatically, overturned.

Demonstrating the allure of Ballard's teachings, more than eighty years after his alleged encounter with the Count of Saint Germain on Mount Shasta, devotees of his movement continue to hold an annual event on the mountain – called the *I AM Come!* pageant - which gives praise to the life and teachings of Jesus Christ. Guy Ballard still looms large at Mount Shasta, long after his physical passing.

Silver Shirts and a Silver Legion

Many of the original followers of the I AM Activity were also members of a near-fascist organization called the Silver Legion, whose members went by the title of Silver Shirts, and which was established in 1933 by a William Dudley Pelley, a racist, anti-Semitic character who had a deep admiration for Adolf Hitler and spiritualism. He was also someone that a certain George Hunt Williamson came to know very well.

Williamson - also known, at various times, as Michael (or, according to the FBI, Michel) d'Obrenovic, Ric Williamson, and Brother Philip - was born in Chicago, Illinois in 1926, became entranced by the occult in his teens, and evolved into a significant player on the flying saucer scene of the 1950s. In early 1951, Williamson was thrown out of the University of Arizona; however, having read, and been deeply influenced by, William Dudley Pelley's 1950 book *Star Guests*, he subsequently helped produce the group's monthly publication *Valor*.

TRAVELING THE PATH BACK TO THE ROAD IN THE SKY

At the time, Pelley had been recently released from prison after serving eight-years for his wartime opposition to President Roosevelt and, as a result, was watched very closely by the FBI after he regained his freedom. Pelley, just like Williamson, was fascinated by occult matters and compiled massive volumes of "automatic writing" on contact with allegedly higher forms of intelligence. Pelley became a major influence on the life of Williamson – who ultimately combined his fascination with the occult and flying saucers by trying to contact extraterrestrial-intelligences with a homemade Ouija board. Upon learning of some of the early assertions of legendary Contactee George Adamski, Williamson became a regular visitor to Adamski's California commune; which is what led to his presence at Adamski's most famous encounter of all.

The Ultimate Contactee

George Adamski was born on April 17, 1891 in Poland, and claimed sensational alien encounters in the California desert in the early 1950s – the details of which were told in the packed-pages of a controversial, 1953 blockbuster-book co-authored with British writer Desmond Leslie, titled *Flying Saucers Have Landed*. Before we get deep into things of a long-haired and saucer-shaped variety as they relate to Adamski, let's start at the beginning. At the age of two, Adamski and his family moved to the United States and put down roots in New York. From 1913 to 1916, he served in the military; then, one year later, moved west, began working at Yellowstone National Park, and later took employment at an Oregon-based flour-mill. But the normality of everyday life was not for Adamski. While in Laguna Beach in the 1930s, he founded the Royal Order of Tibet. In other words, long before the relocated Pole maintained he met long-haired aliens in the deserts of California, he was already delving into a lifestyle that some might have seen as alternative.

An article that appeared in the *LA Times* in April 1934 titled *Shamanistic Order to be Established Here* offered an illuminating insight into the life of Adamski: "The ten-foot trumpets of far away Lhasa, perched among perpetual snows in the Himalayan Mountains in Tibet, will shortly have their echo on the sedate hills of Southern California's Laguna Beach. Already the Royal Order of Tibet has acquired acreage on the placid hills that bathe their Sunkist feet in the purling Pacific and before long, the walls, temples, turrets and dungeons of a Lama monastery will serrate the skyline. It will be the first Tibetan monastery in America and in course of time, the trained disciples of the cult will filter through its glittering gates to spread 'the ancient truths' among all who care to listen. [The] central figure in the new movement is Prof. George Adamski...

"'I learned great truths up there on the roof of the world,' says Adamski, 'or rather the trick of applying age old knowledge to daily life, to cure the body and the mind and to win mastery over self and soul. I do not bring to Laguna the weird rites and bestial superstition in which the old Lamaism is steeped, but the scientific portions of the religion.'"

Six years later, Adamski moved yet again – with a group of friends to a ranch near California's Palomar Mountain. Then, in 1944, the group purchased 20-acres of land on Palomar Mountain, constructed a new home called Palomar Gardens, and opened a restaurant called the Palomar Gardens Café. It wasn't too long before Adamski's life became distinctly weird. On October 9, 1946, Adamski and a number of his buddies claimed that while they were at the Palomar Gardens' campground, they saw a huge cigar-shaped UFO. One year later, Adamski photographed the very same craft; once again at Palomar Gardens. Other sightings of apparently-unidentified aerial vehicles followed; but Adamski's true crowning glory came in the final weeks of 1952. And guess who was present: George Hunt Williamson.

Orthon Comes Calling

Greg Bishop, one of the leading authorities on the Contactee controversy, tells the story: "...Adamski left his Palomar mountain retreat at 1.00 a.m. on Thursday November 20, 1952 along with his lifetime secretary Lucy McGinnis and Alice Wells – the owner of the property where Adamski gave lectures on Universal Law and the café where he flipped burgers to pay the rent. At about 8.00 a.m. they met with Al Bailey and his wife Betty, and George Hunt Williamson [a fellow-Contactee, and about who more imminently] and his wife, Betty, in Blythe, [California] just west of the Arizona / California border.

"Turning back on a 'hunch' the group retraced their drive back to Desert Center and took a small highway 11 miles northeast towards the town of Parker, Arizona and stopped. After a meal, the group aimlessly scanned the skies for saucers. Passing motorists slowed to rubberneck at this small

TRAVELING THE PATH BACK TO THE ROAD IN THE SKY

band staring into the sky in the middle of a barren desert. Shortly after 12 noon, a plane passed overhead, causing momentary excitement. The real drama began moments later, when 'riding high and without sound, there was a gigantic cigar-shaped silvery ship.'

"Williamson understatedly asked: 'Is that a space ship?', as Betty Bailey tried to set up a movie camera, but couldn't because 'she was so excited.' According to Adamski, they were anxious not to attract attention to the object, so they didn't point at it and alert other passing cars to this event.

"'Someone take me down the road, quick! That ship has come looking for me and I don't want to keep them waiting!' Adamski yelled, and jumped into the car with McGinnis and Mr. Bailey. About a half-mile down the road, with the craft shadowing them, Adamski told McGinnis to turn off the road. He then instructed the two to 'go back to the others as quickly as possible...and watch for anything that might take place' – from the safe viewing distance of half a mile or more away. After this first craft was chased away by interceptor jets, another 'beautiful small craft' arrived and landed behind the crest of a mountain about half a mile away.

"Soon, he saw a figure waving to him and walked towards it. Suddenly Adamski 'fully realized I was in the presence of a man from space – a human being from another world!' Adamski learned [the being] was from Venus and that his name was Orthon. After some warnings about atomic weapons and wars, and a refusal to be photographed, he returned to his ship and sailed away.

"Adamski waved to his companions to approach, which they did soon after. Conveniently enough Williamson had brought along some plaster-of-paris and proceeded to make casts of the footprints the Venusian had left in the desert floor. According to Williamson...he was 'the first to arrive at the footprints after the contact had been made. I could see where the space being had scraped away the topsoil in order to get more moist sand that would take the impressions from the carvings on the bottom of his shoes. The carvings on the shoes must have been finely done for the impressions in the sand were clear cut.'

"Either Orthon had a weight problem on Earth, or someone had taken extra care in making the impressions. He goes on to state his interpretation of what meaning the symbols hold for those who 'fail to obey the laws of the Infinite Father.' Williamson also stresses that the designs are not 'alien,' since the Earth is 'part of the Great Totality' and ancient symbols of Earth are the symbols of the space beings as well…after this event Williamson seemed to have found his calling, and concentrated on turning out his own brand of Contactee literature – most of it 'channeled' – leaving clear the nuts-and-bolts domain to his friend and inspiration, the other George – Adamski."

The Williamson-Adamski Connection

On the matter of the relationship between Adamski and Williamson, researcher Colin Bennett states: "Adamski was not an educated man, and he used the better-educated Williamson as he used Desmond Leslie, that is as an extra cerebral lung. As such, George Hunt Williamson was the top of Adamski's multi-media head. As they used to say in those days, they both tripped one another out. The Mojave was certainly rich in ancient Indian legends concerning flying vehicles. This was one of the reasons why George Hunt Williamson and the Baileys accompanied Adamski to the desert. It is more than possible that the group wanted to conjure up something like the kind of presence that they thought they had contacted from their automatic writing, and at least Adamski got more than he bargained for. A combination of high intrigue, burgeoning exotic technology combined with the ancient desert and its prehistoric features was not to be trifled with, and a genie came right of the alchemical bottle. All the best books on occultism contain the warning that the attempted raising of images is not to be taken lightly.

"It is important to understand that like Alan Ginsberg and Jack Kerouac, both Adamski and Williamson were fully inspired by the birth of this brave new world. It threaded through them as ivy threads through a house if it is not cut off; and neither Adamski nor Williamson were the kind of men to cut off any kind of speculative growth. Prototypal belief-systems sprouted almost from the top of their heads, and surreal conspiracies were the very breath of their being. Both were breathless Americans in the first nuclear age, and both were as excited as rich kids let loose in a big-city toyshop."

With Williamson's extensive, and convoluted, background now detailed – as well as the reasons behind how and why he became such a key and integral player in the 1950s era of the Contactees – it's time to take a deep look at the crux of the matter: the FBI's interest in the man himself.

TRAVELING THE PATH BACK TO THE ROAD IN THE SKY

The FBI, Flying Saucers, and Communism

To understand how and why George Hunt Williamson became a person of interest to the FBI as a result of his flying saucer-connected claims, it's highly important to note the climate that existed in the United States in the early 1950s. This was, of course, the formative years of the Cold War, the Soviet Union was perceived as being the next big threat, and Communism was seen as downright evil. Thus, when the likes of Adamski started spouting off about the Space Brothers being communist – at the same time he was influencing tens of thousands of people with his book, *Flying Saucers Have Landed* – the FBI immediately sat up and took a great deal of notice. The FBI's surveillance of Adamski commenced in 1950, and reveals the illuminating fact that the FBI considered Adamski to be nothing less than an outrageous subversive.

Now-declassified FBI records on Adamski note:

"According to [a confidential FBI source whose name is blacked-out in the declassified files] Adamski stated that the Federal Communications Commission, under the direction of the 'Military Government' of the United States, has established communication with the people from other worlds, and has learned that they are so much more advanced than the inhabitants of this earth that they have deciphered the languages used here. Adamski stated that in this interplanetary communication, the Federal Communications Commission asked the inhabitants of the other planet concerning the type of government they had there and the reply indicated that it was very different from the democracy of the United States. Adamski stated that his answer was kept secret by the United States Government, but he added, 'If you ask me they probably have a Communist form of government and our American government wouldn't release that kind of thing, naturally. That is a thing of the future – more advanced.'"

One does not have to be a genius to realize that Adamski's assertions that his long-haired alien friends were nothing less than full-on Russia-loving Reds led the FBI to elevate its secret-spying on the man to a whole new level. And, as the files show, it was the following that led J. Edgar Hoover to conclude that Adamski's actions should be classified as a "security matter." The files state:

"Adamski, during this conversation, made the prediction that Russia will dominate the world and we will then have an era of peace for 1,000 years. He stated that Russia already has the atom bomb and the hydrogen bomb and that the great earthquake, which was reported behind the Iron Curtain recently, was actually a hydrogen bomb explosion being tried out by the Russians. Adamski states this 'earthquake' broke seismograph machines and he added that no normal earthquake can do that.

"Adamski stated that within the next twelve months, San Diego will be bombed. Adamski stated that it does not make any difference if the United States has more atom bombs than Russia inasmuch as Russia needs only ten atom bombs to cripple the United States by placing these simultaneously on such spots as Chicago and other vital centers of this country. The United States today is in the same state of deterioration as was the Roman Empire prior to its collapse and it will fall just as the Roman Empire did. The Government in this country is a corrupt form of government and capitalists are enslaving the poor."

The FBI was not impressed at all. And, as a direct result, they started focusing their attentions on many of Adamski's friends and colleagues in the flying saucer field, including George Hunt Williamson. Official surveillance of Williamson by Hoover's G-Men had begun.

The Secret Surveillance of Williamson

In order to understand how and why Williamson was placed under secret scrutiny, it is important to keep in mind the point that Williamson had made claims that his very own Space Brothers communicated with him via Ouija boards. And it is equally important to note that – as FBI records declassified under the terms of the Freedom of Information Act demonstrate – he was investigated by the FBI to determine if he had Communist leanings, or was knowingly or unknowingly spreading propaganda on behalf of the Soviet Union.

Richard Duke – a now very elderly figure who, in the period in question, worked in US Intelligence - says that as far back as 1948, the FBI began to receive reports and stories very similar to those of Williamson – that human-like aliens were among us, that they were communists, and that their means and modus-operandi of contact seemed to utilize the occult, such as Ouija Boards, as well as advanced science.

Duke further states that certain elements within the FBI came to a startling, albeit tentative, conclusion: that the claimed encounters with Communist extraterrestrials had nothing to do with visitors from other worlds but were instead the outcome of Soviet mind control and "brain-to-brain contact" projects, in which U.S. citizens were being "implanted with thoughts" by Russian "mind-soldiers" that led the Contactees to think they were having real-life experiences with aliens who wanted to tell us how wonderful communism was.

Duke explains that the experiences were initially believed to be "stage-managed, psychological warfare" and were simply the effects of highly sophisticated "mind-management and manipulation" by the Russians on unwitting citizens, who may very well have believed precisely what they were saying. Moreover, Duke claims that the FBI believed the Russians had apparently acquired "the skills to do this" from Nazi scientists captured at the end of the Second World War; they had been working to perfect the utilization of such "mind phenomena" for Adolf Hitler, who was indeed known for his deep interest in the occult.

Duke maintains that this theory came to fruition in 1952, specifically after cleared FBI agents had attended "two of seven or eight" lectures that had been held in the Pentagon that year on the utilization of ESP for psychological warfare purposes. That such lectures held in the Pentagon did occur, and that U.S. Intelligence was aware of Hitler's interest in such matters, is not in any doubt.

In 1977, in a document titled *Parapsychology in Intelligence*, Kenneth A. Kress, an engineer with the CIA's Office of Technical Services, wrote: "Anecdotal reports of extrasensory perception (ESP) capabilities have reached U.S. national security agencies at least since World War II, when Hitler was said to rely on astrologers and seers. Suggestions for military applications of ESP continued to be received after World War II. For example, in 1952 the Department of Defense was lectured on the possible usefulness of extrasensory perception in psychological warfare."

Whether or not there was any truth to the sensational claims that the Contactees – including Williamson – were being mind-manipulated by the Soviets, as a means to help spread communism under the guise of UFOs, is a matter of deep controversy. But, true or not, it led the FBI to keep a careful, ongoing watch on Williamson. And much of it revolved around his relationship with a very strange character named Karl Hunrath.

TRAVELING THE PATH BACK TO THE ROAD IN THE SKY

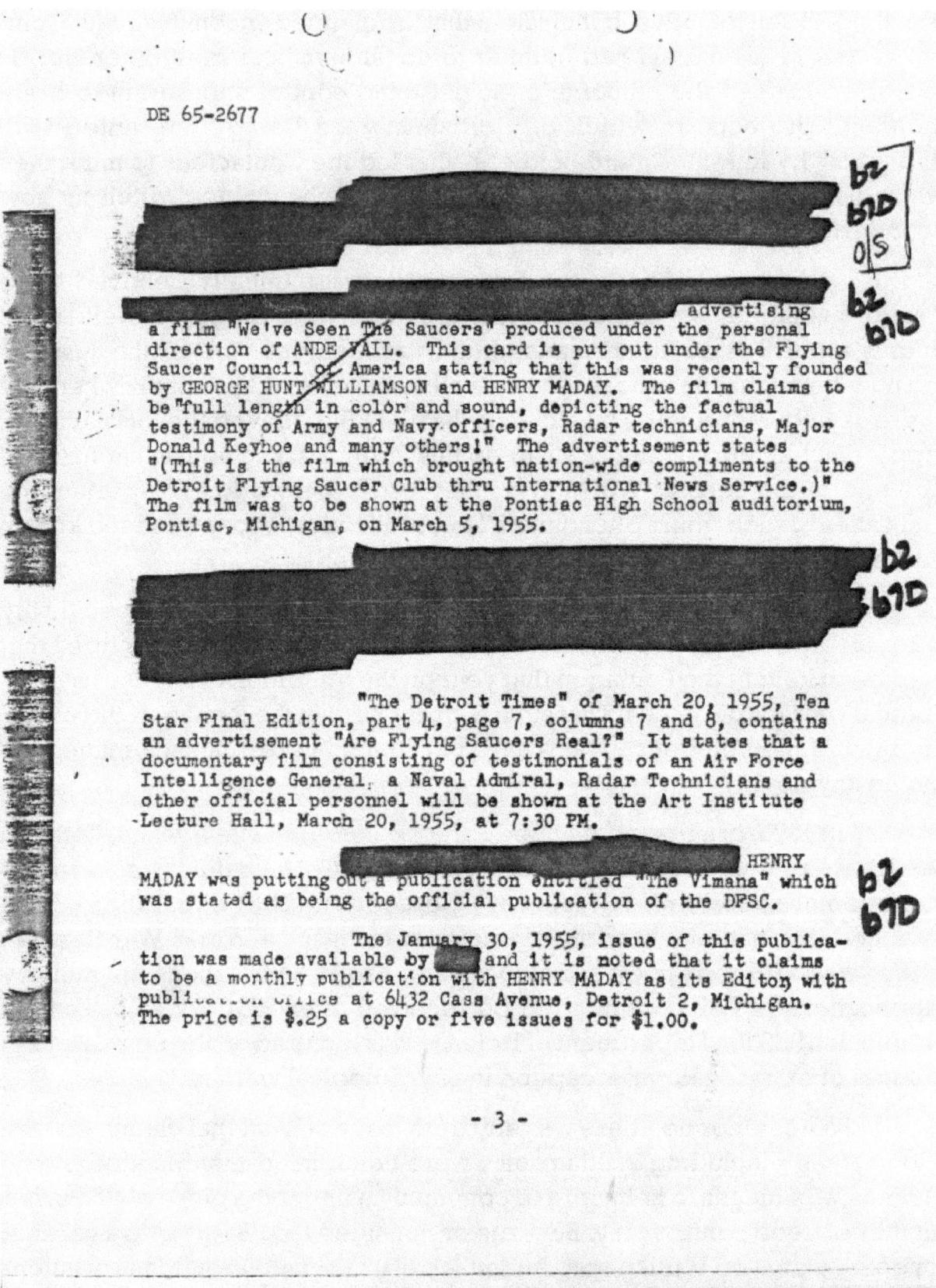

DE 65-2677

[REDACTED] advertising a film "We've Seen The Saucers" produced under the personal direction of ANDE VAIL. This card is put out under the Flying Saucer Council of America stating that this was recently founded by GEORGE HUNT WILLIAMSON and HENRY MADAY. The film claims to be "full length in color and sound, depicting the factual testimony of Army and Navy officers, Radar technicians, Major Donald Keyhoe and many others!" The advertisement states "(This is the film which brought nation-wide compliments to the Detroit Flying Saucer Club thru International News Service.)" The film was to be shown at the Pontiac High School auditorium, Pontiac, Michigan, on March 5, 1955.

[REDACTED]

"The Detroit Times" of March 20, 1955, Ten Star Final Edition, part 4, page 7, columns 7 and 8, contains an advertisement "Are Flying Saucers Real?" It states that a documentary film consisting of testimonials of an Air Force Intelligence General, a Naval Admiral, Radar Technicians and other official personnel will be shown at the Art Institute Lecture Hall, March 20, 1955, at 7:30 PM.

[REDACTED] HENRY MADAY was putting out a publication entitled "The Vimana" which was stated as being the official publication of the DFSC.

The January 30, 1955, issue of this publication was made available by [REDACTED] and it is noted that it claims to be a monthly publication with HENRY MADAY as its Editor with publication office at 6432 Cass Avenue, Detroit 2, Michigan. The price is $.25 a copy or five issues for $1.00.

- 3 -

Williamson FBI Document #1

TRAVELING THE PATH BACK TO THE ROAD IN THE SKY

CONFIDENTIAL

BH 87-4689

████████ made available a file on this case which reflected that the fourth Yucatan expedition ████████ lasted from 12/18/61 until 1/13/62 and was conducted at the site of the Haina, I.D., 25 miles north of Campeche and the collection of shells, tools and ornaments, Obsidian blades, decorated pottery were located. By the date of 2/7/62, ████████ mentioned making arrangements to purchase four Mayan pieces of value -- plate, vase, head of laughing goddess and bowl in bas relief -- plus tow items from Haina, which were apparently brought to Miami by ████████ on 1/14/62. Two 3-legged incense burners were also found in a cave on the Fifth Yucatan trip by ████████ Dr. d-Obrenovic, which were turned over to Mexican authorities.

The file indicated ████████ was interested in securing artifacts from ████████

There was also a letter from a ████████ addressed to WILLIAMSON, who is also known as D'OBRENOVIC, in which he mentioned a carved head being removed from a cave in Yucatan, prior to the time that WILLIAMSON located this cave. The letter indicated that WILLIAMSON had been associated with an ill-fated expeditionary society in Portland, Oregon, in the past. The above-mentioned carved head was apparently taken from a loltun cave in Yucatan sometime in 1961 ████████ was also acquainted with a ████████ apparently, according to the file.

The file also reflected that GEORGE HUNT WILLIAMSON, also known as D'OBRENOVIC, had attended the University of Arizona in 1950-51 and that numerous inquiries had been received by ████████ the University of Arizona, ████████ concerning WILLIAMSON, who has posed as an authority on flying saucers and archaeology

4

87-68228

CONFIDENTIAL

Williamson FBI Document #2

TRAVELING THE PATH BACK TO THE ROAD IN THE SKY

Aliens and Aircraft-Destroying Weapons

Karl Hunrath was a deeply complex, and even mysterious, character with a flair for creating all manner of electronic gadgets and gizmos and who, up until the late summer of 1952, was employed by the John Oster Manufacturing Company in Racine, Wisconsin. There was nothing remotely weird or mysterious about his job, however. The company was focused on the production and marketing of such things as hair-clippers and all manner of kitchen-based, small appliances: toasters, drink-blenders and so on. And Hunrath dutifully did what he was best at: fine-tuning and improving such items in just about every new and novel way possible. But there was something else: Hunrath also claimed to have made contact with aliens who told him the secrets of advanced technologies that could catastrophically bring down US military aircraft from the skies.

In late 1952, Hunrath moved to Los Angeles and wasted no time at all in hooking up with the major UFO players in and around town, as George Hunt Williamson recalled:

"Before Hunrath arrived in California he had become acquainted with another so-called 'genius' - from Ohio. This man called Karl one night saying he had just returned from Japan where he had been working with a Dr. Nagata on electromagnetic experiments. He asked Karl if he could come up to see him since he had heard that Karl was interested in magnetic research. The man came and he stayed four days and nights! When he left, Karl had become an avid saucer enthusiast. Karl said he thought the man was a 'spaceman' because he answered his questions before they were asked and displayed telepathic powers."

Williamson continued: "It was in the winter of 1952 that I first met Karl at George Adamski's on Mount Palomar...During the next few months he visited many saucer researchers including: Frank Scully, Gene Dorsey, George Van Tassel...and he was my house guest in Prescott, Arizona for a week. He was a strange man who would change his mind and ideas from one moment to the next. You couldn't help but like him, but at times a feeling would come over you that made you wish there were a million miles between yourself and Mr. Hunrath. Everyone who came in contact with him had the same experience. He visited saucer researchers as a friend, then, systematically began to spread rumors about them and their work which had no basis in fact. He came to California unknown and soon was stirring up dissension wherever he went. Was it his purpose to cause trouble in the 'hot-bed' of controversy existing among the California saucer enthusiasts? Was it part of a plan formulated by negative forces? Why was Hunrath a brilliant scientist one moment and a not too bright electrician the next?"

These were just a few of the questions that not only Williamson wanted answering. The G-Men were soon knocking on doors, too, and wanting to know what the hell Hunrath's game was. It turned out that, on January 12, Lucy Mcginnis called the soon-to-be-wife of one Jerrold Baker – a handyman at Palomar and one of Adamski's faithful – in alarmed fashion. Adamski, Hunrath, Baker and Williamson had been hanging out at Palomar that morning. All was fine for a while, but matters nearly came to blows when Hunrath started ranting and bragging about how he – thanks to the secret technology the aliens had shared with him - could destroy the U.S. Air Force's aerial armada in a flash. Demonstrating a high degree of astuteness, Adamski became instantly worried and concerned that this information might get back to law-enforcement officials, so he slung Hunrath, Williamson and Baker off his property, ordering them never to return. It wasn't long before Adamski's worst nightmare came absolutely true.

Jerrold Baker's beloved – Irma – was unsure what to about McGinnis' revelations concerning Hunrath and his boasting about being able to destroy American planes, so she erred on the side of what she perceived as caution. That's to say, she picked up the phone, called the Air Force and the FBI, and spilled the beans. The whole damn can. Officialdom moved quickly and right in the direction of George Adamski. On arriving at his home later that very same day, the grim, unsmiling minions of J. Edgar Hoover told the quaking Pole they had heard rumors that he, Adamski "had in his possession a machine which could draw 'flying saucers' and airplanes down from the sky."

Although this was completely untrue, Adamski realized immediately that the FBI agents were actually talking about Hunrath – who, up until the bust-up earlier on that very same day which led to the FBI arriving, had been chummy with Adamski and Williamson for two months or thereabouts - and his wild tale of having created some sort of aircraft-destroying technology.

For the FBI to think that Adamski possessed some form of advanced weapon that could bring significant portions of the U.S. war-machine to a grinding halt was a matter that, for Adamski, practically screamed "Deep Shit!" As a result, Adamski immediately rolled over, and gave up Hunrath's name and all he knew about the man – who he helpfully described to his FBI interrogators as being not "entirely loyal."

Williamson's Revelations

George Hunt Williamson, not surprisingly, became majorly concerned when he learned the FBI had opened a file on Hunrath – the two were, after all, colleagues and friends by now. Williamson also realized, correctly, that if the Feds were watching Hunrath, then they were probably watching him, too. Williamson was not wrong. It was at this time that yet another character came on the scene who Williamson became acquainted with and who was also being spied on by the FBI: Wilbur Wilkinson.

Williamson told the story of Wilkinson as follows: "Hunrath had been in correspondence with Wilbur and convinced him that he should come to the west coast because of important Saucer developments." Wilkinson, always jumping to attention when Hunrath demanded it, did exactly that and secured a job at the Hoffman Radio Corporation, where he was soon promoted to the position of Head of the Inspection Department. Wilkinson, thirty-eight at the time, said Williamson, "had his den and home full of all sorts of electronic equipment, radios, turn-tables, and tape recorders."

And as Mrs. Wilkinson succinctly put it, after their arrival in Los Angeles in June 1953: "Karl was the one who talked us into coming to California because he said he could actually show a saucer to Wilbur."

It was this promise of actual UFO-themed evidence that led the pair – and, on several occasions, Williamson - to regularly hang out in Wilkinson's saucer-dominated den in his new California home, discussing the means by which they would crack wide open the enigma of – and the secrecy surrounding – the UFO controversy. All the while, the FBI was listening carefully and watching closely. It scarcely mattered: as 1953 progressed, the curtain was about to go up on the final act for Hunrath and Wilkinson.

TRAVELING THE PATH BACK TO THE ROAD IN THE SKY

A Mysterious Disappearing Act

On the morning of November 10, 1953, Hunrath and Wilkinson took to the clear, sunny skies in a small plane – containing about three hours' worth of gas - rented from Gardina County Airport, California. The purpose of their flight, to rendezvous at a remote stretch of Golden State desert with fantastically advanced beings from another world that the two had then recently, allegedly contacted via what they were by now calling "mechanical contractions." Don't even think about asking what that means. The pair was not seen nor heard of again. And neither was the aircraft. No skeletal, ragged remains turned up. No tell-tale wreckage was found. *Ever.* Hunrath and Wilkinson were - for all intents and purposes - gone, vanished. In the immediate aftermath of their disappearance, L.A.-based saucer sleuths began to suspect that they were *really* gone. Like *up there* gone.

Ten days later, the *Los Angeles Mirror* highlighted their disappearance in its pages – as well as the attendant theory that their vanishing act was the work of aliens. Suddenly, and not surprisingly, pretty much the entirety of the city's media descended on the Wilkinson home, as George Hunt Williamson noted.

When the press arrived, said Williamson, they found that "Wilkinson's den was lined with flying saucer pictures, weird signs and formulas, which Mrs. Wilkinson said were supposed to be the new interplanetary language. 'Of course, I don't quite go for all the flying saucer talk, but Karl convinced Wilbur they actually existed,' said Mrs. Wilkinson. She then said, 'Karl had tape recordings of conversations with men from other planets who landed here in Saucers.' She showed reporters messages tacked on the wall of the den which were supposedly received by radio from the interplanetary visitors. One was from Regga of the planet Masar."

The photos, said Williamson, were actually some of those taken by Adamski, while the strange formulas and signs "were received by our group working in Northern Arizona, starting in early August, 1952. The tape recordings that Hunrath had were taken during receptions of the Arizona research group."

Was it true? *Were* Hunrath and Wilkinson really invited to take a one-way trip to another, far-away world by benevolent Space-Brothers, as some of their friends and families suspected? Others speculated that the whole affair could be explained away as mere accident. Indeed, several people

TRAVELING THE PATH BACK TO THE ROAD IN THE SKY

offered that nothing stranger than engine-trouble had probably led to terrible tragedy and death on the massive, rugged mountains of southern California. Some, however, weren't quite so sure that the baffling disappearance of Hunrath and Wilkinson was just due to careless pilot-error or mechanical malfunction. But those same souls weren't looking to E.T. for the answers either. They were looking across the border or to the government. And not just the U.S. Government, either.

George Hunt Williamson was one of the more vocal ones on this matter, and who had heard of the Soviet angle: "Some people think the two men went to Mexico, but they didn't have enough fuel for the trip. It has also been reported that Karl is in England and will reappear shortly and also that he has been seen recently in Los Angeles with his hair dyed! He has been called a spaceman, a man possessed of evil spirits, an angel, a member of the F.B.I., and a Russian spy. What he really was no one knows - but we can guess."

And, all the time, the FBI carefully noted Williamson's every word on the Hunrath-Wilkinson affair and, of course, Hunrath's assertions about possessing aircraft-destroying technology devised by aliens. But, with Hunrath and Wilkinson now mysteriously – and forever – gone, the FBI finally turned its attention to other aspects of Williamson's career in the flying saucer field.

The Bethurum Connection

In 1954, Williamson and the aforementioned Al Bailey published their own saucer-dominated volume: *The Saucers Speak*, which focused upon Williamson's attempts to contact extraterrestrials via the alternative mediums of short-wave radio and Ouija-boards. Actar of Mercury; Adu of Hatonn in Andromeda; Agfa Affa of Uranus; Ankar-22 of Jupiter; Artok of Pluto; and numerous others were among the motley alien crew with whom Williamson claimed to have communicated. As a result, Williamson found himself more and more in demand on the lecture circuit.

It was also in 1954 that the FBI sat up and took notice when Williamson planned to speak at an event in Ohio with yet another Contactee, Truman Bethurum. Beyond any shadow of doubt, the number of people who can claim aliens wrecked their marriages is infinitely small. But, such claims have been made – the most memorable being that of construction-worker Bethurum.

TRAVELING THE PATH BACK TO THE ROAD IN THE SKY

His idea of a close encounter was very different to those of other UFO witnesses: his alleged liaisons in the summer of 1952, atop Mormon Mesa, Nevada with Space Captain Aura Rhanes, a supposed citizen of the planet Clarion, ultimately led his outraged wife to file for divorce!

As for why the FBI took so much interest in the Bethurum/Williamson gig, the answer is very simple. The FBI was *already* keeping tabs on Bethurum, for one particularly interesting reason: he had made certain statements linking his experiences with Aura Rhanes to matters of a communist nature. In Bethurum's own words:

"Two or three fellows who had sons in Korea and who read a lot in the newspapers about the Communist underground in this country, were convinced in their own minds that I was, if making contact with anyone at all, making it with enemy agents. They even went so far as to tell me belligerently that they intended to get guns and follow me nights, and if they caught up me having intercourse with any people from planes, airships of any kind, they'd blast me and those people too."

On a related matter, FBI records demonstrate that in December 1954, the Palm Springs Republican Club contacted the FBI to inquire if Bethurum might be guilty of "trying to put over any propaganda." So, when Bethurum – whose curiously-worded statement about "enemy agents" and "airships" caught the immediate attention of the FBI - hooked up with Williamson, who the Bureau had been watching since his early associations with Adamski, it took the investigation of Williamson to a whole new level. And, as an amusing aside, it also led the FBI to refer to Aura Rhanes in its files as a "ravishing woman commandant"! Even the Bureau, it seems, was infected by Aura's hotness!

The FBI paid careful attention to who - in the saucer scene of the time - Williamson and Bethurum were speaking, what the then-current line of thinking was with regard to their claims of alien contact, and the potential impact of their planned lectures. In other words, both men – unbeknownst to them – were having pretty much their every move watched by the secret eyes of officialdom. And, for Williamson, that continued into the following year, 1955.

TRAVELING THE PATH BACK TO THE ROAD IN THE SKY

"We've Seen the Saucers"

Next on the cards for the FBI was a development that occurred in March 1955. Hoover's agents noted in secret memoranda that, along with one Henry Maday, Williamson had then-recently established The Flying Saucer Council of America, which – the FBI also noted – was championing and promoting a new documentary-style film on flying saucers titled *We've Seen the Saucers*.

More alarming to the FBI: Williamson had apparently got his hands on priceless film-footage of UFO activity that appeared in the film. Reportedly, the footage showed "the astounding sighting at White Sands, New Mexico when two saucers trailed an experimental rocket to an altitude of one-hundred ten miles above the earth, and then speed off at the incredible speed of 7,200 mph."

Of this matter, the FBI carefully recorded that the film at issue "was procured in California by Ric Williamson," one of the man's several pseudonyms.

Williamson, the FBI, and a Crashed UFO

Also in 1955, the FBI noted in its file on Williamson: "...according to an article in the *Detroit Times* on March 10, 1949, Ray L. Dimmick, a Los Angeles businessman, had seen a wreckage of a flying saucer which he said crashed near Mexico City. Dimmick reportedly inspected the wrecked saucer at a secret military installation at Mexico City and was escorted there by Mexican business associates. Dimmick described the saucer as being forty-six feet in diameter. He reported that Mexican officials and some scientists believed it was from Mars or another planet. He was reportedly told by Mexican officials that the Saucer was piloted by a strange type of man twenty-three inches tall. He said the pilot was killed in the crash. Dimmick stated that military and government officials from the United States inspected the Saucer."

The FBI then immediately thereafter turned its attentions to Williamson and matters of a crashed UFO nature: "Ric Williamson and Henry Maday while in Saginaw, Michigan, prior to conducting a Flying Saucer Council program, met a prominent photographer of Saginaw, who stated that his son had revealed to him the following: The photographer's son was stationed at Wright-Patterson Air Base about the time of the incident described in the March 10, 1949 *Detroit Times* above and while at Wright-Patterson Air Base, a huge semi-truck came to the Air Base with heavily canopied material jutting out, of immense size."

Echoing the claims that Wright-Patterson AFB is home to the legendary Hangar 18 – a supposed secret storage-area on-base where crashed UFO materials are held – the FBI noted of the "canopied material" that: "...no one seemed to know anything about it except that it was driven to a far hangar where no windows or accessible doors could be discerned."

Secret Smuggling and Ancient Artifacts

As far as the declassified files are concerned, the next entry in the FBI's dossier on George Hunt Williamson dates from 1962. Its subject matter: the possibility that Williamson had been involved in the smuggling into the United States of priceless Mexican artifacts of an historic and archaeological significance.

By now, the FBI noted Williamson was referring to himself as "Michel D.M. d' Obrenovic or Dr. Michel R. D' Obrenovic." Reportedly, there had been some distinct cloak-and-dagger activity in both Yucatan and Meriva, Mexico, where Williamson had been working alongside staff from the University of Alabama – which, the FBI noted, "has received comments of a derogatory nature concerning the activities of subject d' Obrenovic."

The FBI also recorded for posterity that a confidential source had informed them that Williamson, along with an unknown character whose name is blacked-out in all the Freedom of Information Act-derived files, "have been instrumental in smuggling artifacts from these diggings out of Mexico and it is his understanding that the Mexican Government has made it known that they intend to arrest either if they re-enter that country."

As for the value of the items, said the FBI: "From the information available [two words, possibly a name, deleted] it appeared that possibly extremely valuable pieces, possibly including large pieces of jade and gold, valued at $100,000 have been smuggled out of the country by these individuals, possibly through Miami, Florida, into the United States."

The files also reflect that staff at the University of Alabama became deeply worried about this situation when informed of matters by FBI agents.

TRAVELING THE PATH BACK TO THE ROAD IN THE SKY

They quickly arranged for photographs of each and every one of the 22 items found at Yucatan and Meriva to be taken and then handed over to the FBI, for forwarding to Mexican authorities, who could then try and discern if anything in the collection had been secured by the team illegally – albeit unknowingly to senior staff at the university. Those items included a "Ceramic frog effigy;" a "Skull figure;" a "Laughing head;" a "Small round perforated mirror;" an "Urn from a cave; and a "Ceramic owl effigy."

For a while the FBI deeply pondered on whether or not they should get further involved in the pursuit of a potential crime that had occurred outside of its jurisdiction and in another country – Mexico – but finally dropped the matter; rather fortunately, it must be said, for Williamson. There is one particularly curious aspect of this particular affair: a number of the relevant documents are heavily censored according to category B1 of the Freedom of Information Act. Intriguingly, B1 covers nothing less than matters that may have a potential effect on US national security.

Williamson might have overstepped the line to a degree with his Indiana Jones-style escapades in Mexico in 1962, but they hardly seem like matters that would have had a bearing on issues relative to the national security of the United States. Unless, of course, there are additional files on Williamson that the FBI has still yet to declassify, and which remain behind closed doors for reasons tantalizing and unknown.

And there, so far as we can tell at least, ends the FBI's surveillance of George Hunt Williamson. Enigmatic, controversial and shrouded in mystery until the very end, he died in 1986, a figure by then largely forgotten by, or completely unknown to, the UFO research community of the day. But, maybe, not forgotten by the FBI...

TRAVELING THE PATH BACK TO THE ROAD IN THE SKY

Sources:

Bethurum, Truman & Tennison, Mary Kay, *Aboard a Flying Saucer*, DeVorss & Co, 1954.

Bishop, Greg, *George A, George W. and those "tracks on the desert," Wake up Down There!*, Adventures Unlimited, 2000.

FBI files on George Adamski declassified via the terms of the Freedom of Information Act.

FBI files on George Hunt Williamson declassified via the terms of the Freedom of Information Act.

Kress, Kenneth A., *Parapsychology in Intelligence*, Central Intelligence Agency, 1977.

Leslie, Desmond & Adamski, George, *Flying Saucers Have Landed*, Werner Laurie, 1953.

Pelley, William Dudley, *Star Guests*, Soulcraft Chapels, 1950.

Redfern, Nick, *Contactees*, New Page Books, 2009.

Redfern, Nick, interview with Colin Bennett, July 19, 2009.

Williamson, George Hunt & Bailey, Alfred C., *The Saucers Speak!*, New Age, 1954.

Williamson, George Hunt, *Other Tongues – Other Flesh*, Forgotten Books, 2008.

Williamson, George Hunt, *Secret Places of the Lion*, Neville Spearman, 1969.

TRAVELING THE PATH BACK TO THE ROAD IN THE SKY

About Nick Redfern

Nick Redfern works full-time as an author, lecturer and journalist. He focuses upon a wide range of unsolved mysteries, including the increasingly tedious Roswell affair of 1947, the macabre Men in Black, Bigfoot, UFOs, the Loch Ness Monster, alien encounters, and government conspiracies. He writes for *UFO Magazine; Mysterious Universe; Fate; Cryptomundo*; and *Fortean Times*. He also has a regular, weekly, cryptozoology-themed column at Mania.com titled *Lair of the Beasts*.

His many previous books include *Space Girl Dead on Spaghetti Junction; The FBI Files; Man-Monkey; Monsters of Texas* (co-authored with Ken Gerhard); *Cosmic Crashes; Final Events; On the Trail of the Saucer Spies; Keep Out!; There's Something in the Woods; Strange Secrets* (with Andy Roberts); *Memoirs of a Monster Hunter; Science Fiction Secrets; The NASA Conspiracies; A Covert Agenda; Celebrity Secrets;* and *The Real Men in Black*.

Nick has appeared on numerous television shows, including VH1's *Legend Hunters*; the BBC's *Out of this World*; Fox News; History Channel's *Ancient Aliens, MonsterQuest, America's Book of Secrets*; and *UFO Hunters*; National Geographic Channel's *The Truth about UFOs* and *Paranatural*; and SyFy Channel's *Proof Positive* – in which Nick and the Centre for Fortean Zoology's Jon Downes raced around Puerto Rico in a cool silver-coloured jeep in search of the blood-sucking nightmare known as the Chupacabra.

He lists his favourite things as late 1970s punk-rock and new-wave music, black t-shirts and black jeans, Carlsberg Special Brew, Tennents Super, zombies, chocolate, *Family Guy, The Walking Dead, Night of the Demon, Terrorvision*, the works of Jack Kerouac, the novels of Carlos Ruiz Zafon, *Rammstein, Motorhead*, Abby from *NCIS, Oasis*, a nice cup of tea with lots of milk and sugar, and burned toast with mountains of margarine.

Nick can be contacted at http://nickredfernfortean.blogspot.com

TRAVELING THE PATH BACK TO THE ROAD IN THE SKY

TRAVELING THE PATH BACK TO THE ROAD IN THE SKY

Brad and Sherry Steiger

And So It Was Not Meant To Be!

A Short Commentary By Brad Steiger

In the mid-1980s, I was editor of Atlan, a small publishing company, located in Scottsdale, Arizona. While fulfilling my editorial responsibilities to the publishing company, I also maintained a full writing schedule of my own, producing such books as *The Star People, Unknown Powers, The World Beyond Death,* and *The Seed.*

In the fall of 1985, I received a letter from Michael d'Obrenovic, a name which I recognized immediately as an also-known-as name of George Hunt Williamson. Williamson was the author of such remarkable works as *Other Tongues, Other Flesh, Secret Places of the Lion,* and *Road in the Sky.*

Williamson wrote that he was living in California, and he urged a meeting between us as soon as possible. He hinted that he had a great deal of information that he wished to share concerning material that he had never before published. He knew of my research into the Star People, those individuals who claimed to have activating memories of lifetimes on Other Worlds and of my interest, as I had expressed in *Worlds Before Our Own,* of the prehistory of Earth and the possible role of extraterrestrial intelligences in the process of human evolution.

I understood that he wished to share a great deal of data with me that

TRAVELING THE PATH BACK TO THE ROAD IN THE SKY

he had collected since his last published work in the late 1950s. He concluded by suggesting that he travel to Scottsdale so that we might have a personal meeting. I answered at once, indicating that I would be pleased and eager both to meet him in person and to learn what new research materials and information that he had discovered.

NO COINCIDENCES!

I have long believed that there are no coincidences. About that same time in the fall of 1985, Atlan sponsored a short-story contest as a promotional device to alert the public to our existence on both the local and the national levels. The first prize winner was a personable, white-haired, robust woman, who, as we came to know each other better, acknowledged that she was aware of my work as an author as well as the editor of Atlan. In fact, she told me, she had been among the original members of the George Adamski circle who channeled messages from the Space Brothers in the 1950s. Now I was more than ever eager to meet with Williamson and begin to reconstruct this remarkable period in UFOlogy.

Alas, it was not to be. After a period of a few months of silence from Williamson, I made an inquiry to learn when he would be making arrangements to travel to Scottsdale for our meeting. It was then that I was informed of his death in January 1986. I was left only with the anguished speculations of what could have been if we had been able to meet, share ideas, and perhaps even to collaborate on a new book.

TRAVELING THE PATH BACK TO THE ROAD IN THE SKY

Behold! We shall be shown a mystery; we shall not all sleep but we shall all be changed. In a moment, in the twinkling of an eye, this mortal must put on immortality.

ROAD IN THE SKY

GEORGE HUNT WILLIAMSON

Author of: *"The Saucers Speak!"*
"Other Tongues—Other Flesh"
"UFOs Confidential"
"Secret Places of the Lion"

Ancient Pre-Inca representation of the *Road In The Sky* from Peru. The Jaguar God is placed above the Moon, flanked by two eight-pointed stars. Above the entire design is a circular symbol which archaeologists cannot explain. However, this "disc" represents the coming in ancient times, of the *Illa-Siva* or "light rings", known also as the *Ramba-Liviac* or the "litters of electric energies", the UFOs or "Flying Saucers" of modern times.

TRAVELING THE PATH BACK TO THE ROAD IN THE SKY

TABLE OF CONTENTS
- Foreword—31
- Introduction—32
- Yesterday—37
- Today—165
- Tomorrow—198

TRAVELING THE PATH BACK TO THE ROAD IN THE SKY

FOREWORD

The ancient road system of Imperial Rome and the Inca Sun Empire in Peru were the greatest the world has ever known. Yet, there is another 'highway' that the people of earth have been made aware of from time to time down through countless generations.

The 'highway' is grander and longer but one that never has to conquer the valleys and mountains of the Earth planet. Yet it often touched the green hills of Earth, and the contact was recorded in the most ancient records of humanity to be handed down from father to son, from priest to priest, and from age to age. It is the highway linking the stars together and moving out beyond the known Universe into the infinite vastness of galactic space.

Here is the startling evidence, proven by archeology, linking ancient civilizations and the mysteries of their temple rituals with the remote beginnings of humanity and visitations from Outer Space. It is history that began millions of years ago in a forgotten yesterday and connects the happenings in our skies today with an understanding of the prophecies of tomorrow.

Road in the Sky gives us a glimpse into a fantastic yet factual past, which explains the meanings of many ancient legends and myths discovered by Dr. Williamson after years of scientific research and archaeological expeditions into Central and South America.

TRAVELING THE PATH BACK TO THE ROAD IN THE SKY

INTRODUCTION

The Lords Inca constructed the grandest road that there is in the world, as well as the longest... I believe, since the history of man, there has been no other account of such grandeur as is to be seen on this road, which passes over deep valleys and lofty mountains, by snowy heights and over falls of water, through the living rock and along the edges of tortuous torrents... O! What greater things could have been said of Alexander the Great or any of the other powerful kings who have ruled the world than that they could have made such a road as this... the grandest and longest road in the world!'

Pedro Cieza de Leon, a young soldier and adventurer of Spain, came to Peru a short time after the fall of the Inca Empire. He traveled over the magnificent *Capac Nan*, Royal Road of the Inca Emperors, and he wrote down all that he saw on his journeys. The above words are from the account of his experiences along this fabulous road.

Centuries later, Baron Alexander von Humboldt said:

'...the roads of the Incas were the most useful and stupendous works ever created by man.'

The Imperial Roads of Rome were remarkably similar to the Inca Highways of the Sun Empire, and extended for thousands of miles and existed for centuries. The road systems of ancient Rome and Peru were the greatest the world has ever known, yet, there is another 'highway' that the people of the Earth have been made aware of from time to time down through countless generations.

This 'highway' is grander and longer, but never had to conquer the deep valleys and lofty mountains of the Earth planet. It was never cut through living rock nor washed away by raging torrents, yet, it often touched the green hills of Earth and the contact was recorded in the most ancient records of humanity to be handed down from father to son, from priest to priest, and from age to age.

This highway has always been and always will be; it is a pathway that

TRAVELING THE PATH BACK TO THE ROAD IN THE SKY

links the Stars together and moves out beyond the known Universe into the terrible vastness of galactic space.

The glorious roads of Rome and the Incas are now buried beneath desert sand, and the footsteps of busy mankind are no longer heard moving over the ancient stones... but the eternal *road in the sky* exists today as it did *yesterday*, and it shall know an even greater *tomorrow*.

The Inca Emperors had their highways of the Sun, but the pathway of the Stars goes beyond even the Sun of this Solar System, beyond the suns of neighboring systems, and even beyond the Great Central Sun of the Universe. It is a Royal Road that spirals upward, outward, and onward until it reaches the Citadel of Divine Creation itself.

The roads of Peru knew the marching feet of doomed men; the roads of Rome knew the chariots of destruction and the terrible machines of war. But the *road in the sky* serves another purpose. Its 'chariots' are vehicles of 'light', its 'travelers' are not men on a mission of invasion and death, but are messengers of glad tidings from the distant realms of celestial magnificence. The host on the roads of Imperial Rome and Peru was a conquering host; so also is the Host on the *road in the sky*... a Divine Host that will conquer and invade unto the ends of Creation. This conquest will be a conquest of *Love*.

The travelers along the 'highway of the stars' were in communication with the builders of the 'highways of Earth'—these travelers are mentioned in all the records of past civilizations as the 'gods' who rode the starways in 'flaming chariots' or on 'falcons of gold'.

These travelers along the *road in the sky* are in the skies of Earth today, and their 'golden chariots' have become the modern 'Unidentified Flying Objects'... the 'Flying Saucers'. Their 'highway' is more active today than it ever was in the past... a great Celestial Host moves towards Earth.

Dr. M. K. Jessup has said:

"The background of the UFO is as broad, as deep and as old as the background of mankind. It may very well be broader and older... The more I study and ponder this unlimited subject of Unidentified Flying Objects, the more I become convinced that the background of the UFO is the background of humanity."

Yes, 'the background of the UFO' or the 'chariots of light' is indeed 'the background of humanity': more, much more, it is the background of 'the beginning' of Divine Creation itself.

This book deals only with a short history of the *road in the sky*, and only with a fraction of the background of its swift travelers. However, here is

TRAVELING THE PATH BACK TO THE ROAD IN THE SKY

an account that begins millions of years ago in a forgotten *yesterday*, connects with the happenings of *today*, and brings understanding to the prophecies of *tomorrow*.

I wish to extend my appreciation to the following friends and colleagues for their co-operation and assistance.

Dr. Daniel Ruzo, Lima, Peru: For his co-operation in research and permission to use the photographs in Figures No. 2, 7, 9, and 12.

Mayor General, F.A.P., Fernando Ordonez de la Haza, Director del Servicio Aerofotografico Nacional, and Capitan, F.A.P., Jaime Castro D., Relaciones Publicas, Servicio Aerofotografico Nacional: for permission to publish the photographs of the Peruvian Air Force in Figures No. 26, 27, 28, 29, 31, and 32; and for giving me access to the archives of the Peruvian Air Ministry.

Maria Reiche, German scientist and mathematician: For permission to quote from her reports on the 'Lines of Nazca', and to publish her map which is reproduced in Figure No. 30.

Millen Cooke Belknap, Vista, California: For her ideas on the *Martian Miniatures*, and permission to publish the photograph in Figure No. 40.

Rev. Padre Jose Alvarez, Superior, Mission San Miguel (Dominican), Rio Alto Madre de Dios, and Rev. Padre Miguel Almaraz, Mission San Miguel: For extreme kindness to a jungle traveler and for supplying my expedition with suitable guides.

Yost H. Miller, Amishman, Millersburg, Ohio: For reports of UFO sightings amongst the Amish/Mennonite people.

Dan Katchongva, Hopi, Adviser (Sun Clan), Hotevilla, Arizona, Andrew Hermequaftewa, Hopi, Adviser (Bluebird Clan), Shungopovi, Arizona, David Monongye, Hopi, Hotevilla, Arizona, and Thomas Banyacya, Hopi: For permission to publish several of the Hopi legends and prophecies.

Yusuke Matsumura, Yokohama, Japan: For permission to publish the photograph in Figure No. 43.

This work is dedicated to those who 'discern the signs of God', who have the 'spirit of god' within them and who see the 'handwriting on the wall' for the modern world... they shall become new travelers on the eternal *road in the sky*!

Peru. May 8th, 1958, George Hunt Williamson.

TRAVELING THE PATH BACK TO THE ROAD IN THE SKY

TRAVELING THE PATH BACK TO THE ROAD IN THE SKY

Road In The Sky
George Hunt Williamson

TRAVELING THE PATH BACK TO THE ROAD IN THE SKY

PART ONE—YESTERDAY

Those who have come before us.
- **The Time-Spanners**
- **Last of the Sacred Forests**
- **Beacons for the Gods**
- **The Martian Miniatures**
- **Fossils, Footprints and Fantasy**
- **Evidence from the Silent World**

TRAVELING THE PATH BACK TO THE ROAD IN THE SKY

THE TIME-SPANNERS

'There were giants in the earth in those days...'

(Genesis vi:4)

For those of you who consider the following to be mere fantasy, we begin our revelation of the timeless *road in the sky,* with the established and correct form for all so-called unbelievable tales.

'Once upon a time...'

But far more fantastic than our fairyland opening is the date or age of our story.

Once upon a time *one thousand million years ago!*

You might argue, that if this really is a tale of enchantment only, then why attempt to date it at all? And, you might add that one thousand million or a billion years is a ridiculous figure anyway. But why is it ridiculous? You would tell me that it is not possible because 'authorities' or 'experts' say that man has only been on the Earth for 500,000 or 1,000,000 years at the most. Who, you would ask, would have been on the planet one billion years ago to record any 'once upon a time' event? But where is the *authority* of the 'authorities'? Are not their theories and deductions really only *guesses* woven from 'such stuff as dreams are made of'?' But you would tell me that the 'experts' base all statements on 'fact', and I would tell you that so-called *imagination* has a basis in fact also. It this were not so, then why do we 'imagine' this or that?

You might finally agree that since we are writing of dreamland where there are 'castles in the air', 'happy valleys' and a 'man in the moon', we might as well assign fantastic age to the tale if it enhances the over-all plot. Then you would ask me who the characters are in our story and I would tell

TRAVELING THE PATH BACK TO THE ROAD IN THE SKY

you they are creatures similar to men, only giants about twelve feet tall. You would, of course, want to know what an 'authority' like Webster had to say about 'giants', and you would thumb quickly through the dictionary... ghost... ghost dance... ghostly... ghoul... ghyll... giant... ah, yes! Giant: 'A huge mythical manlike or monstrous being of more than mortal, but less than godlike, power and endowment.' You would tell me that Webster has the final say in the matter when he tells us a giant is a mythical manlike being'.

I would say that giants were manlike beings certainly, but *mythical, never!* You would state that in the ultimate analysis neither a million years ago nor giants matter very much. I would tell you then to read what follows as a conjured up vision of vaporous nothings and be entertained by it. But why do picturesque tales move us? Saurat says:

Had there never been an Atlantis, had there never been any giants, the calamities and the resurrections embodied in these images are imprinted very deeply in the texture of our soul and of our innermost feelings. Our dreams are evidence of that fact. In his heart each one of us carries a lost Paradise, an Eve bereft of her Adam, a ruined universe of submerged continents. The old tales move us very deeply because we recognize in them the same nostalgic desires, as in the souls of our predecessors upon earth. *And what indeed is Truth if not that which men have always believed in?*

Prepare yourself then for an 'old tale'—a very old tale!

Once upon a time, one thousand million years ago, there was a planet that had taken up its orbit around a star (sun) and this planet was at last ready for inhabitation. For countless ages it had moved through space a hot and flaming body of cosmic matter. Then it began to cool, and wind and rain bathed its surface... storms raged in the seas and skies of the new world... erosion took place... land surfaces took form... 'beasts, creeping things, and fowls of the air' appeared. Finally, a virgin planet was ready to receive another form of life. This planet today we call Earth.

Remember, Webster says a giant is a 'huge manlike being of more than mortal, but less than godlike, power and endowment.' This is a good definition of the migration that arrived from out of space one billion years ago to become the first intelligent race on Earth that was not human, but was of the race of original *true* man.

In various contacts, the occupants of the UFOs have stated that they are not human. While they look like us physically, they claim they are members of the true race of man. They are men, we are human or *hu-men.* On Earth, mankind is at last graduating from its beasthood to its angelhood, and some individuals on this planet will no longer be human, but will belong to the race of man as the age nears its end.

It is interesting to mention here something from the study of the evolution of Chinese writing. This is shown in the 224 Primitive Characters found on the Bronzes of 2,000 B.C., traced through the successive stages of the Ku Wen or Old Forms moulded in metal, Ta Chuan or Greater Seal (800 B.C.) and Hsiao Chuan or Lesser Seal (200 B.C.), written with black varnish on strips of wood, and their transformation into the modern brush-written forms. Character No. 54 is HU which means : *tiger.* It is represented by a head, claws and stripes. What a perfect description of the HU-man Race. We on Earth are Tiger-Men, still marked by our inheritance from the beast when 'the sons of God saw the daughters of men that they were fair; and they took them wives of all which they chose.'[1] In this connection, it is also interesting to note that the Sphinx at Gizeh, which is part man and part animal, has the Egyptian name of HU.

How the early race that arrived from outer space is related to the space visitors of our day is not known, but members of this race, the first to achieve civilization upon the Earth, were called Cyclopeans, and are known in the secret, arcane knowledge as the 'L' Race, or simply, the "El's".

Before coming to the Earth they traversed space following all the great cycles of Time; they were 'Titans' who rode the starways—and they still do in another dimension-and sought always the best 'pastures' of space for their 'flock'. They were the first builders on Earth and are the Immortals of our legends, the God Race or Elder Race that preceded hu-man beings.

The Greeks speak of the period of the 'gods' whom we call 'giants'. The Cyclops (Kyklops, lit., round eyed) to the Greeks were gigantic monsters having one eye in the middle of the forehead and were more or less of obscure origin. We know of one through the Odyssey and others through the Greek stories of the workshops of Hephaestus (Vulcan) under Mt. Etna. The epic poet Homer spoke of the Cyclops as shepherds. The Greeks also tell us that the Cyclops grew powerful by industry underground and invented the thunder and are fabled to have forged thunderbolts for Zeus. The *underground* connection for the Cyclopeans is very important as we shall see later.

Some of the "El's" were true Cyclops in that they had only one great central round eye in the middle of their forehead. Others had two eyes like hu-man beings, and still others had the development of the psychic 'third eye'. They were about twelve feet tall and they were 'male' and 'female', but not as we think of sex differentiation today. Before coming to Earth they had colonized much of what is known as the Milky Way Galaxy—thousands of suns and worlds came under their direct influence. They usually preceded other highly intelligent life forms to a world after it was ready for inhabitation. Once they took up existence on a new planet, they attempted to leave behind what we shall call great 'libraries' in their deep, underground empire of enormous cities. In these 'libraries' tiny crystal records contain the history of the Universe, and are enclosed in a magnetic field that, at times, finds an affinity with some 'sensitive' person living on the Earth today. Certain students call this 'tuning in to the *library*, or the little red-brick schoolhouse'. In this way, the "El's", were Planet Preparers, for they always left a legacy behind for the future races that would eventually follow them as masters of a world.

It has been written :

Here in the secret caverns, their original homes, the vast might of their ("El's") being echoes titanically with every reverberating footstep upon the polished floor. That mirror polish is the perfect finish and the perfect reflector of both light and sound. One wonders why they went to so much trouble to have such polished surfaces. But that mirror polish was their method of showing off by continuous revealing reflection the slightest shift of Earth's rocks about them. The slightest crack would be detected upon those walls, and the Cyclopeans immediately would seal off such cracked portions of their underworld cities forever from occupancy.

The so-called myths of the ancients were not far from wrong when they spoke of the *underground* industry of the Cyclops and how they lived *under* Mt. Etna. As for their inventing thunder, they must have utilized some great cosmic energy or force. What radiant cities they dwelt in—and they still exist—no one lives there now, but every hall and library and every moving part of every piece of 'El' equipment and fantastic scientific device is still in perfect order exactly as it was when the "El's" were there millions of years ago. There are many of these labyrinthine cities under the surface of our planet. One is, indeed, under Mt. Etna, and there is another city, even greater in extent, under Lago de Titicaca in South America.

TRAVELING THE PATH BACK TO THE ROAD IN THE SKY

The "El's" were not exactly three-dimensional beings as we are today, but they were definitely physical creatures in a physical world. Their language, if we can call it that, was completely different from anything known on Earth today, with the possible exception of the Bantu languages which constitute the most important linguistic family in Africa south of the Sahara. This family of about one hundred languages and dialects is spoken by 50,000,000 people in equatorial Africa and consists of peculiar 'click' sounds.

The Cyclopean "El's" used no spoken words, but communicated with each other by a strange system of similar clicking sounds which sounded very much like a swarm of bees at a distance, but more staccato. These sounds are still heard on Earth today by certain 'sensitives' when they tune in to the 'libraries'. Later, the 'click' sounds became a plaything of poets, a relic of their distant past, for they were replaced as a means of communication by devices utilizing powerful penetrative rays which revealed their thoughts to each other. During the end of their last period on Earth they used telepathy without the need of devices of any kind as helping aids.

The "El's" were true frequency beings in that they operated according to certain rays or frequencies. Their music was the unadulterated music of the spheres—still, the fantasia of the ancient "El's" resounds throughout the polished halls, and weird nocturnes reverberate in violent crescendos throughout hundreds of crystalline prismatic levels in 'El' cities. It is claimed, however, that hu-man will surely die if he hears these sounds, for they are strange electronic rhapsodies reserved for the 'gods'. The combined thoughts of all 'El' beings comprise their symphony of life : their world beneath the surface of what we call our planet was a kaleidoscopic scene of changing hue and reflected luminosity, a 'holy of holies' that no mere Earthman could live through.

For countless ages, after their arrival upon the Earth planet, the "El's" had been attempting to achieve a Timeless condition, that is, to reach a place where they could not only create by mere Thought, but also escape the binding chains of physical existence, to break for ever the ties that bound them to physical planets and systems—the conquest of Matter, Energy, Space and Time. They searched for the secrets of Timelessness that would make them Immortals so they might march across Time and the Stars unfettered and free.

The Earth planet was the last world they colonized in the Milky Way

TRAVELING THE PATH BACK TO THE ROAD IN THE SKY

Galaxy, for soon after their arrival here they achieved the power of Creative Thought. They conquered physical matter and became the legendary 'gods'. They could mentally project any amount of matter in any degree of density or intensity to any place on Earth at any time. They constructed a Control Room which we might call 'Earth Central'—although it was not in the centre of the planet—at their underground city near Lake Titicaca, which now lies between Bolivia and Peru.

The Rio Desaguadero flows from Lago de Titicaca into Lago Poopó. Two hundred thousand cubic feet of water per minute flow into Lake Poopó, and from the *only known* outlet only two thousand cubic feet of water per minute flow. This would seem to indicate that Poopó is constantly rising and expanding, yet it hasn't risen a foot in centuries. This is a great mystery to scientists who have claimed that evaporation is the cause. They might be right if they were talking about Lago de Coipasa to the west which is surrounded by the Salar de Coipasa or Salt Lake. However, Poopó is a beautiful freshwater lake. After the water enters Poopó, great quantities of it drops underground into caverns that honeycomb the entire Lake Titicaca area. But most of the waters of Lake Poopó now flow like a River Styx of the lower world past the glassy, scintillating cities of the 'troglodytic' "El's". The Cyclopeans used this subterranean area when they arrived on Earth, although at that time there was no Lake Titicaca or Lake Poopó.

The 'El' Control Room was not the usual type with great dials and scientific gadgets, but a council chamber where the greatest 'El' minds gathered to perform their experiments in Creative Thinking. From this chamber, the Earth could be made to move on its axis, if necessary. Millions of years later, the 'Sons of God' arrived on Earth and they, too, had the power of creative thought, but they misused this divine power and the Great Abomination or Great Adultery took place—the 'fall of man' on this planet. The 'El' Race, however, applied the power correctly and in accordance with Universal Law.

There is an interesting connection between the "El's" and some of the words in common usage today. For instance, take Hell, made up of H and ELL. H is the eighth letter of the English alphabet and came through the Latin from the Greek H (eta) which was derived from a Phoenician letter, corresponding to Hebrew *cheth,* that stood for a strong guttural aspirate. In English, its sound is usually that of an aspiration or breathing. Now it is interesting to note that H is the symbol of the Greek *spiritus asper* or rough breath-

TRAVELING THE PATH BACK TO THE ROAD IN THE SKY

ing, and also is the *eighth* letter of the alphabet. When we combine the H (rough breathing) with ELL we get our word for the place of the dead or the abode of evil spirits. What does this mean?

We learn more when we realize that the word *aspiration* can designate an act of breathing or a breath and also an act of aspiring, a desiring ardently, a strong wish, or a longing for what is elevated or above one. This connection of breathing with aspiring gives us a key, for did not the 'El' Race *aspire* to the condition of Timelessness? And did they not become *elevated* through their eventual conquest of MEST?

The "El's" were *underground* and they had to dive into their own souls (the rough breathing) and experience the inner 'hurricane', then penetrate beyond that region of fury, and meet the divinity within their own beings. The 'penetration' beyond that 'region of fury' (now known to us as Hell) constituted 'El' *aspiration. The* word HELL can symbolize the "El's" (ELL) when they were going through their period of 'rough breathing' or struggling for Timelessness (H), or it can also symbolize their desire at the same time to seek something higher and greater, to tower, to soar, to aspire (H). We find the connection today with the place of punishment for the wicked after death as they suffer in a state of misery. This corresponds to the Cyclopeans as they conquered self or the primitive mind (ID); they were 'punished' by themselves as they labored in their *underground* world to be elevated to a state of non-materiality. Do not the souls in Hell also struggle in their 'sea of fire', their 'region of fury', or their 'inner hurricane' to be free of their torment? The similarities and correspondences are obvious to the diligent researcher. Hell is, to us, a place of the *dead,* because the "El's" left their *underground* home and it became a vacant, lifeless place except for the movements of its complicated devices—devices no longer necessary when Creative Thought was used. And so, we have our word HELL (H plus ELL).

We find also that the word *hurricane* (beginning with an H) stands for tempest. In Spanish it is huracan; in French it is Ouragan; in Russian it is Uragan; and in German it is Orkan. Behind these words stand other names, figures of mythology, such as Basque ORK-eguna (day of the thunder-god, Thursday, Thor's Day), and in the Groeden Valley (Austrian Alps) we find ORC-o, the giant of hurricanes. Then there is the Latin ORC-us (hell) and the Greek ORG-eia (orgy). There is a definite tie-in with tempest, wrath, anger, fury, orgy, hurricane and hell. All of these have been derived from the 'inner hurricane' or 'rough breathing' (H) of the 'El' Race as they *aspired* (H) to

TRAVELING THE PATH BACK TO THE ROAD IN THE SKY

lift themselves out of the world of MEST. Therefore, Hell to us is always *underground* and a place of 'fire'. The "El's" were 'underground' figuratively in that they were controlled by matter and also literally from the standpoint that their great cities were beneath the surface of the Earth. All of this is fascinating when we consider the beginning of things on our planet, and the "El's" of a billion years ago certainly can be called the true 'beginning of things'.

Everywhere we turn to study language we find connections. Take the word HA, for example. It is an exclamation expressing surprise, joy, or grief. When repeated, *ha, ha,* it expresses laughter, satisfaction, or triumph. A is the first letter of the English alphabet and comes from the Latin A which was derived from the Greek A (alpha), which in turn was derived from the first letter of the Phoenician alphabet. *Alpha* stands for the first or the beginning, or the chief. Therefore, while H ('rough breathing') plus A ('the beginning' with the "El's") gives us HA as an expression of *grief,* we also find that H (as a symbol of aspiration) plus A (symbol of 'the first or chief' or "El's") gives us HA as an expression of surprise, joy, laughter, satisfaction, and triumph. The very words we speak today come to us out of a dim, forgotten past where words were never spoken; the *aspiration* of the 'El' Race and its great *triumph* over MEST has more to do with our daily lives than we suspect. Of course, the "El's" never used words, but remember it is the *sound of* H, for instance, that is important.

In connection with other words using H, we could mention HADES (Hell) made up of the HA (grief) we mentioned above and DES which stands for *destruction, desolation,* descend, desperate, *desert,* desire, despair, despise, *despoil,* despondent, destroy, etc.

Also, we must remember that H is the great hieratic symbol of the Lost Continent of Mu.[2] And, remember, Mu went down beneath the waves into a 'region of fury' to suffer for her wickedness. So, H is her proper symbol for her period of 'rough breathing' and also as her symbol of aspiration when she will again rule among nations as she rises from the bottom of the Pacific Ocean.

After attaining the power of Creative Thought, the "El's" went a step further and actually annihilated MEST (for themselves, that is), for no longer did they have need of the Earth world or the great Galaxy it belonged to. They were at last free, they became true members of the Thought Universe,

TRAVELING THE PATH BACK TO THE ROAD IN THE SKY

the Theta Universe. H-ELL for them was something quite different than our concept of *hell* today. It is interesting to note that *hell* in German means : bright. And the Time-Spanning of the "El's" was indeed wonderful and bright.

We mentioned before that H, as a symbol of *spiritus asper,* or 'rough breathing', was also the *eighth* letter of the alphabet. Why is this connection important? What is the significance of the number eight? If we were studying a chart of the 'Spectrum of Awareness' We would discover nine levels :

ONE: (The sense of Individual Awareness, survival of Self).

TWO: (The sense of Future, survival through Life continuance individually).

THREE: (The sense of Direct Telepathic Translation, survival through Groups of all types).

FOUR: (The sense of Time Scanning, survival through Mankind as a whole).

FIVE: (The sense of Stabilization, survival through affinity with Life).

SIX: ("The sense of Inspection, survival through Matter-Energy-Space-Time).

SEVEN: (The sense of Purpose, survival Affinitive—purpose in Theta).

EIGHT: (Thought Universe—Universal Time—Thought beyond physical existence, survival through Supreme Entity).

NINE: (The Energy Universe).

The Thought Universe is THETA (eighth letter of the Greek alphabet) UNIVERSE because it is the eighth level of progression in individual life-form awareness. The seventh level is Sense of Purpose, based upon the concept of Thought and Energy Universes, and is the apparent upper limit of Physical Organism Awareness. After achieving the power of Creative Thought, the "El's" had no choice but to take the next step and move into the eighth level of Thought beyond physical existence—the conquest of MEST. Now they are free to move into the ninth level of the Energy Universe—union with the Creative Spirit—at-one-ment.

It is very significant, therefore, that H (as a symbol of the 'rough breathing' or labor of the "El's" and also their 'aspiration') is the eighth letter of the English alphabet corresponding to Theta, the eighth letter of the Greek al-

TRAVELING THE PATH BACK TO THE ROAD IN THE SKY

phabet. The H symbolized the Cyclopean struggle to achieve the *eighth level* or the Thought (Theta) Universe. They were, therefore, not in Hell, but were "El's" in H (ELL in H)—underground to work into level eight or H (eta).

Actually, the "El's" were not known as "El's" until they achieved the Theta condition. Before this they are referred to as the Cyclopean or Elder Race. It was their *method* of leaving physical existence and conditions that gave them the name of "El's". Through the secret use of the Ninety Degree Phase Shift they abandoned the Earth and the entire Galaxy and left it quite vacant for hu-man-ity.

A ninety degree angle forms the letter 'L'. Therefore, when you all them "El's" you are referring to *a symbol* of their Race and not *really* a name. The Cyclopeans were EL-DERS before the Phase Shift, that is to say, they were EL's-*DEFINED*, they had definition for they represented the upper limit of Physical Organism Awareness (they were expressing themselves in organic, physical form on the Earth! When they entered the Theta Universe they lost their definition, they were no longer defined, so the EL-DERS became, simply, "El's".

What is a ninety degree phase shift? Frankly, I do not know. However, it may have some connection with the crossing of light lines of force. T in the English alphabet comes through the Latin from the Greek (tau), which took it from the Phoenician (Hebrew taw). T is the symbol for T-IME. If we take our English T from Time, and relate it to the Greek Tau and from there relate it to the Tau Cross of antiquity and then place two of these crosses on top of each other (or four 'L's' or ninety degree angles joined together) we arrive at a simple cross symbolic of the crossing of light lines of energy! Is this just a part of the secret of the "El's"? Do we find the letter T in Time because it is the symbol of the achievement of a timeless state? Also, the number four stands for the Four Great Primary Forces, the Creative Forces of the Universe emanating from the Creator. Our formula, then, is something like this:

4 'L's' (90° angles): = ✚ when joined together,

2 opposing T's or double Tau's: ╤ when joined together,

1 simple Greek cross: ✚ = symbol of the crossing of light lines of force. *(Timelessness?)*

Occupants of the UFOs claim that Time is nothing but a *magnetic field*. Therefore, the crossing of light lines of force or energy may be definitely

47

TRAVELING THE PATH BACK TO THE ROAD IN THE SKY

connected with the Theta Universe or the conquest of MEST.

Now let us look at some other very simple symbols:

(1.) | = First Cause   }

(2.) L = Extension} LIFE

(3.) O = Infinity   }

Symbol No. 1 represents the Cyclopeans when they were ELDERS (with definition); Symbol No. 2 represents the same beings when they became L's ("El's"), or extended into the Theta Universe; Symbol No. 3 represents that ahead of the "El's" or the ninth level or Energy Universe (Infinity).

Now, let us do some simple addition with the separate symbols:

| : First Cause (Beasthood) + — : Extension (Angelhood, or is it *angle*hood?) + O : Infinity (Christhood, Godhood) = Å.

We find that our formula leads us to one of the oldest symbols known to the Earth, the *Circle* Cross. First Cause added to Extension and then added to Infinity gives us a crucial point at the centre of our Circle Cross. Remember, above, we had the Double Taus joined to give us a simple cross (light lines of force), and now if we add the Circle of Infinity we find a very appropriate symbol for the eventual entry of the Cyclopean Race into the Energy Universe or level nine.

An even more startling comparison is realized when we find that the symbol for T in the Minoan or Cretan language is: ¢q or: Å. We also realize that the Circle Cross is appropriate, indeed, as a symbol for level nine, for it is the *ninth* letter of both the Phoenician and the Greek alphabets. Phoenician: Å; Greek: Å or:

⊙

The above ideas are only guesses, but did the "El's" escape the magnetic field they were expressing themselves in with physical form by somehow utilizing light lines of force?

In a further study of the two words: ELDER RACE, we come up with a most interesting deduction. Remember, the word EL-DERS applies to the Cyclopeans before they entered the Theta Universe and became simply: "El's". ELDER RACE can also be written : L-DR-RAYS. Since the "El's" were frequency beings operating according to certain *rays,* we can easily see how rays became *race.* Now let us go a step further and break down the letters of L-DR-RAYS (Elder Race).

L=Light DR=Darkness R = Radiation A = Absorption Y=(Symbol of kind of action taking place) S = (The same as Y, only standing for Phase)

Light and Darkness are *Primary Polarity* and Radiation and Absorption are *Secondary Polarity* (whose action we sense as color or hue). Y and S are understood as symbols of the kind of action taking place if we place these letters on their sides. The formula then is:

```
L —  /    R    ~
     \    A
```

```
Light —   /   Radiation   ~ Phase (motion)
          \   Absorption
```

Y shows the action of Light (Radiant Energy) upon the organs of vision enabling them to sense color or hue through Radiation and Absorption. S shows the Phase or Motion which can easily stand for the Phase Shift of the Cyclopeans. Also, this can easily mean that L-DR-RAYS were Color, Hue, or Ray Beings. I believe there is some connection here with the word HU-MAN, for it can also be: *HUE*-Man. Of course, the Cyclopeans were not Hu-men which means: Tiger-Men and applies to hu-man-ity on Earth today. But the connection with Hue-men and Color-Men is most interesting. Furthermore, we find in the study of languages that H oftentimes was written like a Y:

Sinaitic Script: H = ⌄ ⌄

Thamudene: H = Y

TRAVELING THE PATH BACK TO THE ROAD IN THE SKY

Saftaic : H =

Abyssinian : H =

Therefore, the letter Y in L-DR-RAYS (our formula above), can take on the value of H (Theta) or Eight, and this symbolizes the Cyclopean entry into the Thought Universe. Also, Beings can be: Be-in-g's, or: Be-in-gravity.

Orin T. Lewis of Long Beach, California, received an interesting communication some years ago, and we give it here merely because it may have something to do with the "El's".

We are not of the world you are in. We are in a different type of place. We are in one of many other *streams of time.* The opposite polarity of Cg og // B $_{14.}$ This is the way you would write it in your letters. It means that there will be an event in the past which has happened in the future and you will meet it coming the other way, but we know it now. C is Contra, g is moving time, // is the operation of a non-time factor, *og* is non-moving time, and B is the other term for a known time which in your case is one of 14. This is the time of the great awakening and its Symbol is B. There are other times now in motion (magnetic fields?) which were begun by the great opening when the old world was again tipped.

This may be the time of the *great awakening,* but at this point I am thoroughly confused. How about you? Anyway, if you will study the simple symbols given above you will come away with some interesting answers in connection with the great Time-Spanners or "El's". If you don't come up with anything, remember, this is a 'once upon a *time'* tale!

Many words today have been derived from the name (symbol) of the most ancient 'El' Race. You only need to look in your dictionary to discover this truth. Read the meaning of the following words with the "El's" and their achievements in mind and you will be quite surprised:

TRAVELING THE PATH BACK TO THE ROAD IN THE SKY

ELaborate

Wrought out with great care; Studied; painstaking.

ELan

(French *éloncer* : to dart, hurl, rush forth) Ardour; eagerness for action; dash.

ELan vital

Literally, vital living force (French). In Bergsonian philosophy it is the creative force within an organism which is able to build physical form and to produce growth and necessary or desirable adaptations.

Elapse

To slip or glide away; to pass, as time.

ELastic:

Capable of being readily stretched, expanded, flexible, yielding, accommodating, readily recovering from depression oi exhaustion.

ELate

Lifted up or elevated, to put in high spirits, brought out, raised exalted.

ELated

Exalted in spirit, exultant.

ELd

Age, esp. old age. (Archaic: old times: antiquity); Derived from , ald, eald, old.

Elder

Older; of the greater age or of earlier birth; senior, elder times aged person.

ELdest

Oldest.

ELdritch

Weird, uncanny, unearthly (Scotch).

TRAVELING THE PATH BACK TO THE ROAD IN THE SKY

ELeatic

(Pertaining to ELea, an ancient city). Designating a school of Greek philosophers founded by Xenophanes of Colophon who resided in Elea. Doctrines are developments of the conception of the universal unity of being. (Unreality of motion or change).

ELect

Picked out, chosen, select or choice; chosen by God for eternal life, to select for divine mercy or favor, esp. for salvation.

ELection

The choice by God of individuals, as for a particular work, or salvation or eternal life.

ELective

Appointed, bestowed, choosing.

ELector

One who elects or may elect, or has the right of choice.

ELectra complex

The Oedipus complex in females; so called because of Electra's love for her father.

ELectric

Pertaining to electricity; consisting of, containing, producing, derived from, or produced or operated by, electricity. Electrifying; thrilling, stirring.

ELectron

The most elementary charge of negative electricity.

ELectrum

An amber-coloured alloy of gold and silver known to the ancients.

ELegance

Elegant quality, refinement.

TRAVELING THE PATH BACK TO THE ROAD IN THE SKY

ELegant

Excellent, fine, superior.

ELegy

A poem of lamentation for the dead.

ELement

One of the simple substances or principles (fire, air, water, and earth) formerly believed to compose the physical universe.

ELementary

Pertaining to, or treating of, the elements or first principles of anything; rudimental.

ELephantine

Like the elephant; hence, huge; ponderous.

ELeusinian mysteries

Religious mysteries at ELeusis, in ancient Attica, in worship of Demeter and Persephone.

Elevate

To lift up to a higher position; to raise; to exalt; ennoble.

ELevation

Loftiness; grandeur or dignity; nobleness.

Eleven

A cardinal number, ten plus one.

ELeventh hour

The last possible hour for doing something.

ELf

One of a class of imaginary beings, esp. from mountainous regions, with magical powers, given to capricious interference in human affairs.

ELicit

To draw or bring out or forth.

TRAVELING THE PATH BACK TO THE ROAD IN THE SKY

ELigible

Worthy of choice; desirable.

Eliminate

To get rid of; expel; remove; exclude.

ELite

The choice or best part of, as a body or class of persons.

ELixir

An alchemic preparation for transmuting base metals into gold, or for prolonging life : *elixir vitae,* or elixir of life. The refined spirit; quintessence.

ELl

An extension to a building, usually at right angles to one end.

ELl

A measure of length, now little used, varying in different countries: in England and her colonies equal to 45 inches, and the old Dutch or Flemish ell is 27 inches.

ELocution

Style or manner of speaking or reading in public.

ELohim (Sometimes El or Elah),

God, or gods; a term used in the Hebrew Scriptures. The first of the three primary names of Deity, a uni-plural noun formed from El, strength, or the strong one, and Alah, to swear or bind oneself by an oath, so implying faithfulness. Elohim=Strong One.

ELoign

To remove afar off; to convey to a distance, or to conceal.

ELongate

To draw out to greater length; lengthen; extend.

ELope

To run away, escape.

TRAVELING THE PATH BACK TO THE ROAD IN THE SKY

ELoquent

Movingly expressive.

ELse

Taking the place of, or different from.

ELsewhere

Somewhere else; in or to some other place.

ELucidate

To make lucid or clear; throw light upon.

ELude

To avoid or escape by dexterity or artifice.

ELul

The twelfth month of the year in the Jewish calendar.

ELusion

Act of eluding, evasion, clever escape.

ELusive

Hard to express or define; eluding clear perception or complete mental grasp.

ELutriate

To purify by washing and straining or decanting.

ELysian

Blissful; delightful.

ELysium: (*Also* Elysian Fields).

The place where the good dwelt after death, located in the Western Ocean or in the lower world. Abode or state of ideal delight and happiness; paradise.

Also, we find many names in the Bible using the EL (Eli; Elijah; Elias; Elisha; Elisheba; Elishua; Elizur, etc.). The word for THE (masculine) in Spanish and other languages is: EL. The word: OLD came from the more ancient word: ELD (therefore, we can see where we derived OLDER from ELDER or,

TRAVELING THE PATH BACK TO THE ROAD IN THE SKY

in connection with the Cyclopeans, the *Elder* Race was the *Older* Race). In Electra's love for her father we see the "El's" union with the father in the eventual entry into the Energy Universe (Infinity). It is curious to note that ELL, the measure of length, adds up to a 9 whether we take the English 45 inches or the Dutch 27 inches.

An Elohist is the writer (or writers) of one of the major strands or sources of the Hexateuch in which God is characteristically referred to as Elohim instead of Yahweh or Jehovah. When we read the Old Testament we must keep in mind that Elohim, Yahweh and Jehovah are not three names for the one God, but are actually three distinct Beings. Elohim is the most ancient name for God after El. Yahweh was a tribal god of the ancient Hebrews and is quite different from the Christian Jehovah.

We find our EL again in the strange words of Jesus Christ upon the cross (Eloi) in Mark xv:34.

There are also many words that begin with L that are significant, such as: Life; Love; Live; Levitate (to rise or float in the air by reason of lightness, or, now usually, through some alleged supernormal power that overcomes gravity); and Leviathan (something huge and formidable of its kind). Of course, there are many, many more examples, but those listed will give you some idea how the "El's" and their Phase Shift to Timelessness have influenced everything about us today.

Several years ago, Master Kuthumi (Koot Hoomi Lal Singh) of India made a most interesting statement that refers directly to the "El's".

Over the planet (Earth) stands the great Presence of the Beloved Elohim, *Cyclopea.* His radiation covers the entire Earth.

Also, it has been said that 'in the atmosphere above the planet stands the Elohim, *Hercules,* who represents Cosmic Force and Fire'.

At a strange place called Huayti, about forty kilometers from Arequipa, Peru, there is a great ruin of unknown origin, but there is no question that it was built by a race far older than the Incas. On a granite rock near the ruin we find petroglyphs that unquestionably refer to the 'El' Race. (See Fig. 1).

TRAVELING THE PATH BACK TO THE ROAD IN THE SKY

Figure 1

Startling as it is, we find a member of the 'El' Race or a Cyclopean standing on top of a great bird. He wears some sort of a short tunic. It is obvious that this Being is highly developed for he stands on top of the ancient and sacred sign for one of the Four Great Primary Forces (The Builder), and we can see that this sign is really in the form of an L or a 90° angle (Shaded). Since the 'El' stands on top of the great bird we know that he has conquered MEST or that he has become a master of gravity and levitation. His great head contains only one eye—a round one directly in the centre—therefore, we know he is a Cyclops. (This also symbolizes the 'Third Eye' of a great Spiritual Being). He wears a nimbus of radiant light containing Four Rays. (Made up of eight lines.) This symbolizes the fact that the "El's" conquered the Four Conditions of Matter-Energy-Space-Time, and also the fact that they were in perfect harmony with the Four Great Primary Forces of Creation. Both of the arms of the 'El' are extended. The right arm is receiving Cosmic Energy from space, and the left arm is directing this energy to various places. This symbolizes the fact that the "El's" achieved the Power of Creative Thought, for the figure is 'pulling in' Cosmic Energy with one hand and molding it into various forms with the other hand. The rectangle is an ancient symbol of the planet Earth ("To the Four Corners of the Earth')

TRAVELING THE PATH BACK TO THE ROAD IN THE SKY

and here we find it surrounded by *eight* rays. In its centre is the *eighth* letter of the Phoenician and Greek alphabets. The eight rays and the eighth letter stand for the entry of the "El's" into the Thought or Theta (8) Universe. The fact the eighth letter is in the centre of the Earth indicates the underground cities of the "El's" where they went through their 90° Phase Shift. The eight outflowing rays indicate the fact that the "El's" left the Earth planet to enter a Timeless condition. You will notice that one of the rays is forked like the letter Y. This indicates that the next achievement is the entry into the ninth level or the Energy Universe (Infinity). Remember, also, we showed that, in many languages, H oftentimes was written like a Y, so we have the value of *eight again (8* itself is a symbol of infinity.) There are also two lines formed like an S—this is the Motion which stands for the Phase Shift of the "El's". And finally, we find two symbols of the Circle Cross, the *Ninth* letter of the Phoenician and the Greek alphabets. Of course, this indicates the *ninth* level or The Energy Universe.

This ancient engraving upon the granite rock is in the very same area where the "El's" had their underground empire. The city of Arequipa, Peru, is very close to Lago de Titicaca and evidently some Pre-Inca Race had racial memory of the Cyclopeans and therefore made the record in stone.

Here, then, is the story of the mighty "El's". They have pointed the way for hu-man-ity on the Earth, but no one on this planet will ever become an 'El', simply because we do not belong to the Cyclopean (Elder) Race. However, in order to fulfill our proper destiny in the Divine Scheme of things we must also conquer Matter-Energy-Space and Time. The present plan of the Universal Hierarchy is as follows :

The production of a subjective synthesis in hu-man-ity and of a telepathic interplay which will eventually *annihilate Time.*

We will not become "El's" but we will follow the 'gods' through the 'womb of Time' to be unfettered and free: for this we were created, for this we live, and for this we shall be ELevated to beyond the stars.

The amaranthine crystalline world of the great Time-Spanners lies imperishable, incessant and ceaseless beneath our feet as perfect as it was the day after the world was made'—the 'day' they arrived on the first *road in the sky* following the great cycles of Time. Now that *road* for them has become an unending radiance that draws them out eternally beyond galactic space, beyond the ancient starways, for them there is no night and there is no day, there are no stars, no earth, no crime, no check, no bad nor good, no change, no *Time.*

As we follow, traveling the *road* of many forgotten *yesterdays,* may our aspirations be whipped by the winds of Timeless lands from whence comes the forbidden secret of the "El's".

[1] See Genesis vi:2, and the chapter entitled The Migrants, in *Other Tongues—Other Flesh*, by Dr. Williamson.

[2] See James Churchward's *The Lost Continents of Mu.* (Neville Spearman).—*Editor.*

TRAVELING THE PATH BACK TO THE ROAD IN THE SKY

LAST OF THE SACRED FORESTS

'In the high places of our land, dwelt the Giant Gods *in the days of our ancient fathers.'* (Huanca Indian legend of Peru, South America.)

'I WAS in a great subterranean hall—it appeared as though it had been hewn by the hands of a colossus—there were deep niches in the ancient walls which contained scrolls and scripts beyond count. I was alone, there was no sound. Over everything hung the atmosphere and odor of hoary age—how remote in the past I do not know! I had been to this chamber before many times, but I desired to know the name of this forgotten depository of the ancient ones. Suddenly, for the first time, I heard a voice within me say "Masma, Masma, Masma!" That this place was real, I was certain, and that it held a key to the mysteries of the world!'

The year was 1905, the place was the city of Andahuaylas, Peru, and the man was Pedro Astete. His description of a tomb-like place above comes from his now famous *Dream of Masma* known in Peru as *El Sueño de Masma*.

Pedro Astete was born in Lima, Peru, November 7, 1871. He studied in New York, Madrid, and traveled to various parts of the world to pursue his greatest interest—'Numbers, Signs, and Letters' of the ancient and secret science. Any mystery, large or small, was his special delight. He was a very colorful personality and lived in an equally colorful place in the old house of 'La Calle de Polvos Azules', or 'Street of the Blue Dust', a place he almost never left after his years of traveling were over. A great balcony looked out over the Rio Rimac that now passes close behind the Presidential Palace in Lima. Here he had a magnificent view of the lofty Andes where, thousands of years ago, a race of great intelligence left footsteps in Time.

Astete was a great scientist who, like many before him, was not appreciated during his lifetime. He died in Lima, January 5, 1940. He wrote volumes of information on the lost and ancient science, but little has been published.

Dr. Daniel Ruzo, a friend of Pedro Astete, and a well-known researcher of Peru, has published one of his books *(Los Signos Develación del Lenguaje de los Símbolos,* 1953). Dr. Ruzo believes Astete experienced far more than a dream; he feels certain that this man was teleported or projected to an actual location beneath the surface of the Earth.

Dr. Ruzo used the word 'Masma' as a key to attempt to locate the area in the 'vision' of his friend Astete. Here is where one really becomes confused, because all over South America there exists a great ancient collection of many races representing many migrations. It is nearly impossible to separate them, classify them, and to study them. For instance, the only 'Masma' in Peru is a tiny Quechua Indian village north of Jauja in the Departamento de Junin. Could there possibly be a connection? It still is not known, although there is something most curious about the name of the village: Masma. Masma is the seventeenth Patriarch in the Bible after Noah. What possible connection can there be between a character out of Holy Scripture, a 'dream' of a Peruvian in 1905, and a tiny, forgotten, almost deserted Indian village? I do not know, but there are many Hebrew place-names in Peru and other parts of the Continent. This is only one unexplained mystery, and South America apparently is the 'Mother of Mysteries'; she literally abounds in them. For example, is *Ophir* of the Bible really Peru, and is *Yectan* really Yucatan, Mexico? Some of these questions I hope to answer soon. I think we will discover that many of the Old Testament Bible characters also represent races and lands.

Perhaps the word 'Masma' in Astete's 'dream' has nothing to do with known places, but represents something else. Because of the strange figures seen from the air and on the ground near the hills of San Cristobal (not far from Lima) on the coast of Peru, Dr. Ruzo believes the subterranean depository may be there. Fantastic monoliths are in the mountains of this area, although it is difficult to study them now because of their ruined state due to thousands upon thousands of years of erosion.

Dr. Ruzo continued to search for the elusive 'Library of the Great Ones'. Finally, in 1952, he made a discovery high in the Andes that some day will place his name beside the immortals of exploration. Its importance is so overwhelming he might just as well have discovered the Great Pyramid at

TRAVELING THE PATH BACK TO THE ROAD IN THE SKY

Gizeh. For twenty-five years Dr. Ruzo had explored the mountains and the coast of his country to study and photograph giant stone figures made by a vanished race. These figures, isolated and partially destroyed, were not considered important, and sufficient proof was lacking.

In 1952, Dr. Ruzo heard about a remarkable monolithic carving that existed high on a plateau overlooking the village of San Pedro de Casta. This plateau is called 'Marcahuasi'. It is three kilometers long by one kilometer wide and is located between the Santa Eulalia and the Rimac Valleys. San Pedro de Casta is 9,800 feet above sea level and the plateau itself is a little over 12,000 feet.

The remarkable monolithic carving that Dr. Ruzo heard about is undoubtedly the most important figure on the plateau. (See Figure 2).

Figure 2

It faces Lake Shotoc and is over twenty-five meters in height. The oldest name Dr. Ruzo can find for this enormous carved head, is 'Peca-Gasha' or 'the head of the narrow pass'. Undoubtedly, this is not the original name, but is used by the natives of the area at the present time. Also, Dr. Ruzo has photographed this head over three hundred times at different times of the year and from different angles. At least sixteen anthropomorphic figures are carved on the 'Peca-Gasha' and they apparently represent several different races.

In the early part of 1957, I met and talked with Dr. Ruzo at his home near Lima, Peru, and I became convinced that the evidence he had accumulated through the years of research was indisputable. Through the kindness of this fine man, arrangements were made so that my expeditionary party, then working in Peru, might visit the fabulous plateau.

On June 7, 1957, we made our way on foot and on horseback over tortuous Andean trails to San Pedro de Casta and from there on up and up and up to the plateau itself. The native people of the village far below, descen-

TRAVELING THE PATH BACK TO THE ROAD IN THE SKY

dants of the Huanca Indians, fear the plateau because they say it is an ancient place of 'magicians', 'wizards', or 'Giant Gods'. Their ancestors, the Huancas, held their sacred rituals of 'Huari' at Marcahuasi. The word *huari* in the Quechua language means: giant or strong. Formerly, the 'Huarinas' (virgins in the worship of the god Huari) danced at the monolithic altars of Marcahuasi, casting their shadows upon stone figures carved in the days when the Earth was young. There are two altars that must have been used. One of these is now called 'Mayoralas'. It is located over a hundred meters above an abyss, and the gigantic stones which form it face the sunset. The modern name of 'Mayoralas' is one applied to the maidens that sing and dance in the ritual festivals during the first week in October every year far below in San Pedro de Casta. The ancient name for the virgins was 'Taquet' ('to sing' in Quechua) and this is also another name for the stone altar whose stones apparently were carved to represent giant creatures in the act of singing. The figures are placed in such a way that special acoustic effects are permitted. This was part of the plan of the ancient builders who wanted the religious chants to be amplified.

The other altar of importance is called 'Cancaucho' and faces the sunrise. It is so gigantic it could hold a large modern army in front of it. On a little hill near this altar there is a king or priest sitting on a throne with his hands folded in prayer.

Figure 3 below shows 'Cancaucho' with its weird, snow-white facing.

TRAVELING THE PATH BACK TO THE ROAD IN THE SKY

Figure 4 is the author exploring the surrounding area. (The altar is in the right background.)

Why the festivals are no longer held at Marcahuasi is not known, unless it is because of the fear of the place in general. Formerly, the 'Huarinas' were virgins; now the natives have dispensed with that requirement. Men of the village below say that the first night of the ritual in October is secret, and no white man may ever witness its dances or hear its strange songs, performed in hidden valleys in the surrounding hills. The second day the fiesta is held in town, and the local Catholic priest officiates, since it now has all the appearances of a Christian celebration, although it is, in reality, a ritual to the worship and adoration of 'Huari', the most ancient of all gods in this area. More of him later on.

We were greeted by all kinds of friendly people in San Pedro de Casta who followed us up to the plateau. There were women in curious hats and bright attire, naked, dusty children, teachers from the local school, and important politicians.

Figure 5 shows some of our friends with their families.

TRAVELING THE PATH BACK TO THE ROAD IN THE SKY

Figure 6 is the great 'PecaGasha' itself with a swarm of friends at its base. This will give you an idea how colossal it really is.

The entire plateau is covered by a coarse, dry vegetation and is also covered by fog most of the time during seven months of the year. However, between May and September the sun turns it into a delightful place, although the nights and early mornings are very cold.

The first thing that caught my eye after I was made speechless with the sight of the 'Peca-Gasha', was a cement block with a bronze plaque. It read:

ASOCIACION PERUANA DE ASTRONOMIA

MARCAHUASI:

LAT : 11° 46 40, 9 S

LONG: 76° 35 26, 3 W.

CAP. J. SAMANEZ C.25 IV 1954

The Peruvian Association of Astronomy determined the magnetic declination of the plateau and an aerial photograph was taken which is now in the archives of the Peruvian Air Ministry. Dr. Ruzo has been studying the relationship of the symbols represented in all the stone figures and the mathematical relationship among the figures themselves. There is no question that the position of the sculptures on the plateau and surrounding the little lakes on top indicates a general pre-established plan of the ancient priests and master builders. At the four cardinal points of the plateau we find the most outstanding and important carved figures.

I spent many days on horseback, traveling over the entire area of Marcahuasi. I can give you here only a little of what I saw, for to really appreciate and be thrilled by the plateau, you must see it for yourself—words are inadequate. Ouspensky, in writing of the Sphinx of Egypt, said:

"... it had seemed to me that it would be necessary to approach it with the full equipment of a knowledge different from ours, with some new form of perception, some special kind of mathematics..."

If Ouspensky had ever seen Marcahuasi, he would have immediately realized that his words were even more fitting for Peru than they were for Egypt, for we must also approach the strange monoliths of the plateau with a 'knowledge different from ours... a new form of perception... a special kind of mathematics.' If we don't, we are liable to go mad.

There are magnificent artificial lake systems and large dams and canals. On the stones rising from the ancient water level are carved figures that once cast curious shadows on the surfaces of sacred lakes. Strangely enough, there is a small lake on the plateau today called 'Black Lagoon', and out of its centre rises the perfectly carved head of a scaly dinosaur-like monster as if it were just breaking the surface, resting its enormous, ponderous body on the bottom.

After studying hundreds of carvings on the plateau, Dr. Ruzo reached a startling conclusion. But the evidence was all there. Gigantic altars that could accommodate only very large life forms. How large? At least *twelve* feet tall. Therefore, Ruzo believes Marcahuasi holds important keys to the world's ancient mysteries—it is possibly the last 'Sacred Forest' in such a state of preservation. One of the great 'Sacred Forests' of whispered antiquity where the 'gods' met in council to decide the fate of the world.

When you view the figures on the plateau you feel you are looking at some long-forgotten museum of the 'Giant Gods', for it seems that everything ever created is represented here. There are all kinds of great birds and animals from lions and elephants to camels and penguins—all of which never existed in South America.

Figure 7, 'The Lion',

TRAVELING THE PATH BACK TO THE ROAD IN THE SKY

And **Figure 8**, 'The Group of Elephants'.) In Figure No. 8 you will find the elephants (one going away from you and others leaning against him) in the centre of the photograph. To the extreme left you will notice several stone burial 'chulpas' (tombs) of the Incas.

There are countless human faces representing all the races of mankind. (See Fig. No. 9, which is called 'La Negrita', the colored woman.) Many great stone heads bear strong resemblance to those found on Easter Island in the Pacific Ocean, for they possess the same features with the stone hats and all that the Island statues are famous for. There is another curious figure exactly like Easter Island representations. It is a great carving of a headless man with a gigantic bird head attached to the end of his spine.

TRAVELING THE PATH BACK TO THE ROAD IN THE SKY

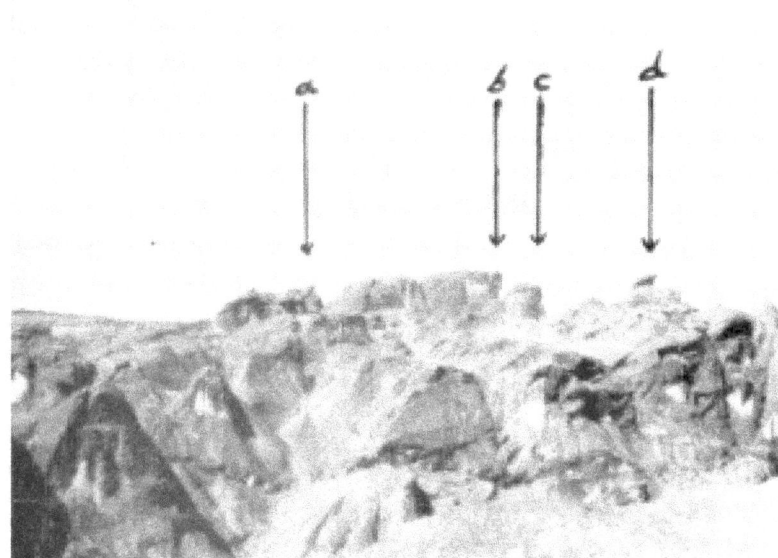

10

Obviously, ancient religions are represented, for there are many sphinxes in evidence. (See **Figure 10**, and look at the photograph with a magnifying glass. *a.* is called 'The Warrior's Helmet'; *b.* is called 'Elephant Head'; *c.* is a pair of magnificent sphinxes that appear to be Grecian, for they have the faces of women; and *d.* looks like a great 'Toad'.)

11

Figure 11 also gives you a close-up view of the same great 'Warrior's Helmet'.

Thoueris (Ta-urt), the Egyptian goddess represented as a hippopotamus, was supposed by priests at Thebes, where she was worshipped as Apet, to have given birth to Osiris. She is always shown leaning on an amulet which represented the blood of Isis and is similar in shape to the *crux ansata,* the Egyptian ankh, sacred emblem of Eternal Life.

12

See **Figure 12** for the Marcahuasi 'Thoueris'

TRAVELING THE PATH BACK TO THE ROAD IN THE SKY

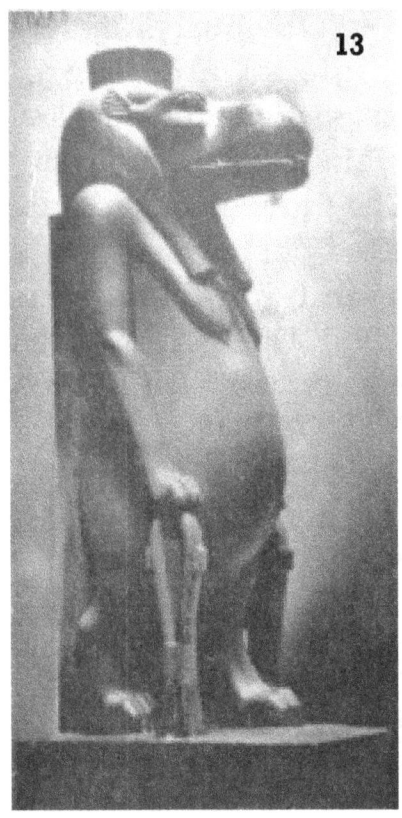

Figure 13 is the Egyptian Thoueris in the Cairo Museum). When the light is just right, the typical headgear, features, arm, and even the sacred amulet are plainly visible on the Marcahuasi goddess.

Figure 14 is of 'The Turtle'. This great monolith looks out towards the west, and one gets a magnificent view of the Pacific Ocean from this point. This great figure has been 'guarding the way' for thousands of years, long before the Incas were ever heard of, long before Pizarro plundered an Empire, long before you and I  knew existence. What tales he could tell if he could but talk to us!

TRAVELING THE PATH BACK TO THE ROAD IN THE SKY

Figure 15 is of a strange carved face in front of the 'Cancaucho' Altar.

When we get a side view of this face **(See Figure 16)** a most unusual effect is discovered. There are really two faces in one. If you look at the front of the carving only, you will see the face of an Old Patriarch, kind and wise, but, if you look at the whole figure and view the great depression near the top as an eye, you find you have the opposite, a hideous and sinister face, a 'prince of devils!'

TRAVELING THE PATH BACK TO THE ROAD IN THE SKY

Figure 17 is called simply, 'The Lovers', since we find two figures locked in a tight embrace and kissing.

Some of the carvings of Marcahuasi appear to be natural at first instead of artificial. That is, they could be the weird result of erosion over thousands of years and not man made. There are several reasons why they appear this way on first study. First of all, if the ancients wanted to portray a man in stone, they wouldn't choose a group of stones that had more the appearance of a dog or bird, etc. They would first find the rocks that in a general, rough way had the outline of what they desired in the final product.

Natural igneous rock formations of crystalline texture (granite; diorite) would have their original shapes roughly adapted by having only one feature carved on them; others would be carved so that from different angles of observation, three or more distinct figures could be seen. Now, after thousands of years of destructive action caused by erosion (for the stones are now profoundly weathered) the features added by the builders have almost disappeared, and the stones have nearly reverted to their original appearance of being nothing but 'stones'.

Therefore, we have two main reasons why several 'experts' have called the discovery at Marcahuasi "Ruzo's Folly"! They don't realize that the figures appear natural—of course, they have only studied photographs of the area since they wouldn't take the time to examine the evidence first hand—because the ancients chose those formations that had the original outlines of what they desired to create. This gave the entire piece of art the appearance of having 'grown up out of the ground'. They only depended on their sculptural techniques when it was absolutely necessary to complete the figure so that it would be easily recognizable. The second reason is that the so-called 'authorities' do not realize the fantastic age of the images and therefore don't take into account the fact that erosion has almost destroyed that which intelligent beings carved in the rock formations. The ancients wanted everything to remain as *natural* as possible, for they felt they could not improve on that which the Creator had brought into existence. How much better our world would be if we had the same feelings today.

Dr. M. K. Jessup, former astronomer at the University of Michigan and explorer of note (Mexico and Peru) has informed me that the amount of time necessary to produce such erosion in the great carved figures is staggering. He says at least 100,000 years would be required and more likely 1,000,000. Here, then, is perhaps one of the great clues to the identity of the designers and builders of the 'Sacred Forest'. Who could have possibly constructed these figures at such an early date?

The ancients built enormous stone platforms for the express purpose of viewing their creations—several of these have been located recently on the plateau. The figures were never meant to be seen from all angles at once. The builders desired that only a section of each group be viewed at one time. Therefore, they constructed observation platforms that fixed the point of view. So ingenious and inventive were the designers, so adroit at their labor, that they were able to perform miracles on the plateau by the clever utilization of light and shadow falling upon the completed figures and their surroundings.

TRAVELING THE PATH BACK TO THE ROAD IN THE SKY

Many of the monoliths were never meant to be observed except during certain, fixed hours of the day, or of the month. Others were meant to be observed the entire year through and still others require an extreme angle of sunlight—or moonlight—to be visible and meaningful at all. Yes, many of the images only can be appreciated in the twilight when no sunlight falls upon their surfaces. Many carvings were meant to be purely solstitial in that they appear only at a solstice in June or December of each year.

Several of the larger groupings of figures are definitely related to each other, since they stand in the four cardinal directions of the plateau, and since it is possible to draw straight lines connecting three or more points of importance. Many of these lines, if lengthened, indicate the rising or setting of the sun.

Perhaps the most predominant feature in the figures, and one which definitely proves sculpturing by an intelligence, is the treatment of the eye formation. Many of the statues have three or even four eyes, but from a distance they present only two eyes, no matter what angle you observe them from.

In the centre of one group of figures, one can observe the great reclining form of a very old man. He is attended by two women who stand over him. Also, there appear to be several animal forms which could easily represent the Four Elements of the ancients. Dr. Ruzo discovered something about these particular figures that makes us pause in amazement at the intelligence of the designers. When a photograph of the figure of the old man is taken, and the negative is projected on a screen, you see the face of a handsome young man with hair falling over his forehead, and he looks at you with a virile, proud and noble expression. How could the ancients portray a senile and ugly old man and know that a photograph taken thousands of years later would change him into a youthful creature in the bloom of his manhood? This I call the mystery of the 'Methuselah of Marcahuasi'!

Originally, there must have been many petroglyphs and pictographs at Marcahuasi but, unfortunately, these have almost all been erased by the effects of time. However, when the light of the sun strikes some of them at a certain angle, five and six pointed stars, circles, triangles and rectangles show up. Others can only be viewed in very subdued light.

There is one pictograph painted on the neck of the giant 'Peca-Gasha' that has been well preserved, due to its location under the protruding chin of the figure. With a make-shift ladder I climbed to this point to study the design in detail. It is made in a strange way—small black dots have been used to form the lines of the design. (See Fig. No. 18.)

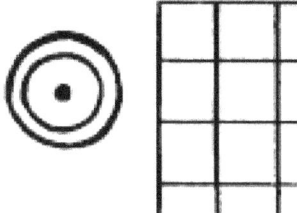

Figure 18

The larger square contains sixteen smaller squares, and it is flanked by two circles. Each of these circles has another circle within it and in the centre a dot. All lines of the design are in black, except the second line within each circle which is in yellow. This square of sixteen smaller squares has been observed on rock formations throughout the world, and I have even observed it in my explorations in the Mohave Desert of the State of California in the United States. One possible clue to the meaning of this pictograph may be found in the fact that the two circle designs are the same as the ninth letter of the Greek alphabet.

Dr. Ruzo says of this simple drawing: 'This squared design, a two dimensional space sub-divided by crosses repeated at regular intervals, is the central figure of Pedro Astete's work, *Los Signos*'. What a strange story begins to unfold! Astete 'dreams' of a fabulous depository of an ancient race in 1905 and in his research comes up with the idea that all symbolism or symbols of the past, present and, of course, future can be traced to the basic design of the 'Sixteen Squares'. Then, in 1952, forty-seven years after his 'dream' and twelve years after his death, his friend finds the 'Sixteen Squares' exactly reproduced on the greatest stone carving of a hitherto scientifically unknown plateau of the High Andes. What is the answer? As they would say in Peru: 'Quien sabe, señor?' But it seems most likely that Astete—and even Ruzo, etc.—was guided in his work by an unseen intelligence. Could this possibly have been at the direction of the vanished 'El' Race? We will look at the possibilities a little later on, staggering as they may be.

Figure 19

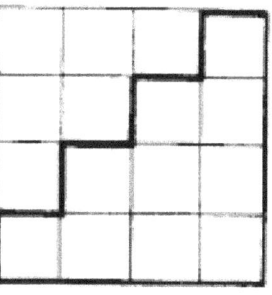

The design of the 'Squares' is undoubtedly the highest symbol of a very ancient mythology : it was placed on the heads of the Egyptian gods, it was engraved on important monuments the world over, and it is found in a very ancient monolithic ruin near Cuzco, Peru, former

TRAVELING THE PATH BACK TO THE ROAD IN THE SKY

capital of the Inca Empire. It should be pointed out that the well-known 'Stair-Step' design or design of 'Evolution' found in all symbolism-especially in Mexico-is only a secondary symbol of the 'Sixteen Squares' being only one of the possible symbolic expressions within the 'Squares'. (See Fig. No. 19.)

Figure No. 19 clearly shows us that we have four steps to climb to reach the top. Does this 'top' symbolize the conquest of the four conditions, MEST, or the harmonization of an individual with the Four Great Primary Forces? It is obvious that the 'Stair-Step' design, long thought to be one of the very earliest symbols on Earth, is not as old as the 'Sixteen Squares' from which it must have been derived.

Also, at Marcahuasi, near one of the strange altars that must have accommodated a creature at least twelve feet tall, due to the distance from the head rest to the foot position on top of the altar, we find another symbol. (See Fig. No. 20.) The four squares within a larger square again symbolize the Four Great Primary Forces working also within the Earth.

Fig. No. 20

Figure 20

Besides geometric designs, unusual glyphs or characters have been discovered on the plateau. (See Fig. No. 21.) One is very similar to the early Chinese characters SAI: to walk slowly; and PIEN: to separate. Most of these characters seem to be grouped around what may be tombs. Great stone slabs have giant faces carved on top of them, and these may be the faces of those buried in the crypts. However, these may be what is known as 'false tombs'.

Figure 21

Most of the people today at San Pedro de Casta are not even aware of the existence of such fabulous figures high above them on the plateau. However, there are some legends, and one of them says that during a certain ancient period the great sorcerers and healers gathered together on the plateau and that there is a rock now which represents each one who attended the council. Another story tells of the 'Caris', the

hard-working men, and the 'Quellas', the idle, lazy men. The people believe that there are stone images of these men on the plateau. When Dr. Ruzo first went to Marcahuasi he located stone figures portraying these two types of men. The 'Caris' are shown with a great burden on their backs (the *aguayunco),* and the 'Quellas' are shown lying on the ground, asleep.

Cristobal de Molina says in his *Relacion de las Fábulas y Ritos de los Incas,* that, 'Tecsi Viracocha, the Incomprehensible God, came along the mountain road visiting and inspecting all the provinces to see how they had begun to multiply and to accomplish what he had ordered them. He found some rebel nations that had not fulfilled his orders, and a large part of these he turned to stone into figures of men and women, with the same dress they were wearing.' This conversion into stone took place, says the legend, at Tiahuanaco, Bolivia; Pucara; Jauja (very near Masma); Pachacamac; Cajamarca, and other places.

It is an interesting fact that the 'Incomprehensible God' is used and that in the above places today one can see giant stone figures, but, because no one understands them, they say the 'gods' turned people into stone. Yet, it may be that the 'gods' of *yesterday,* the 'Elder Race' created on the Marcahuasi plateau and elsewhere an ancient museum—a time capsule, so to speak, that depicted the future animals, the races of mankind and their religions, and the symbolism of the future world that was to follow them millions of years later! Fantastic? Yet, were they not called 'Planet Preparers' and were they not 'Incomprehensible'?

There is another story that says Tupac Inca Yupanqui, one of the great Inca Emperors, traveled to Jauja where he visited some very ancient buildings, and the people there told him these had been built by some very brave strangers who were white, very *tall,* and so invincible and valiant that only *time* could overwhelm them. Obviously these ruins were Pre-Inca if the Emperor of the Inca Empire knew nothing about them. Also, remember, Jauja is very near Masma, that strange little village that bears the name from Genesis and from Astete's 1905 'vision'. The legend says 'very tall' beings created these things and only 'time could overwhelm them'. We begin to get clues that 'overwhelm' us, too, but we must move on. Who was *tall,* and who was *overwhelmed by Time?*

The early Huancas and their conquerors, the Incas, spoke of many places in the land that had been the former homes or locations of 'magicians', wizards', and 'Giant Gods'. Legends of the 'Corisapra', or the 'Golden Beards', are widespread throughout South America. In the old records of the city of Andahuaylas, Peru, among the family names of Indians, the surname 'Corisapra' is repeated over and over again indicating a blonde and bearded people in Peru in ancient times and undoubtedly in the very area of Andahuaylas. Remember, again, that Pedro Astete had his now famous 'dream' in this same city in 1905. Is there any connection? Perhaps not, but what if tiny Andahuaylas is located over a great subterranean chamber once occupied by the 'El' Race? There are so many loose threads to bring together in this matter that it is almost impossible to concentrate on it. Surely, it could drive one literally mad? Complicated mystery upon mystery becomes a barrier to our research.

There are several reasons why the 'El's' may have had something to do with the figures of Marcahuasi. First of all, of course, there is the fantastic age of the granite formations themselves. Also, there are no house remains on the plateau which correspond to the age of the monoliths. Remember, the 'El's' lived underground. Astete saw 'scrolls' when he had his 'dream'—and the 'El's' used no written word—only tiny crystals which contained thousands of items of information. These constituted their historical records, etc., and they were 'played back' to a researcher in their 'libraries' through the use of a magnetic field that would enclose the crystal from their archives. If Astete's subterranean chamber belongs to the 'El's' then why the 'scrolls' on the shelves and in the niches? This appears to be a contradiction but may not be—only *time will* tell.

In the symbols of Marcahuasi we appear to have clues of the Cyclopeans. (See Fig. No. 18.) In the two circle designs we find the symbol of the *ninth* level or the Energy Universe (Infinity) in the *ninth* letter of the Greek alphabet. In the 'Sixteen Squares' we find 8+8=16, and we already know that the symbolism of *eight is* for the Thought or Theta Universe.

Perhaps the 'El's' didn't plan and build the great 'Forest' of Marcahuasi, but maybe it was constructed at a later date by those who retained some kind of a memory of the 'Elder Race'. This could have been through 'sensitives' of the day who tuned-in to the underground 'libraries'.

There are figures with only *one great eye* on the plateau, and the legends and traditions point to the fact that 'Giant Gods' lived there. If it wasn't the 'El's' then *who* or *what* was it? And we have more evidence than legendary evidence. For we have the mute, unbelievable altars that could accommodate nothing under twelve feet in height. I am convinced these were not sacrificial altars, but were used in temples that were both centers of religious and spiritual devotion as well as scientific laboratories.

The god 'Huari' of the Huancas was evidently a Hercules or a culture-hero of these people. Very likely he had been a giant king or being in the dim past. Like his Greek counterpart, the Huanca 'Hercules-Huari' was celebrated for strength. The *huaris,* or 'great ones', were the ancestors of the aristocrats of the tribe, and were regarded as specially favorable towards agricultural effort (perhaps because of the underground 'El' accomplishment. The 'El's' sprang from the soil into the Theta Universe, and this symbolized growing things and bountiful crops that had to come from the soil also?). The *huaris* were called the 'gods of great strength', and many libations of *chicha* (strong drink) were sacrificed to them by the priests. Ancestors were deeply revered, a memory of the 'Elder Race'?

The fact that the worship of 'Huari' and the *huaris* was widespread can be seen in the names of towns, etc., today in Peru : Huari; Huariaca; Huaribamba, etc. Memory of the Huancas is found in such place names as : Huancayo; Huanacupampa; Huanca; Huancabamba; Huancane; Huancano; Huancape; Huancapon; Huancarama; Huancaray; Huancaraylla; Huancarqui; Huanca-Sancos; Huancaspata; Huancavelica; Huancaya, and many others.

Monstrous stone figures, carved into fantastic shapes, enormous altars for giant beings, faces, signs and symbols that only become visible during certain times of the year when the sun or moonlight strikes them at the right angle, any of these things alone is quite enough to stir our sense of imagination and make us thrill to the happenings of a long forgotten *yesterday,* but there is more on Marcahuasi and about Marcahuasi that is even yet more incredible.

Something literally 'out of this world' seems to be hovering over the plateau. One night the view of the moon was beautiful and I joined several native youths who were sitting next to the great bulk of 'Peca-Gasha'. Then my ear immediately caught something I had heard before, while exploring, but because of the wind howling around the plateau and the figures, I never paid much attention to it before. Undoubtedly, the sound of the wind had drowned it out so that it was not too noticeable.

An eerie humming sound filled the cool crisp night air. I asked the

TRAVELING THE PATH BACK TO THE ROAD IN THE SKY

boys if the sound was made by crickets, and they politely informed me that there were no crickets anywhere on the plateau and there never had been—it was too high. Then I asked them if the sound was made by any animal they knew about. Again they informed me politely that the sound was not made by any known animal. I could readily see that the boys didn't want to talk about the sound, for they had been laughing and enjoying the evening until I had drawn their attention to the odd droning coming from the great carved head towering above us. Now they were quiet, and appeared most uncommunicative. I asked them more questions which they didn't answer for a long time—we all just sat there, engulfed in the steadily increasing pitch of the sound. Finally, one of the youths told me that their ancestors spoke of the sound, but said they didn't know what it was either!

I listened to it again carefully; it was so loud it could have been taperecorded on the spot. What did it really sound like? It was like a swarm of bees at a distance, yet like crickets too—much more *staccato* than bees. Then the thought struck me like a demoniac thunderbolt; of course, the strange clicking sounds of the 'El's', this is what it must have sounded like. A chill went up my spine that was not altogether caused by the coolness of the Andean night. I got up and walked over to a point where I could look down into the valley below, and I beheld a sight I shall never forget, like a 'Punch-and-Judy' show or a pantomime the shadows cast by the carved figures high up on the plateau were turning into the forms of men, animals and mythological creatures in the valley beneath me. What great race conceived these things? Here was something outside of human ability to understand—a peek into another dimension! Who carved stones so that at certain angles they would change shape and cast shadows at twilight into low valleys, so that when the moon moves across the night sky, strange and fantastic forms go through thousands of motions as if they were alive? As I turned to go to my sleeping bag, I glanced back for the last time to see a shadow-figure that looked all the world like a little hook-nosed humpback 'Punch' emerge from the rocks below. *The monoliths of Marcahuasi*—figures of another world we will never fully comprehend. The words of Ouspensky burned in my brain: '... it had seemed to me that it would be necessary to approach it with the full equipment of a knowledge different from ours...'

In other parts of the world the strange humming sounds have been reported, and some 'experts' have declared it is the action of the wind. However, there was absolutely no wind of any kind the night I heard the sounds

TRAVELING THE PATH BACK TO THE ROAD IN THE SKY

coming from 'Peca-Gasha', and the wind will not answer the question of what is causing such noises in different stone figures throughout the world. It is usually associated with objects made of granite. Let us remember that granite was the sacred rock of the Egyptians and other ancient people. Why was it considered sacred? It is just possible that the great stone figures of Marcahuasi are in reality some kind of fantastic batteries, but for what purpose? In each figure there are thousands of quartz crystals displaying a piezoelectric effect due to the tremendous pressure of the crystallized substances. It is stated that the humming sound is getting louder year by year at Marcahuasi and at other places in the world. Why?

During the time of the 'El's' on (or I should say *under*) the Earth our planet was bombarded with a certain intensity of Cosmic Rays. I believe that a decrease or an increase in intensity will cause widespread changes on the planet, such as the size of animal and plant life, etc. Scientific calculations show that at the present time the electron count has speeded up and the Cosmic Ray bombardment of our world has increased fantastically. Perhaps the humming sound will continue to increase until the Cosmic Ray intensity is the same as it was during the time of the builders of the Marcahuasi monoliths. At this time, when the intensity is exactly right, the tombs and subterranean chambers of the plateau may open and reveal their 'time-capsule' contents. Is there a cosmic *lock* on the secrets of Marcahuasi that will open in accordance with that which is written: '... for there is nothing covered, that shall not be revealed; and hid, that shall not be known.' (St. Matthew x:26)

The name Marcahuasi is evidently a name that came from the time when the Inca army occupied the area of the plateau. Because of its strategic position, it was the ideal location for a fortress. In Quechua, 'Marcahuasi' means: 'house of two stories'. This describes the headquarters building of the Inca military colony that lived on the plateau shortly after 1350 A.D. and established the rule of the Empire of the Sun over the entire region. The Incas knew nothing about the giant stone figures and the conquered Huancas only had their strange legends of 'Giant Gods'.

There are also stone 'chulpas' (burial tombs) near the fortress, built either in series, isolated, or in a two-storied arrangement. These tombs, which contained the splendid mummies of important military leaders, have all been violated. Evidently the Spanish did a thorough job of plundering when they arrived on the plateau shortly after they had murdered the Inca

TRAVELING THE PATH BACK TO THE ROAD IN THE SKY

Emperor Atahualpa at Cajamarca, Peru. Today, they stand as mute evidence of man's insatiable lust for gold.

During our exploration of the plateau, we came upon a cave that had obviously been used for ancient burials, for in its entrance we found many skulls and pieces of clothing that had been made from llama and alpaca fur. This cave is in a beautiful place that overlooks a valley thousands of feet below. As we sat down to rest in front of the cave, I noticed an artificial stone or adobe wall that ran in front of the original, or natural granite wall of the cave. Suddenly, an exciting thought came to me: could it be possible that the Spanish didn't find all the tombs at Marcahuasi, that some might still be intact, untouched since the time the soldiers at the fortress buried their dead in them? Of course, I had no hopes of finding objects of gold or silver, for poor soldiers didn't own such costly and precious material. While I sat looking at the man-made wall which passed over the natural wall, I had an idea. Would the Incas have gone to all the trouble of building an artificial wall in front of a perfectly good natural wall? In other words, why were there two walls on top of each other, unless—unless the natural wall behind the first Inca wall was not solid, but had a hole or entrance in it that would lead to—to what? I sat quietly while these thoughts went around in my mind. Finally, I thought it was fanciful to think of such a thing, and yet the possibility was there.

Before we left the area, I had one of the native men with me remove several of the stones from the adobe wall; quickly we saw that the cave wall behind it was not solid as I had suspected, and there was a large cavity there. As we peered into the dusty interior we found that we had discovered an unopened tomb! I could see by the dim light that there were many mummies lying on the floor of the crypt. Later we learned they were of young soldiers who had been attached to the fortress on the plateau, and since there were remains of women and children also, we realized these must have belonged to the families of the same soldiers.

Figure 22 shows a workman on the right holding a complete

mummy in front of the newly opened tomb, and the author on the left holding the mummy bundle of some long-dead warrior. In front of the cave you can see countless skulls, parts of mummy bundles, etc., that came from the interior where the cave had been sealed up with stones by the Inca owners.

Figure 23 shows the author with two of the finds from the new tomb (that's me on the right!). Notice one of the mummies is still tied with the ancient rope that encircled his body preparing him for burial.

I had an experience in the deepest part of that tomb which I would like to relate. We had removed all of the mummies but one. This one was deep in the tomb and it was impossible to stand up in this area for it was only about three feet high and very narrow. The odor of the centuries was overpowering and the atmosphere very oppressive—fine dust was on everything. I was as excited as though I had found another 'Tut-ankh-amun' and crawled into the tomb and bent down in the small area to remove the last mummy-bundle. I had come to Marchuasi to look at giant stone figures, not to excavate a tomb, so I had no tools with me to do a proper job. I had to use my hands to dig around the mummy to free it of the debris of centuries.

While I was engaged in this work, I suddenly felt a terrific pain in the right side of my head. At first I thought something had fallen from the ceiling and hit me, but that was impossible for the ceiling was barely an inch from my head as I bent down to work. I continued to excavate, but a pressure began to build up in my head and I found myself with the most awful headache I have ever experienced, and I have had very few in my lifetime. Finally, I could work no more for the pain was so great I could hardly see what

TRAVELING THE PATH BACK TO THE ROAD IN THE SKY

I was doing. I stumbled out of the cave-tomb and went to bed to remain there for two and a half days.

During those days of confinement I ran a high temperature and the headache continued. Natives coming to look at the sick 'gringo' would shake their heads and say, under their breath: *'Soroche.'* This means altitude or mountain sickness, and we were nearly 12,400 feet above sea level. However, my headache had nothing to do with 'soroche' and besides I didn't have the other common symptoms of the condition.

A few hours before I got up in the middle of the third day a native brought me that last mummy I had been working on at the time of the awful headache. He wanted to show me the pieces of the woolen poncho and part of the soldier's array of weapons that had been attached to the outside of the mummy-bundle of vicuna hide. This was all interesting enough, but as the man turned to go, I saw the right and back side of the mummy, a part I had never seen because I was unable to complete the excavations in the tomb several days before. What I saw made my blood run cold. In exactly the same place on the head where I had had my terrible headache, the mummy's skull displayed a great gaping hole that must have been caused by some ancient adversary's powerful stone war club.

What did all of this mean? I really don't know. However, I have heard it explained that in haunted castles and places where violent deaths have occurred—either accidental or as a result of murder—not always is the discarnate entity itself doing the 'haunting', but only the 'astral shell' that stays on going through similar motions it knew during the entity's last moments on Earth. Because of the nature of the death through violent means, something takes place which is very much like taking a picture by letting light fall on sensitive film or photographic paper. The entity may have long since gone on to his heavenly reward, or whatever his fate was to be, while his 'astral double or shell' continues to 'haunt' the death area year after year.

Is it possible that in the unopened tomb, where no one had been since the day the mummy was placed there, the 'astral shell' of this ancient Inca soldier was still around, hovering over the former body, and, if so, did this 'shell' still contain all the impressions of battle, wounds, agony and eventual death that had actually occurred many centuries in the past? Is that why natives in Peru today are, as they say: '... more afraid of the dead in tombs than of dying.' And if all this is true is it possible that somehow I got in rapport

TRAVELING THE PATH BACK TO THE ROAD IN THE SKY

with that 'shell' through my enthusiasm over the discovery? Did I actually feel the dying pains of a young Inca warrior who died on the battlefield serving 'Lord Inca' on his throne in Cuzco? Was it a battle where the Inca army defeated the Huancas of the Marcahuasi plateau? Perhaps we will never know these answers.

Having accepted the reality of UFOs, or ships from other worlds visiting the Earth now and in the ancient past, I have often wondered as I viewed portions of the 'Capac Nan', Royal Road of the Incas, in various isolated parts of Peru, if the travelers ever looked up to see what we see in our skies today? Did the young *chasquis,* or runners, who were 'chosen from among the most active and swiftest of all their tribesmen' hurry along the greatest highway of the ancient world, encountering heights of 15,000 feet, did they ever pause for a moment to look up in wonderment at a swiftly moving *unidentified flying object?* And did they report breathlessly later to an official of 'Lord Inca' at one of the highway stations or *tampus* that they had witnessed a sacred sight—the *Illa-Siva or* 'light rings', the *Rampa-Liviac* or 'litters of electric energies?' I believe they did, and I am now preparing a book that will reveal this and other truths about the unknown and mysterious beginnings of the Inca Empire.

The travelers along the greatest known road in the world were *in communication* with the travelers along the greatest 'highway of the stars', the *road in the sky* that this book deals with. Here is a correlation that excites us and makes us pause and wonder.

There are other people in the world who are vitally interested in Marcahuasi and its great monoliths. On July 12, 1957, H. S. Bellamy wrote the following in a letter to Dr. Ruzo from Vienna :

These things (the Marcahuasi figures) are really astounding, although I am afraid I know nothing further about them than what I have learned from your book (*La Cultura Masma),* I am fully prepared to regard them as genuine monuments left by a people that have long since disappeared.

Mr. Bellamy is well-known for his books : *Moons, Myths and Man; Built Before The Flood; The Calendar Of Tiahuanaco,* and many others.

On September 1, 1957, Peter Allan, Mr. Bellamy's co-author of *The Calendar Of Tiahuanaco,* wrote to Dr. Ruzo from England:

Congratulations on making a discovery of the greatest importance.

TRAVELING THE PATH BACK TO THE ROAD IN THE SKY

After reading your book and having spent hours studying the photographs, it seems to me that the culture of Marcahuasi may well be of such an extreme antiquity that it might profitably be studied in the light of our findings in respect to the Tiahuanaco monuments.

Prof. Henri Bac of France wrote:

I have read and re-read your inspiring book on *La Cultura Masma* which interests me very much because it supports my own theories on Atlantean migrations...

The distinguished geographer, lecturer and explorer, Dr. Joseph Grellier, professor of the School of Anthropology in Paris, France, wrote:

The archaeology of Peru presented by Dr. Daniel Ruzo, the fifth of January, at the Sorbonne (University of Paris) for the Ethnographical Society of Paris was a brilliant lecture on the Marcahuasi Plateau which he has studied since 1952. During a conference which I gave last Friday in the Louvre, under the auspices of the Society of Comparative Civilization, I presented his colored slides. This excited much emotion as well as interest.

Dr. Grellier is the discoverer of the sources of the Orinoco in South America, and since 1949 he has been studying the geography of Colombia and Venezuela. He is a well-known authority on the effects of erosion, and he claims that the stone figures of Marcahuasi could not possibly be natural.

Prof. Pierre Legallic, noted scientist and lecturer of France, wrote:

... these vestiges (at Marcahuasi) are not in places of habitation but in places where many people used to gather... places of reunion like Jerusalem for the Hebrews and Mecca the holy city of the Moslems... the assemblage of monuments in this area depicts a sacred work like the caverns, crypts and grottos known throughout the world to be places of pilgrimage only. One can see at Marcahuasi a 'Sacred Forest' or a hidden grove or wood of countless European legends... the only one that remains so well preserved.

Dr. M. Martigny of France, professor of the School of Anthropology, wrote:

I am very interested in your work. Would you be able to send me a text of your investigations so that I might present it to the Ethnographical Society? I am certain that my colleagues will greatly appreciate it as well as I. We will study the possibility of organizing a scientific expedition to the

TRAVELING THE PATH BACK TO THE ROAD IN THE SKY

area of your discoveries.

Dr. Antonio Pampa y Pompa, secretary of the National Academy of Sciences of Mexico and director of the National Institute of Anthropology and History wrote :

I congratulate you for the form and depth of your research. I recently made a very dangerous journey to the hill of Meco (Cerro del Meco) and had the satisfaction of observing similar monoliths in their original position... I have come to the conclusion that these are not natural but made by man (intelligent beings). They are very similar to the Sphinx. Therefore, I will appreciate your communications which I shall make known to the Academy of Sciences. You and I will form two units of investigation in America studying this prehistoric cultural expression.

Prof. Denis Saurat, author and lecturer of France, wrote:

The more I look at the photographs and read and re-read your book, the more I am impressed by your astonishing discoveries. You give extremely important information which appears to me to be decisive. I am going to give a conference in December in the Centre Universitaire Mediterranen, and I will utilize your material as documents for I intend to discuss your findings thoroughly.

I don't believe the distinguished gentlemen quoted would gather at the Sorbonne or the Louvre or the Mexican Academy of Sciences to view and study 'Ruzo's Folly' if he had nothing but photographs of granite masses, badly eroded, and showing not the slightest indication that they were ever carved.

Throughout the world scientists are beginning to recognize similar discoveries. In Mexico there are the monolithic constructions of Malinalco, and the "Guanajuato Frogs' are not freaks of nature, but were carved by a highly intelligent race in ancient times. There are great carvings on 'Sugar Loaf' at Rio de Janeiro, Brazil, and others in Italy, Spain, France, etc.

Recently I received several letters from Rome that are of extreme importance in connection with the discoveries at Marcahuasi. Prof. Costantino Cattoi and his wife Maria Mataloni Cattoi, both research scientists and archaeologists, write that they have discovered in certain places there is a strange concentration *underground* of electro-magnetic energy. And they have further found that where this energy exists gigantic stone figures like those of Marcahuasi are found, and they have further noted that there is a high frequency of UFO sightings in the same areas. When I first read this information all I could think of was the monoliths of Marcahuasi and their strange humming sound like the 'click' of the 'El's'.

Prof. Cattoi has a photograph of a UFO hovering directly over an enormous carved stone head. He has studied and photographed hundreds of such figures for over forty years and has discovered lions, dragons, and even the one-eyed Cyclops. Again, we are reminded of Marcahuasi and the one-eyed 'Elder Race' beneath Lago de Titicaca.

Prof. Cattoi is a retired Italian Air Force colonel, one of Italy's most decorated airmen. In 1923 the 36th Italian Geological Congress praised his pioneering use of the airplane in archaeological research. In 1929 he met his wife while conducting excavations in central Italy. At the present time he is one of the directors of the Latin Academy of Science and Art in Rome.

He is the discoverer of the ancient Etruscan city of Capena which he located twenty miles north of Rome, and in 1932 a royal decree changed the name of the modern city near the ruins from Leprignano to 'Capena' in honour of Cattoi's discovery.

Cattoi and his wife discovered an older 'Capena' about seven feet below the surface close to the Etruscan Capena. This discovery was never revealed because of strange 'mysteries' at the place. There are in existence vertical pits and several tunnels and chambers, one on top of the other in levels. This indicates a vast underground city. Cattoi believes that this great city is connected by tunnels with another subterranean city beneath the ancient city of Rome itself.

The early Christians did not build the Catacombs of Rome, but only used them for safe places in which to meet and be buried.

After his work at Capena, Cattoi was requested by the Antiquities and Fine Arts Department of Trapani and Marsala (Sicily) to attempt to locate the ancient city of Lylybeus. After working for one year, on December 25, 1931, Cattoi announced that he had located the city in the 'Stagnone di Marsala' (the Great Pond of Marsala). His announcement caused a general surprise and a major upset among historians and archaeologists. 'Authorities' and 'experts' saw their theories challenged and they refused to recognize Cattoi's discovery. Because of this attitude it is just as well that Cattoi didn't announce *everything* he had found under the waters of the 'Stagnone'. Stranded on the

TRAVELING THE PATH BACK TO THE ROAD IN THE SKY

sand bottom of the pond, he and his wife discovered two large 'boats' that appeared to be made of 'bronze'. Nearby they found a large mural or wall painting now mostly covered with a lime formation. This painting depicted a map of the ancient city of Lylybeus and strange, undecipherable hieroglyphics that may be of the original language of Earth. Also in the 'Stagnone' area Cattoi discovered many stone Tau's or T's, and we already have discussed the possible meaning of the 'T'.

In the vicinity of Trapani (Sicily) Cattoi and his wife located a great hill that had been carved as a monstrous 'Sphinx'. This is one of the many great sculptures which 'experts' have called 'freaks of nature', but Cattoi claims it was originally a magnificent work. The 'Trapani Sphinx' has the head of a dog, and because of this and other factors Cattoi connects it with one of the principal gods of EgyptThoth (Tehuti), whose name means 'the measurer'. The Greeks identified this god with Hermes and he was known to the Romans as Mercury, messenger of the gods.

An interesting correlation is realized when we read the words of Dr. Ruzo:

'We have seen many figures of *dogs* or of *dog heads* on several peaks of the Andes of Peru... its outline against the sky is a very common sight to the traveler.'

The dog was the most important sacred symbol of the Huancas and because of this was identified with the god 'Huari'. Evidently, the dog was sacred over most of ancient South America in the dim past and finally he was revered in the Marcahuasi area only by the Huancas. I believe this indicates that the religious or spiritual 'Mecca' for the worship of 'Huari' was at Marcahuasi, and the dog continued to be revered only at the site where its cult was the strongest. Many dogs and dog heads can be seen today on top of the Marcahuasi Plateau, adding their mute evidence to all the other monoliths of forgotten time.

In September, 1954, Cattoi discovered the city of Cosa, which he located on the bottom of the Tyrrhenian Sea near the Island of Giglio off the Italian coast. Cattoi claims Cosa is ancient beyond belief and that he knows that scattered within, or near this and other sunken cities in the Mediterranean Sea, are many space ships or UFOs which didn't have time to escape from the doomed cities when they suddenly sank beneath the angry water.

On May 5, 1955, Cattoi discovered another great 'Sphinx' on Mount

TRAVELING THE PATH BACK TO THE ROAD IN THE SKY

Argentario near Orbetello, Italy. Again, the figure is related to Thoth (Hermes-Mercury) and the discovery is even more important when one realizes that the ancient legend says that Mercury (Thoth-Hermes), the 'divine teacher' left the very same Mount Argentario on a falcon or hawk with golden wings and reached Egypt bringing along the Book of the Sacred Word and the divine teachings on science, art and agriculture.

Prof. Cattoi has found a strange figure on the 'Sphinx'—the body of a child wrapped in a blanket with the head of a baboon. Remember, baboon's have *dog-like* muzzles. And of the two animals sacred to Thoth, the cenotaphalas is most important to our discussion here. This animal is the *dog-headed* ape and in Egypt always was grouped in numbers *of eight* when they attended Thoth, he also appeared as a *dog-headed* ape and this made a total of *nine.* The cynocephali were called 'watchers for the dawn', and nine of them were said to open the gates in the west for the setting sun, and each is then called by a name: 'Opener of the Earth', 'Soul of the Earth', 'Heart of the Earth', etc. They are thus represented in the illustrations to a work frequently inscribed on the walls of royal Theban tombs, relating to the passage of the sun during the hours of night, and called 'The book of that which is in the underworld'. In the judgment scene represented in papyri of the *Book of the Dead,* and on the walls at Der el Medineh, a cynocephalus is seated on the balance in the middle of the beam of the scales in which the heart of the deceased is being weighed, while Thoth stands by with palette and reed pen waiting to record the result. In this case the cynocephalus may represent equilibrium, which would naturally be a quality of the god Thoth (Hermes-Mercury).

Here, again, we have a mystery that is similar to the mystery of the connection between Astete's 'dream' of 1905 of 'Masma', the Patriarch of Genesis called Masma, and the small, isolated Indian village of Masma in Peru. As in that mystery, we again find apparent correlation, but just what does it all mean? It has been so garbled by centuries and even millennia of tradition and legends that it is almost impossible to sift out the real original meaning or happening. However, there is enough evidence to give us much to think about. What is the connection between the carved Peruvian dog heads of the Huancas and the dog-headed 'Sphinx' of Cattoi and the dog-headed ape the sacred symbol of the god Thoth?

First of all, the cynocephali numbered *eight* and were called 'Watchers for the dawn'. This reminds us of the eighth level or the Thought or Theta

TRAVELING THE PATH BACK TO THE ROAD IN THE SKY

Universe. Also, the title 'watchers' is most significant, for those on an eighth level (as the 'El's' are now) are 'watchers for the dawn' in the sense they are watching or waiting for the ninth level or the Energy Universe (Infinity). When these eight dog-headed apes joined Thoth, they became *nine* and they 'opened the gates in the west for the setting sun'. The significance here is obvious, Thoth as 'the measurer', symbol of equilibrium, standing for the attainment of the *ninth* or Energy Universe. Also, the apes were given names such as 'Heart of the Earth', etc. All of this symbolism reminds us of the 'El's' and their passage from the *seventh* level to that of Theta. The 'El's' who lived underground and the apes called 'Heart of the Earth', etc. 'The book of that which is in the underworld' may refer specifically to the *underworld* of the 'Elder Race' or the Cyclopeans. In other words, we may find that which we have called 'most ancient', the religious symbolism of Egypt and other ancient civilizations is only *effect,* built on top of an actual happening that is millions of years older. Therefore, the passage of the 'Elder's' into the Theta Universe when they became true 'El's' would be *cause.* In the strange, unknown symbolism of the world, as it appears in the so-called myths of gods and demons, we find confirmation of a fact that goes back to the very beginnings of the planet Earth. For another example, look at the *frontispiece* of this book. In this design we have a Pre-Inca representation of the great *road in the sky* from Peru, South America. The Moon here is flanked by two eight-pointed stars. The Moon was especially connected with Thoth as 'the measurer' and as a great lunar deity he wore the lunar crescent-in this symbol from Peru we find the lunar crescent also, and we find the Jaguar God (or is it a dog-headed creature?) with three horn-like projections coming out of the front of him (and above him) and we find four of these projections coming out of the back of him. In Egypt there were ten chief mythological localities with gods ruling over each one. Thoth is connected with the *third* and the *seventh* localities. In the Peruvian design we have the symbol of *three* above the head of the creature (three horn-like projections) and when we add all the projections together we get *seven.* The *seventh locality* could refer to *seven levels* of our 'Spectrum of Awareness' we discussed in our section on *The Time-Spanners.* Thoth, as god of the seventh locality (level), which was the 'Place of judgment' to the Egyptians, was the guardian of the way which led to the eighth level or the Thought-Theta Universe. Therefore, he is always represented in the judgment scenes in Egypt where he records on his palette the result of the weighing of the heart of the deceased (to see if they were suitable to pass on to the Theta or eighth level from the seventh

TRAVELING THE PATH BACK TO THE ROAD IN THE SKY

level (locality) which was the locality (level) known as the 'Place of judgment'?). Remember, the seventh level is Sense of Purpose, and is the apparent upper limit of Physical Organism Awareness. Because of this inner meaning of the symbolism spoken of above, it is obvious why the Egyptians transferred to their own doctrines the original happening of the 'El's' going from the seventh level which was physical existence to the eighth level which was non-physical existence and made it pertain to the Egyptian dead in the seventh locality which was the 'Place of Judgment'. Here also, is the proof that in 'dying' we are really 'living' for when the 'Elder's' lost their physical equipment they didn't really 'die' but found true life in non-physical existence. I think we may discover that what we call 'life' is really *death,* and the death we fear much may be *living* at its fullest.

Also in our ancient Peruvian symbol we find two eight-pointed stars (8 + 8 = 16). Notice each one is made up of a four-pointed star and a simple Greek cross making a total of eight points. This could symbolize the Four Great Primary Forces revolving around the circle in the centre which is First Divine Cause. The crossed lines of the cross can stand for crossed lines of light energy and when combined with the Four Great Primary Forces a total of *eight* is reached. Also, you will recognize the dotted circle in the centre as the *ninth* letter of the Greek alphabet. Above the entire design is a disc which I believe stands for the coming, in ancient times, of the 'light rings' (Illa-Siva) or the 'litters of electric energies' (Rampa-Liviac) known also in Quechua as *Quilla-Anca* or 'Moon Eagles'. (The UFOs of today.) Remember, Thoth as *a lunar* deity left Mount Argentario on a hawk (eagle) with golden wings. Does all of this add up to the fact that Thoth originally came from outer space as a Teacher to humanity on Earth? I have already stated that I believe Osiris of Egypt and Apollo of Greece were spacemen. [See *Other Tongues-Other Flesh.*]

The whole picture gets more complicated as we study it, but there is a connection between the 'Flying Saucers' of the past and present with the 'El's' and with the legends of mankind that were used to build up a theology that attempted to explain God and the supernatural. Wherever we look into the mythology and symbolism of Egypt, Phoenicia, Greece, Rome, or the various ancient civilizations of South America, and indeed, the entire world, we will find references and symbols that unquestionably relate back to a time in the most dim past of millions of years ago when the EL-DERS became simply the 'El's'. I believe the 'sensitives' of past ages in past great civilizations have 'tuned in' so to speak with the centres of magnetic energy that are the 'El' 'libraries', and that through this medium they have brought information to their people. They were the oracles of the ancient world, the inspired prophets who made known the divine purpose and revealed the sacred mysteries. Perhaps they did not really know where they obtained their information, but obtain it they did, and religious creeds and doctrines were based upon it throughout the world from Thebes to Athens and from Rome to Cuzco. The entire conception of Hell whether it's called Sheol, Hades, Tartarus, Gehenna or just simply 'underworld' is bound up in the happenings of the 'Elder Race' when this Race left the Earth from its *underground* Empire. The whole idea of Lords of the *underworld* and judges of the *dead* developed out of an occurrence that took place in 'the days when the Earth was young', the 'beginning of things' for our planet.

In respect to all of this, the much distorted account of Nebuchadnezzar's dream related in the fourth chapter of the Book of Daniel might be understood in a new light. The king saw 'a tree in the midst of the earth, and the height thereof was great'. (Daniel iv:10). 'The tree grew, and was strong, and the height thereof reached unto heaven, and the sight thereof to the end of all the earth: The leaves thereof were fair, and the fruit thereof much... (Daniel iv:11,12). Then the king saw in his vision: '... behold, a *watcher* and an holy one came down from heaven...' (Daniel iv:13). Later we read: 'Let his heart be changed from man's, and let a beast's heart be given unto him; and let *seven* times pass over him. This matter is by the decree of the *watchers,* and the demand by the word of the holy ones...' (Daniel iv:16,17).

The Akawais of British Guiana have a legend that says the great world tree which the creator, Makunaima, caused to grow in the *middle* of the Earth bore all manner of wonderful fruit.

Could Nebuchadnezzar's 'tree in the *midst* of the earth' represent the same thing as the 'tree in the *middle* of the earth' from British Guiana? And could that possibly relate to the *underground* cities of the 'Elder Race' and the fantastic power and force that was built up there over countless ages until the Power of Creative Thought was realized by the Cyclopeans? Remember, 'the tree grew, and was strong, and the height thereof reached unto heaven.' Did not the 'Elder Race' 'grow' and become 'strong', and did not their 'height' appear to 'reach unto heaven'? 'Wonderful fruit' was on the 'tree' according to the Bible and to the Akawais. The 'Elder's produced such 'fruit' also in their accomplishments. The exchange of a man's heart for a

TRAVELING THE PATH BACK TO THE ROAD IN THE SKY

beast's heart could refer to the later Great Abomination or Adultery on the Earth when MAN (the 'Sons of God') became HU-MAN (children of the 'daughters of men'), and mankind lost the Power of Creative Thought. Then we read that *seven times* must pass over him. Could this mean that anyone wishing to enter the Theta or Thought Universe of level eight, must first pass through the *seven* levels of Physical Organism Awareness or the 'seven times'? And who are the 'watchers'? Remember, the eight cynocephali of Egypt were also called 'the watchers'. The 'watchers' *decree* the matter, or the entry into Theta (8), but the 'holy ones' *demand* it by their word. The 'holy ones' could easily be the Great Primary Forces or Universal Laws that the Infinite One has put into effect for they are immutable, unchangeable, and would, therefore, *'demand* by their word'.

And now, for a moment, back to Professor Cattoi and his discoveries in Italy. At the present time he is excavating parts of petrified bodies of giant beings on Mount Argentario, the place we have already associated with Thoth. He has also found remains in Albania, Greece and Libya. Cattoi says:

The great rock sculptures are concealing their age-old secrets ... their 'language' (their meaning) is largely unknown because it is the 'magic language of animals', written with symbols representing animal and human forms carved in stone to remind those of a far future time of the precepts of the original 'wise men' who received them from the messengers of God. I believe that Thoth or Mercury-Hermes actually traveled to various parts of the ancient world starting from Mount Argentario wherever he went a gigantic carving was left of his own symbol the Dog. Sometimes there are *two dogs* shown... I believe this is because Isis came down to Earth from the star Sirius (the Dog Star) in the constellation Canis Major (larger dog) bringing with her the seed of wheat, the great cereal grain. The dog carving is found in many places in Europe and there is even an example in Karakorum, Siberia....

Was Mercury-Thoth's 'falcon with gold-feathered wings' the same as the Peruvian 'litters of electric energies' or 'light rings'? Did the gods of antiquity come down from the stars themselves on their glorious *road in the sky* to enlighten hu-man-ity on Earth? The thought is intriguing and there is much proof for it.

So, in Italy, we have Giants, UFOs, and Monoliths; in Peru we have exactly the same thing. Cattoi has found areas where there is a concentration

TRAVELING THE PATH BACK TO THE ROAD IN THE SKY

underground of electro-magnetic energy; at Marcahuasi I was fascinated by the humming monoliths. Cattoi says there are 'Flying Saucers' or UFOs on the bottom of the Mediterranean Sea near sunken cities; in Peru we have symbols that may be related to Mercury-Thoth who we believe was a being from space. And Cattoi has located hundreds of gigantic sculptures in Italy; at Marcahuasi and elsewhere there are many more identical in shape, technique used and evidently meaning—if we but knew that *meaning*.

What else is at Marcahuasi? Perhaps it would be better to say: 'What isn't there?' There are stones carved that have the appearance of monstrous catapults that could have been designed for some battle between gigantic creatures; there are figures of all kinds with strange hats, halos and cones on their heads; there are great reptiles too, dinosaurs belonging to some antediluvian world (Cattoi found many of these in Italy, etc.); there are fish carved to rise out of the centre of some artificial lake; there are sinister cloaked figures with dark hoods and demons and monsters and men; there are shadows that become condors, llamas and bats when the light is just right; there is a great altar where a priest could see the sun rising over an army of enormous toads; there are irregular, truncated tetrahedrons placed in fantastic positions; there are fish with little human faces and there are men with animal faces; there are giant men and dwarfed men and headless men. What madness is this; who conceived this fantastic 'forest' of stone?

I remember one rainy day I rode out from the 'Peca-Gasha' where we made our camp to another part of the plateau. I was deep in thought and let the horse go where he pleased. He wandered into a dead-end canyon, and when he jerked to a standstill, I was rudely brought out of my state of reverie to look up at a gigantic hand in front of me. At the very end of this dead-end canyon the monstrous figure of a hand had been carved as though some great being were on the other side reaching his hand over like we would reach into a cookie jar. After my surprise, I settled down to study this sculpture and suddenly realized there were six fingers instead of five! Later, Dr. Ruzo told me he called this figure 'La Mano'. The fact a hand was carved there at all was startling enough, but the six fingers! I have also found countless six-fingered beings in dancing positions carved on gigantic slabs of stone from a 'Temple of the Wind' on a hill overlooking the Rio Sechin in the Casma valley of Peru. I am going to have a great deal to say about this temple in future works, for it is fantastically ancient and of great importance. (See Fig. No. 24.)

TRAVELING THE PATH BACK TO THE ROAD IN THE SKY

Figure 24

Dr. Ruzo also discovered something recently at Marcahuasi that is definitely a symbol of the 'El's'. He found a tomb with the figure of a man on top of it and on his chest was carved a large 'L' or 90° angle or the main symbol in the mysteries of the Freemasons.

Is there anything else we could say about Marcahuasi that would make it any more fantastic or wonderful? It doesn't seem possible that there could be anything else; yet, there is, and something that makes everything else on the plateau pale into insignificance.

When I looked at an aerial photograph taken by the Peruvian Air Force and now in the files of the archives of the Peruvian Air Ministry, I saw more great figures, signs, lines and symbols. These can never be seen from the ground, like

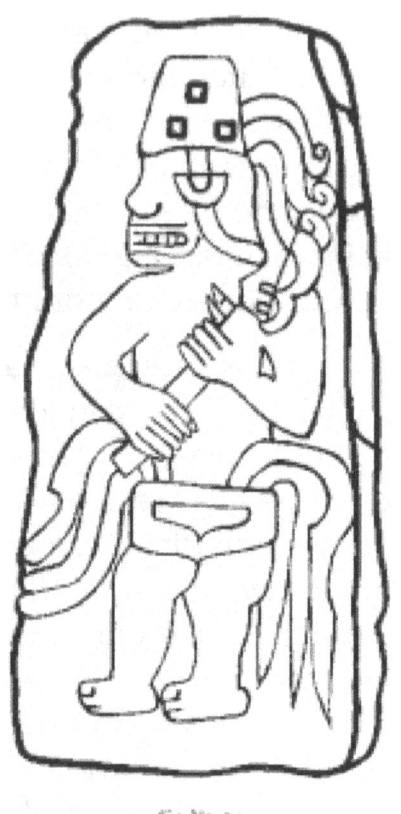

Fig. No. 24
"La Mano", with six fingers

the man who can't see the forest for the trees when he is in that forest on the ground, but if he ever gets above the forest he will see it in its entirety. We must also observe our 'forest of stone' at Marcahuasi in the same way. These figures observed from high in the air are in no way to be confused with the giant carvings we are writing about that exist on the ground; they are completely separate and were for another purpose. When we are on the ground we cannot possibly make out their outline. Therefore, the ancients couldn't see the figures they were making for this purpose unless they, too, were able to go above the ground to do the viewing. But how could ancient people do that? Some 'experts' may say that they climbed to higher positions around the plateau and observed the construction of the figures from there. This is possible although it would take centuries for them to put a stone in position and then climb a mountain to see how it looked, climb down again and add another stone and then climb up again. A lot of work requiring a lot of time, but it could have been done, However, there is one point that I must mention that immediately destroys that 'expert' opinion. You see, there is *nothing* higher around Marcahuasi to climb up to and to look down from. Then what is the answer?

TRAVELING THE PATH BACK TO THE ROAD IN THE SKY

Did the ancients have some kind of airships? This doesn't seem likely in this area. Were they able to jump up high enough to view their handiwork? This isn't likely, either. Then what is the answer? Like the man who said he climbed a great mountain simply 'because it was there' we must deal with this fact in the same way. The fact is *there,* and it is undeniable, there are astronomically perfect lines laid out on the ground, a great network of strange figures (one looking for all the world like some old Chinese priest in a flowing robe), never meant to be seen from the ground. So, we have the *fact,* but what is the *answer?* In exactly the same location as the *male* lion on the ground (see Fig. No. 7) there is, when viewed from the air, a great figure of *a female* lion. Maybe the ancients weren't up in the air but somebody or something was.

Is it possible that these figures that only have meaning and are only visible from the air served as markers or beacons for the 'litters of electric energies' or UFOs arriving from outer space?

This, then, is the story of the monoliths of Marcahuasi that started in modern times through a 'vision' of one Pedro Astete in 1905. The unknown designers and builders of this great city with a tremendous population where no one ever lived could be called 'The Masma Race', 'The Huari Race', or simply 'The Giant Race'. Were they really the EL-DERS before they became 'El's'? It doesn't seem likely because while the figures are very old (100,000 to 1,000,000 years) it is almost inconceivable that they could have existed for nearly a billion years and not be completely destroyed by time. Yet, anything is possible. However, I believe the ancient creation at Marcahuasi is some sort of a fantastic 'museum' that was built by later races after the advent of hu-man-ity on the Earth. Here they placed those figures that would serve as prototypes for the creatures of ages to follow them. Is that part of the answer to the mystery of the 'Methuselah of Marcahuasi'? Was this carving made to show that man would be born, reach manhood and then die in future time on the Earth? Is this the symbolism of the old man turning into a young man or *vice versa?* If they were not 'El's' at Marcahuasi, who were they? They were giants, that we do know, standing at least twelve feet in height. I believe they constructed their strange 'Mecca in Stone' over an area that had been occupied by the 'Elder Race' before its conquest of MEST, and that somehow their 'sensitives' serving in the temples as oracles were able to tap the 'magnetic libraries' and thereby learn the history of the 'El's'. Of course, this all would have been several hundred thousand years ago.

TRAVELING THE PATH BACK TO THE ROAD IN THE SKY

Their 'museum' must have been dedicated to the memory of the 'Elder Race' and to the future of hu-man-ity on Earth; in other words, to those of us who live on this little planet, love here and die here.

I hope we can learn something from the great mysteries carved in solid granite.

Figure 25 is of the sunset on the plateau, and we close this section of the book with the symbol of the great stone carving in this photograph. The figure appears to be an old 'Patriarch' with his well-set features, his stern mien and his large stone hat. He has watched that same sun set over the plateau thousands upon thousands of times. He is the symbol of that which was created here, still and quiet, and waiting, waiting, waiting.

Again we have traveled the highway of *yesterday* and viewed the monoliths that touched the *road* to the stars in the last of the 'Sacred Forests'.

As Dr. Ruzo would say: '... the atmosphere enfolds us, there is an air of suspense that leaves our mind naked and transports our souls to the past—Marcahuasi, over twelve thousand feet about the thundering sea—Marcahuasi which towers above the Pacific, and which awakens in the depths of its visitors the most profound human emotions.

TRAVELING THE PATH BACK TO THE ROAD IN THE SKY

BEACONS FOR THE GODS

'We must make our creations great upon the land that the sky gods may view them.' (An ancient legend of South America.)

'Look, what in heaven's name is that?'

'What are you talking about? Where?'

'Down there—down there on the desert-on the sand!'

"I still don't know what you're talking about. What do you see?'

'Can't you see those hundreds of radiating lines? They look like some kind of pathways or roads, and yet..."

'Good God, now I see them! What could they possibly be? And look over there, on the right, those aren't lines, they look like figures of great birds...'

'And there directly beneath us is the figure of a man wearing a big crown!'

'I don't know what those things are, but when we land I intend to ask a lot of questions. Those perfectly straight lines almost look like *beacons!*'

The above conversation took place between two pilots who were flying their plane about 4,000 feet above the area between Nazca and Palpa, Peru, several years ago. Nazca is 471 kilometres south of Lima and not far from the coast of Peru.

The radiating lines, animals, platforms and abstractions the pilots saw that day were nothing new under the Peruvian sun, but had actually been on the eternally rainless southern desert for hundreds and hundreds of years and fill hundreds of square miles of that same desert.

TRAVELING THE PATH BACK TO THE ROAD IN THE SKY

Figure No. 26 will give you an idea of what those two men saw that day for the *first time* from the air in modern times. The photograph was taken north of Nazca on January 4, 1945, at an altitude of 3,000 feet by the Peruvian Air Force. [This, and all other photographs of the 'desert beacons' is through the courtesy of the Servicio Aerofotografico Nacional which gave me access to the archives of the Peruvian Air Ministry and permission to publish their excellent aerial photographs.]

The strange delineations of the barren plains and tablelands near Nazca are in an area that was once the very centre of a highly evolved culture. To the north is Paracas where archaeologists have found 2,000 year old textiles in hundreds of caverns. Mummies were wrapped in textiles that are of such fantastic and imaginative beauty that scientists claim them to be some of the finest weavings in the world. This area also supported the Nazcas, a 'shadowy people' whose identity was revealed by their magnificent pottery of polychromic colors and adorned with stylized representations of animals, birds, monsters and gods. The ancient people of the beautiful textiles and also those of the elaborate and colorful ceramics lived on the coast of Peru

TRAVELING THE PATH BACK TO THE ROAD IN THE SKY

hundreds of years before the coming of the Incas who wished to found an Empire.

The astronomically perfect lines and figures must have meant nothing to the Inca conquerors and invaders. In fact, I doubt very much if they ever saw them at all for they laid their great twenty-four-foot Aide coastal road—the Royal Road of Lord Inca—right through many of the patterns and pathways. This is our first proof that the lines and figures were not made by the Incas, and were, in fact, unknown to them.

In the last few years, many theories have been presented to explain the origin of this 'mystery on the desert'; all of these theories are contradictory. The most popular idea was that the straight lines led to Pre-Inca buried treasure of the Nazca people. Another theory said the figures must have something to do with the riddle of the mummies that were found at Paracas. Yet another said that the pathways were in reality part of an ancient road system, but when they were traced and followed, it was discovered that they led to nowhere, for they begin and end in the desert. Another idea said that the lines had formerly been irrigation ditches.

Dr. Paul Kosok, historian of Long Island University, was the first scientist to make an investigation into the mystery, in 1941, and proved the delineations could never have been roads, treasure indicators or agricultural furrows.

For centuries travelers have traversed the desert on their way from one valley to another and have crossed over parts of the great patterns thousands of times yet, they knew not what they were crossing over. Again, it is a question of not seeing the forest for the trees. I believe the Nazca people knew something about these lines and figures but I do not believe they were the designers or builders. After the conquest of these people by the Inca army, the patterns were nearly forgotten. And if there were one or two of the priesthood amongst the Nazca who retained the secret, this knowledge was completely obliterated by the coming of Don Francisco Pizarro, the murder of the Inca Atahualpa and the conquest of the Empire of the Sun in 1533.

The Spanish were too concerned with the plundering of sun temples and convents of sun virgins to pay any attention to marks on a dusty desert. It is very doubtful if they would have noticed them anyway.

Civilized men have come from all over the world since the day of Pizarro to pass back and forth over the Nazca-Palpa area, but no one ever

TRAVELING THE PATH BACK TO THE ROAD IN THE SKY

knew what he was walking over. Only from an aeroplane can the absolutely straight lines and borders of elongated surfaces be appreciated. The dimensions are astonishing for only small fractions of them can be seen unless one is very high in an aeroplane. The arrangement is a curious one of stars, groups of parallels and zigzags, all appearing as though they had been created on some gigantic drawing-board.

One scientist who viewed the immense patterns from the air said:

Below us stretching out in all directions on the flat grey plain of flint rock was a vast network of drawn lines. A series of rectangles as wide as airfields and long straight lines... some originating from a single complex, others from no source at all... went off in every variant of the compass to fade away at the end into nothing. There were lines, triangles, circles of all sizes appearing at frequent intervals. As we looked down fascinated at the bewildering maze spread beneath us, we realized that we were looking at yet another of the great mysteries of the southern Peruvian deserts, this time at the so-called 'Lines of Nazca'.

Actually, the gigantic designs are very shallow surface depressions. The light color they display was produced by a very simple process. The plains and mountains of this region are exceptionally rich in iron, and therefore the characteristic color is reddish dark brown. This color has been produced by oxidation and the effect of thousands of years of daily morning dew followed by excessive heat. Therefore it does not go deeper than one or two inches. Underneath this color are yellowish white stones and gravel.

The contrast stated above made it possible for the builders to use the level surfaces as if they were enormous 'blackboards'. White designs could be produced on a very dark background by simply removing the upper layer of dark stones. Such stones were disposed of by being heaped up on both sides of the cleaned surfaces.

German scientist and mathematician Maria Reiche has made a very thorough study of the 'Lines of Nazca' and in her report she says :

Being absolutely superficial, it is remarkable how these mysterious tracings have remained intact for over hundreds, maybe even thousands of years. Erosion has not had its effect in this region, so that every stone seems to have remained in its place since time immemorial. This is due to a special geographic and climatic situation, which is unique on the Peruvian coast.

TRAVELING THE PATH BACK TO THE ROAD IN THE SKY

As a rule, the Andes rise up to their great height from a narrow strip of coastal plains. These desert plains and the adjacent foothills are exposed to the winds from the sea. The winds deposit on the plains large amounts of sand, while to the foothills they carry enough moisture to support in the sunless season a temporary vegetation of bulbous plants which dries up every summer forming a layer of earth and humus.

In this region, the succession of coastal plains and mountains is interrupted by a tableland, twelve hundred feet above sea level, which is protected from the ocean winds by a range of elevations about three thousand feet high which runs along the coast. This tableland, the principal site of the ancient tracings, does not belong to the mountainous region with its occasional rainfalls, nor to the coast with its months of moist sunless weather. It forms a separate geographic and climatic unit, absolutely dry and with eternal sunshine, except for an occasional mist in the morning.

Coming by bus from the north, the traveler notices clearly the sudden transition, as he enters from a region which is often cloudy in winter into the full sunshine of a strangely picturesque landscape, where the dark violet-black mountains and plains in their fascinating contrast against the ever blue sky, seem to proclaim the great mystery they enclose.

The patterns have remained intact over thousands of years because of the unusual climatic conditions in this area. The limited space on the top of plateaus is usually completely covered with the complicated designs composed of short sharp turns or angles. Look closely at **Figure No. 27** and you will see literally hundreds of them going in all directions as far as the eye can see. You will also notice irregular lines going in and out of the original tracings—these are the tracks left by the cars of today. This photograph was taken in the Valle del Ingenio on January 4, 1945, at an altitude of 4,000 feet.

The sites of the great designs comprise a strip about forty miles long from north to south and about one mile wide. Also, there are many other designs in isolated places in the adjacent mountainous region at the bottom of dry valleys.

Maria Reiche says:

We find tracings on top of small hills, on terraces halfway up the slopes of the deep valleys and behind mountain ranges. These ancient people must have been on a constant search for dark even surfaces, for it would appear that wherever there is a spot, no matter how small, it has been put to use for

TRAVELING THE PATH BACK TO THE ROAD IN THE SKY

TRAVELING THE PATH BACK TO THE ROAD IN THE SKY

the designs.

Figure No. 28 shows the Pan-American Highway as a dark band in the foreground running across the entire picture. This was taken north of Nazca the same day as the photograph in **Figure No. 27**, and at the same altitude. Notice the immense lines and pathways near the centre of the photograph. Some end at the base of a small hill, and others actually go on over the hill.

The Servicio Aerofotografico Nacional has a number of vertical photographs whose scale (1/5000) is three times larger than that of all the other photographs it has taken. Through careful study of these large-scale photographs many startling details have come to light, details which never could have been detected from the ground nor on the smaller scale photographs. One discovery using this method was of the figures of 'gods', large drawings in stone of great beings with enormous crowns on their heads and headdresses displaying rays or halos.

A tremendous amount of labor went into the making of the delineated fields. Maria Reiche says she does not know how the work was done nor with what tools. She hopes that some time an illustration will be found on pottery that will give us a clue to how it was done and with what. It is a well-known fact that many phases of ancient life are found depicted on pottery.

There are indications that the size of the delineated surfaces was standardized in some way. When one considers the technical skill needed to create these figures and lines, one realizes that the Spanish, the Incas and those just preceding them could never have accomplished it. First of all, there is the problem of the enormous amount of labor required. Second, the perfectly straight lines and borders cross great distances, cutting through many valleys and passing over plateaus without ever swerving from their original direction. Here is a feat of engineering equal to none. Third, think of the technical ability necessary to solve the complicated problem of the transfer of the elaborate figures from models (which must have existed) to a scale at least one hundred times greater.

Maria Reiche says:

It is hard to imagine how these ancient people with their limited knowledge could have projected these complicated patterns with such precision on the desert .. it is difficult to conceive how the people with their rudimentary implements could have produced something so complicated and technically involved. Only a race with a considerable amount of intelligence and perseverance could have succeeded in transferring animal and ornamental motifs from their pottery to the ground of the desert in exact proportion.

I don't believe the 'ancient people with their limited knowledge' had anything to do with the figures or lines outside of the construction of some very crude and much smaller copies. I believe ancient people with a great deal of knowledge were the designers and originators and that it was all created several thousand years before the Nazca or Paracas cultures existed.

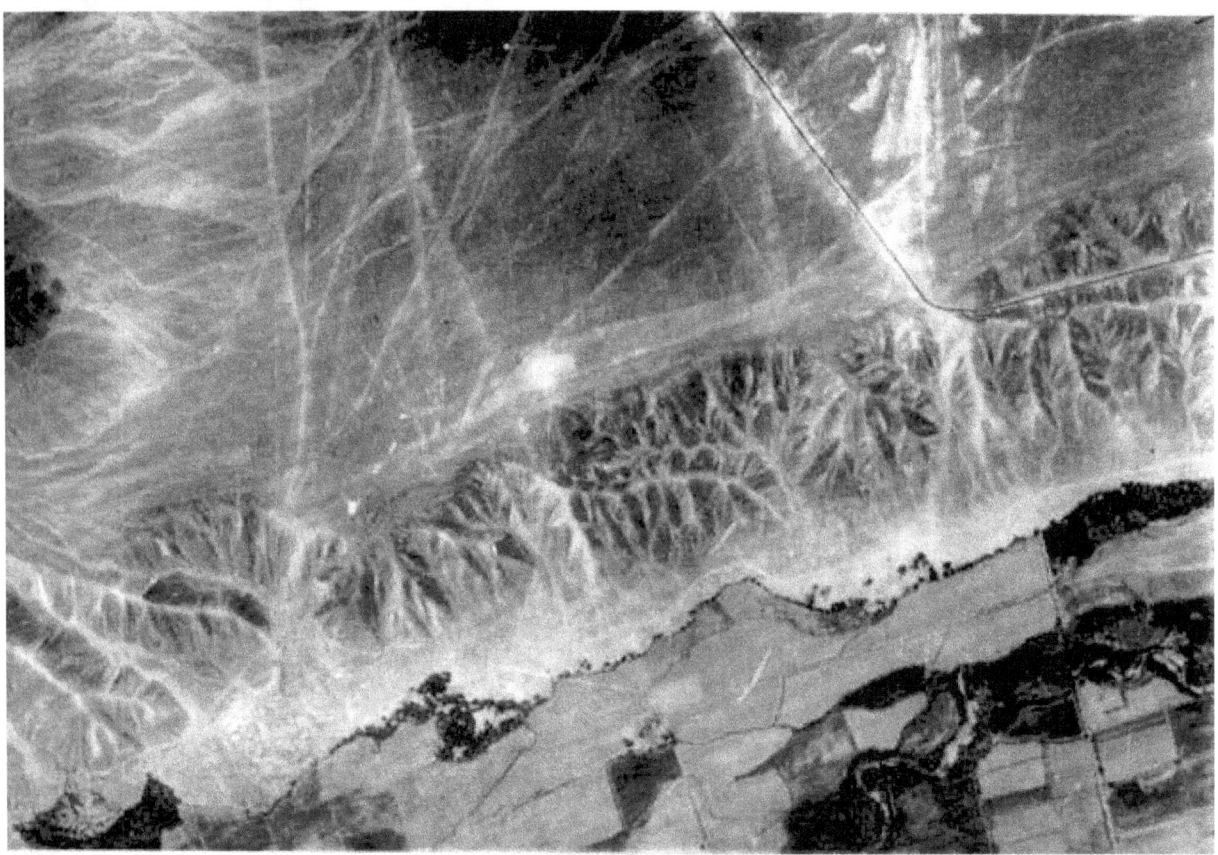

In some places there are irregularly shaped white surfaces or patches. At one time these were an important part of the tracings. They are not dug out like the rest of the designs, but are on the same level as the dark surface. **Figure No. 29** (above) shows some of these inexplicable white areas in the upper right of the photograph taken by the Peruvian Air Force on October 9, 1947, in the vicinity of the Rio del Ingenio. The black band in the upper right is the Pan-American Highway which cuts through a great rectangle in the top of the photograph. The irregular white lines are car tracks.

TRAVELING THE PATH BACK TO THE ROAD IN THE SKY

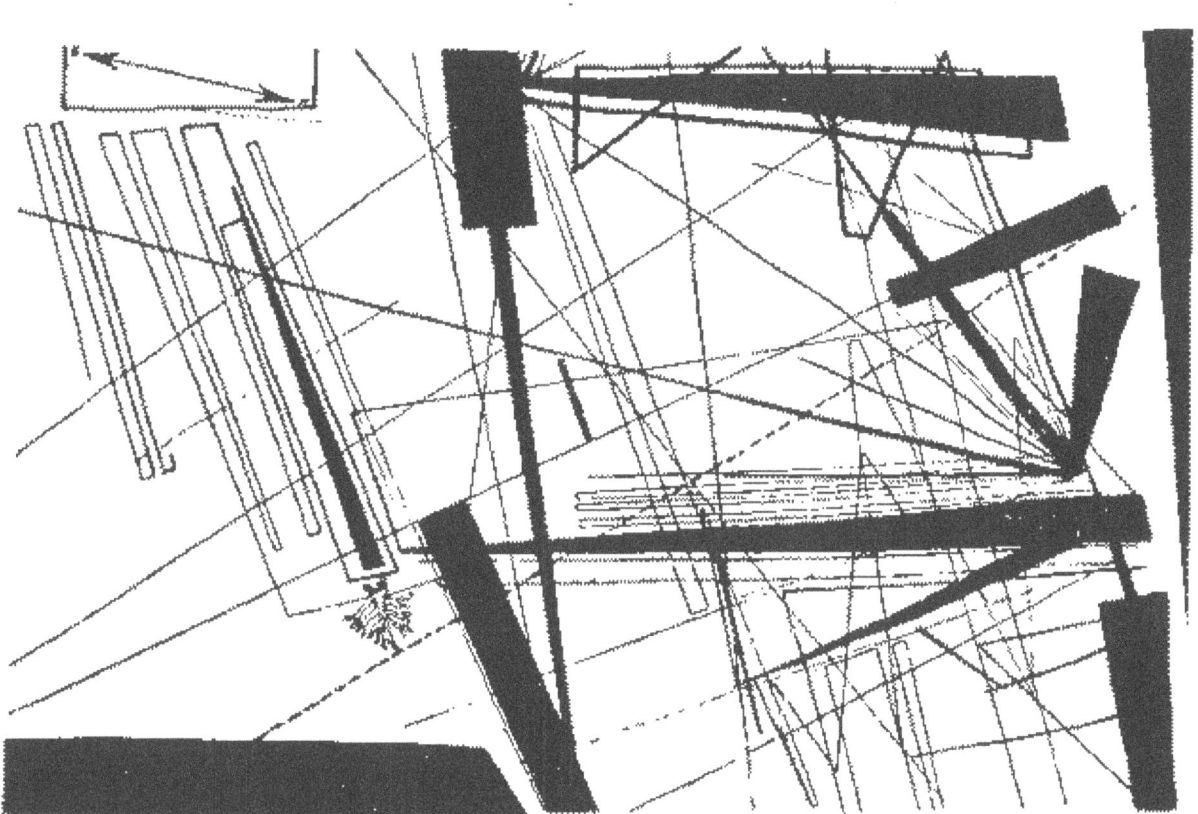

Fig. 30. A detailed map of the region which shows on the photograph in Fig. 29.

Figure No. 30 is a detailed map of the region which shows on the photograph in Figure No. 29 (1 inch= 250 yards). This will give you a better idea of the terrifically complicated delineated surfaces and lines. This map was drawn by the mathematician, Maria Reiche, who gave permission to reproduce it here. (The dotted line is the Pan-American Highway.)

The theory currently popular is that the designs were connected with very ancient magical ceremonies and a calendar system and that the tracings had an astronomical use. I believe that this is true in part, but by no means offers a complete explanation. Commenting on this theory, Maria Reiche says:

The existence of lines which divide the year in two halves by mark ing the 21st of June and the 21st of December is not sufficient proof for the astronomical meaning of the tracings. There are too many different directions, many of these, although very close to solstice directions, are outside the course of the sun. They could find their explanation in certain extreme rising and setting points of planets. Likewise, the great variety of other directions could be interpreted as representing the rising or setting of certain

TRAVELING THE PATH BACK TO THE ROAD IN THE SKY

heavenly bodies. To decide which these were and in what centuries they rose and set over the tracings, would be very difficult because of the great number of different possibilities of such an interpretation.

Dr. Paul Kosok, Professor of History at Long Island University, saw the sun setting exactly over a narrow line, on June 22nd, the solstice date. This led him to believe that this particular line was traced for the special purpose of marking this date. Therefore, he suspected other lines were made for the purpose of fixing exact dates of the year. He believes the tracings form a gigantic calendar and says that 'a reliable calendar was a vital necessity for an agricultural people like the ancient Nazca, whose economy was based on irrigation from rivers which carry water only during certain months of the year. One can think of no better reason to justify the immense effort put in the tracing of these designs, whose complicated pattern would reveal the enormous difficulties overcome by these primitive people in making a calendar.'

Astronomers object to an observation made today that is applied to ancient times, since the sun's setting point was then at an angle equivalent to at least one-eighth of the sun's diameter further north. However, Dr. Kosok has contributed greatly to our knowledge and understanding of the 'Lines of Nazca'. Undoubtedly, the astronomical meaning is *part* of the answer.

Would all of this prodigious amount of work covering a period lasting many centuries have been accomplished merely because primitive people were interested in astrology (including the development of a solar calendar and the determining of the solstices)? Would the Nazca people have gone to all that trouble just to see the sun set or rise over narrow lines? Can their abundance or lack of water for irrigation purposes explain the patterns adequately? Can religious ceremonies alone explain the mystery? I believe all of these answers are true to an extent, but behind the 'mystery on the desert' is something far more ancient and far more important than the whims of Nazca agriculturists, priests or astrologers.

One of the great unanswered questions about Nazca is: Why were the patterns made so immense? This would not be necessary just to view or mark extreme rising and setting points of heavenly bodies. We may find one answer to this in an ancient legend which says:

'We must make our creations great upon the land that the *sky gods* may view them.'

TRAVELING THE PATH BACK TO THE ROAD IN THE SKY

What is the real meaning behind this statement? Is it just the fact that the ancient people made such gigantic patterns merely to let the 'sky gods' know the Nazca were watching for the time when the water should be coming to them so that their crops would be well irrigated? Was this to be a reminder to the 'sky dwellers' so that they wouldn't neglect their 'Earth children'?

I still don't believe these people would have gone to all that work just for the 'sky gods'. They could have attracted the attention of these 'gods' by elaborate rituals and ceremonials and through fasting and prayer. Cultural groups throughout the world who performed ceremonies for needed rain did not construct such immense patterns but made supplications to the 'sky gods' through complicated rituals, etc.

The Hopi Indians of Arizona in the United States have need for great amounts of rain every year for their crops for they live in an arid region of the American Southwest. This is a problem for the Hopis of today as it has been for centuries in the same area. However, the Hopis never turn the surface of the surrounding desert into an immense drawing-board. The reason for this is because these Indians have a totally different concept of 'rain gods' and how to attract their attention. We will be discussing this later.

I believe the statement from the legend is much more ancient than the Nazca people. It must have originally meant, literally, exactly what it says. In other words, there were actually 'sky gods' and somehow they were connected with the necessity for constructing the mystery lines. After this occurrence, the later cultures interpreted the 'sky gods' as those 'dwellers in the heavens' who would or who would not give them water when they needed it for irrigation. The real meaning was lost in antiquity, and the legend took on new meaning with the later people who inhabited the same area. These later people, including the Nazca, actually constructed some designs on the desert themselves, but they are completely different from the earlier delineated surfaces and perfect lines. For the most part the Nazca creations are birds, spiders, fish and a few human forms. The later designs are all *figures* that need only to be viewed from an altitude of a few feet to take on meaning and be completely visible. This altitude can be anywhere from about five feet above the ground on up to four or five hundred feet. The animal figures cannot be distinguished from high altitudes of several thousand feet. Many of these are several hundred feet in length, but Maria Reiche studied them by using a twelve foot and a six foot ladder. Also, a five foot stool was used

TRAVELING THE PATH BACK TO THE ROAD IN THE SKY

because it 'was firmer than the ladder and could withstand a strong wind'. Later, the mathematician used a helicopter of the Peruvian Air Force to view and photograph the animal figures. She is, indeed, an amazing woman-she climbs *outside* of the helicopter while it is in the air to take the pictures herself. One cannot help but admire her stamina and dedication to the study of the 'Lines of Nazca'.

Let us now go back in time, starting with our modern era. We know present-day engineers didn't construct the designs (absurd thought) since there is no record of it, and besides, our highways have been placed *over* the older lines and figures.

We know the Spanish conquerors didn't make our 'Lines of Nazca' for they walked over them and there isn't even one word to be found in their chronicles that would indicate they ever saw the designs. Besides, they didn't come to Peru to construct animal and geometric forms on the sandy desert.

The Incas could not possibly have been the builders since they placed their roads over the immense patterns also, and their legends do not speak of them at all.

Now we come to the first place in history in our 'looking backwards' view where we find a people who knew something about the 'mystery on the desert'. These people were the Nazca. They not only inherited the land from their ancestors but they also inherited many legends that had been built up on ancient traditional evidence. They came into the land peacefully and they were the first people to learn of the existence of the most ancient delineated surfaces. The Incas, remember, came as invaders and conquerors, so did the Spanish, and a conqueror never learns the real secrets of a land, he is only able to capture the outward, visible wealth. In fact, usually, the conqueror remains in the new land to finally become the 'conquered'.

The Nazca retained knowledge of astrology and astronomy from generations of priests who had received the arcane secrets from their forefathers. This ancient knowledge came originally from one of the greatest civilizations the world has ever known. In the interior of South America there existed thousands upon thousands of years ago an empire called 'Land of the Jaguar (Tiger) King', known in the old chronicles as 'Paititi'. After the destruction of this Empire by catastrophe, the remnant of her people traveled over the great Andes Mountains of the west and entered into the desert areas of the Peruvian coast. The Nazca people were the descendants of a part of this remnant that had been saved in the very early days. Therefore they were the guardians of the ancient knowledge.

They knew about the delineated surfaces that were there when they arrived in the area, but they could not possibly duplicate them. However, they knew that somehow the lines had originally served some astronomical and directional purpose because of the legends that had been passed down to them. One of these, already referred to, spoke of the 'sky gods' and that the people made their 'creations great upon the land' so that these 'gods' could easily see them from their vantage point in the heavens. The Nazca could not possibly know what the real meaning behind this legend, and others, was. The 'sky gods' to them became simply 'rain gods' because their economy demanded it. The 'sky gods' of a greater antiquity were those divinities who would supply them with water when they needed it provided the people attracted their attention with sacrifices and adoration.

Of course, the Nazca never viewed the gigantic designs from the air, but they could see a small fraction of them by tracing them for long distances on the ground. How did these primitive people know the lines were there when the later Incas and Spanish were ignorant of the fact? This is not a contradiction, for, as already mentioned, the Nazca had the traditional evidence that had come with their ancestors on their journey over the Andes. Those ancestors had carried the secret knowledge with them and they knew they were traveling to the area of the 'great creations upon the land'. They decided beforehand on this and were headed for this area-to them it was a pilgrimage. The Incas and Spanish on the other hand never came looking for 'great creations upon the land' unless it was creations of gold and silver and conquest. The *motive* was entirely different. If you come into a new land with a blessing that land blesses you in return by revealing its secrets to you. But if you come with a curse and intend to subdue the land, the doors of revelation are closed to you, and you never find the real treasure, only the golden baubles on the surface that are the playthings of would-be conquerors.

The ancient legend to the Nazca became a Divine Ordinance, a commandment from the ancestors they revered, and they, too, had to create the 'great creations upon the land'. We have already discussed how a true happening of the dim past will later take on new ramifications (Apollo, Osiris and Mercury-Thoth became 'gods'). So, the 'sky gods' to the Nazca were 'rain gods'. These people lived in an area where sowing and planting time

TRAVELING THE PATH BACK TO THE ROAD IN THE SKY

started abruptly and unannounced some time in November or December. From one day to the other the water came and filled the wide riverbeds of the Peruvian coast, which during previous months had been absolutely dry or containing only a tiny stream. The waiting for the water must have reached a state of fear, for if it didn't arrive in time, the year would advance to the point where they could no longer plant and harvest their crops. To overcome this uncertainty, the Nazca decided to follow the commandment of the ancient tradition. They must also build 'great creations on the land' so the 'sky or rain gods' could see them and know that the Nazca needed water. It was to be a reminder to those who dwelt in the 'heavens'.

As stated above, the Nazca could not duplicate the ancient perfectly straight lines going in all directions, so they transferred from their pottery, the figures of birds, monkeys, and spiders, and placed them on the ground. The great delineated surfaces or pathways are always on level ground (sometimes extending on over small artificial or natural hills, however), but the animal figures, etc., are traced on slopes. Maria Reiche has noticed that later generations in the area of the designs made frequent changes, for some designs overlap others and therefore must have been built later. Miss Reiche also says: '... if one could find a higher point of observation, one would be able to see how they (lines of the figures) continue...' For that purpose she used the ladders. Now, the Nazca could also have observed the construction of their animal figures from specially built stone and adobe platforms which could have been removed later. Mounds of heaped up stones have been found in connection with the designs which may have been related to these points of observation made by the Nazca people. However, these people never were able to get to an altitude of three, four or even ten thousand feet. They couldn't possibly have built a 'Tower of Babel' to observe the older creations.

Pottery fragments are found everywhere on the ground near the tracings, but 'their designs show a great variety in style' which indicates they belong to many different periods. A stone was found containing a typical Nazca pottery motif, a snake head and a small trophy head. The painted pottery of these people has the same motifs as the gigantic animal figures traced on the ground; therefore, there is no question who made *them,* but what of the delineated surfaces the Nazca could never properly see?

The Nazca constructions are few and were 'copies' of the older work in that they apparently (to the Nazca) served the same purpose. They were not

TRAVELING THE PATH BACK TO THE ROAD IN THE SKY

literal copies of the lines, etc., for the Nazca creations were entirely different in form, etc.

Therefore, we must go back in time to see what or who preceded the Nazca, to get at the real *cause* of the mystery. When we study the Nazca people and their accomplishments we only are arriving at *effect,* for they represent the effect of something out of the dim past that necessitated the building of the lines and surfaces originally. Their attempts and beliefs were a *degeneration* of a more highly evolved science and understanding that was known to their predecessors.

Who the 'predecessors' were we do not know, but that they existed there is no question. As already mentioned, the earlier race constructed only delineated surfaces and astronomically perfect lines; they never made crude animal forms. Also, their creations had to be viewed from a very high altitude, no 'stools' or 'ladders' or 'mounds of earth and stone' would reach the necessary height. Also their designs were always placed on level ground whereas the Nazca forms were generally placed on slopes where they could be viewed by the people more easily on a higher elevation. As Maria Reiche says: '... standing before such a slope or on an opposite elevation, one can sometimes distinguish the figures on it clearly...'

The delineated surfaces are usually central features around which all other forms are grouped. This is so because the Nazca built around the older tracings they had found on the ground while observing a small fraction of their total area.

Now if the later Nazca 'rain gods' actually were real beings who came to Earth in the past, and were called in the legends 'sky gods', then who were they? This is a much more important question than who were the designers and builders of the lines, for it answers the great question of the entire mystery: Why were the immense patterns made?

Did the strange surfaces and lines serve as markers or *beacons* for something arriving from outer space since they must be observed from high in the air, and only then take on visibility and meaning? Was the great labor expended to place signal stations on the coast of South America? If so, for what purpose? Warning? Guidance? Indicators? Many questions are raised here that demand answers.

Tracings are found in other parts of the coastal region. They are not as well preserved as those around Nazca and Palpa because of the peculiar

TRAVELING THE PATH BACK TO THE ROAD IN THE SKY

geographic location and the climatic conditions present in the latter area. Ten miles north of Lima and over three hundred miles north of the Nazca area patterns have been found. Reports have come from Chile that similar designs are there. In the Casma valley of Peru not far from the carved stones of the six-fingered dancers (**see Fig. No. 24**), there are more immense patterns. Facing the Bay of Paracas (the area of the riddle of the mummies), Peru, etched into a sandhill on the cliffs of the bay is the monstrous symbol called 'Tres Cruces'. It is over six hundred feet high and is unquestionably a 'Tree of Life' symbol. It faces the sea and directly north-south. It was made by four feet of sand being scooped out of the ground. Almost nothing is known of the people who buried their dead in the caverns of Paracas. There are no remains to be found of their cities or dwellings where their rich fabric was woven. They lived temporarily on the Bay of Paracas while they prepared their dead for internment in the stone crypts. Is the 'Tree of Life' symbol etched in the sand related to them? Could it possibly have been a guide or *beacon* to those who came from some unknown land in the sea and stopped only long enough to bury their dead? This is another of the great mysteries of the Peruvian southern desert.

We have already discussed the figures visible from the air on the Marcahuasi Plateau in Peru. In the United States designs are found that are more like the Nazca animal forms than the delineated surfaces and lines. In Ohio the 'mounds' or patterns were made of low, compact walls of earth. This was necessary since the designs were subjected to a more rigorous climate than is found in Peru. In the American Southwest many other designs have been found recently, in fact, such signals or *beacons* for the 'sky gods' are found all over the planet Earth and there is reference to them in countless legends. The true happening was later distorted and became an integral part of ancient theological beliefs and the 'sky gods' were added to the enormous pantheon of the ancients. The figures and lines are well preserved in Peru in the area of Nazca-Palpa because of the geographical-climatic situation there.

Another startling discovery, that very definitely has a connection with our 'Lines of Nazca', was made only recently by the men flying in the B-52's of the United States Air Force. These men were at very high altitudes over the area of the Great Pyramid at Gizeh in Egypt. Suddenly they noticed on the ground, which surrounded the Great Pyramid itself, many perfectly straight lines extending out into the desert, and going in every direction.

TRAVELING THE PATH BACK TO THE ROAD IN THE SKY

These lines were never observed by the travelers passing by the Great Pyramid for centuries, nor were they seen by low-flying aircraft, but the B-52 flies very high, and because of this the tracings were observed for the first time. Did I hear someone say 'The plot thickens?' Indeed it does, indeed it does!

In Case No. 24 of the Museo Nacional de Antropologia y Arqueologia (National Museum of Anthropology and Archaeology) in Magdalena Vieja, Lima, Peru, there are two pottery pieces from the Mochica culture of Peru. These Pre-Inca objects represent men with wings on their backs. They are ingeniously strapped on, with the straps clearly held by the left hand of each figure. The straps go from the wings and cross in front of each man. Evidently the ancient Mochica people of the northern part of Peru had legends that spoke of the time when men flew in the skies above. And because of this they immortalized the happening by depicting it in a stylized form in ceramics. It also reminds us of the tale from Greek mythology where Icarus and his father escaped the Cretan labyrinth by means of wings made from feathers. Icarus flew too near the sun, the wax of his wings melted, and he was drowned in the sea. What do Mochica pottery figures have to do with Icarus and his escape from the labyrinth? There is mystery upon mystery in this strange land that all of her conquerors, Inca and Spanish alike, were never able to unravel.

Figure No. 31 is of the area about two miles north of Palpa. The photograph of the flat-topped long ridge between the Rio Grande (to the right) and the Rio Palpa (to the left) was taken by the Peruvian Air Force on January 4, 1945, at an altitude of 3,000 feet. In the background is the Pan-American Highway winding up the ridge and down again. (Looking south-east.)

We mentioned before the overlapping of different designs which seem to be the result of corrections or additions which have taken place at a later period. In the centre of the photograph in Figure No. 31, two delineated surfaces can be seen completely overlapping or crossing each other. There is also another important example of 'overlapping'. This is seen in the foreground of the photograph, where exist ancient stone ruins, clearly visible on the flat topped ridge. If you will look closely you will see where the ancient city was built directly over the immense lines and surfaces. Here is absolute proof of the great antiquity of the patterns or 'Lines of Nazca'.

If you will look even more closely you will see yet another example of

TRAVELING THE PATH BACK TO THE ROAD IN THE SKY

'overlapping' that may turn out to be the answer to the entire mystery, and then again, it may be nothing at all. Whatever it turns out to be don't let the 'experts' tell you it's nothing but a large grasshopper resting on the ridge!

When I was going through hundreds of photographs in the archives of the Peruvian Air Ministry, I came across this photograph. My eye was immediately caught by the extensive ruins, then I noticed that they had been constructed over the great surfaces. As I traced the largest surface out from the ancient city towards the centre of the photograph, my glance came to rest on something very strange and out of place at the very end of, and centered in the middle of, the great surfaced area. This 'strange something' was much whiter than anything else around it, and stood out clearly against the darker surface of the prehistoric pattern. What was it?

At first I thought it must have been caused during the developing process of the film. If this were so it would not appear on other photographs taken at different times. I quickly turned to the next picture (see Fig. No. 32). Here I found the same white design again which almost appeared to be glowing! That meant it had been no accident in the dark room which had caused the appearance of this 'something'. If it were present in two different photographs taken at different times this would seem to indicate that the 'something' was stationary on the ground. I called to one of the Air Force Captains who was standing by and asked him if he could identify the glow on the ridge. At first, he said it looked very much like the targets that are made on the ground for bombing practice. I handed him a large magnifying glass that was on the table in front of us. He studied the 'something' for a long time. I could see a slight frown developing on his face. Then, very solemnly, he said :

'I thought it might be a bomb target, but it just simply can't be—under magnification it doesn't look like it at all.'

'What do you think it is, Captain?' I said.

'Frankly, sir, I don't know. I wish I did. I have never seen anything like it before.'

If it wasn't a target, then what kind of a stationary object would look like that, I thought, and what would it be doing out on that ridge in such a desolate place, a place of forgotten ruins and still older and forgotten lines? Yet, it must be stationary or a permanent part of the ridge if two different photographs taken at different times indicate it. Then I had an idea. I looked

TRAVELING THE PATH BACK TO THE ROAD IN THE SKY

in the records to see when the two photographs had been taken by the Peruvian Air Force. Both were taken in the same place over an area about two miles north of Palpa at 3,000 feet altitude and *both were taken the same day,* January 4, 1945. Here was my first real clue. Both photographs were taken on the same day in the same area at the same altitude and only a few moments apart! This meant the 'something' may not have been connected with the ridge at all, but may have been an 'object' of some kind that had landed there. The thought is all the more intriguing when you notice that the 'object' is apparently 'glowing' and contains an outer bright ring with a dense shining centre. Under magnification it is even apparently casting a shadow on the ground beneath it. This could mean that it is hovering there.

What kind of a 'hovering object' would be centered in the middle of an ancient delineated surface that looked like some kind of a fantastic airfield, and actually perched at the very end of this field as though it were ready to 'take off' like some weirdly-shaped aircraft? Could it possibly be a modern visitation of the 'sky gods' who need the 'creations great upon the Earth'? Actually, it may be nothing at all, we can't be sure.

However, we are sure of one thing, and that is that there were 'sky gods' who came to Earth in the dim past. But why did they come and what was the necessity of immense astronomically perfect lines all over the world? These 'gods' or heavenly messengers must have been in communication with some highly advanced civilizations on Earth : perhaps these people assisted the 'gods' in the building of the lines and surfaces, or perhaps the 'gods' were only the master architects and the Earth races did the actual building. But what purpose did these patterns serve?

There must be a connection between the discoveries of Prof. Cattoi in Italy, the mysteries of Marcahuasi and the 'Lines of Nazca' in Peru. Remember, Cattoi found areas where there was a great concentration underground of electro-magnetic energy and he discovered gigantic stone figures in the same areas plus the fact that there is a high frequency of UFO sightings in the same places. At Marcahuasi there are the same great monoliths plus the humming sound which also may indicate great underground concentrations of electro-magnetic energy. At Nazca there are the fabulous lines and delineated surfaces that were made 'great up on the land' so the 'sky gods could view them'. Cattoi has successfully photographed a UFO directly over the carving of an enormous stone head! What are the UFOs doing in these areas?

TRAVELING THE PATH BACK TO THE ROAD IN THE SKY

Actually, visitors from space may be doing many things when they visit ancient sites of former civilizations which were the former areas of previous visitation on their part in the forgotten past of our planet Earth.

It is possible that these magnetic centers can be used by the UFOs as 're-fuelling' stations. Space craft do not use 'fuel' as we think of it, but many of the smaller craft never were designed to go through interstellar space. They are carried to the Earth in the interior of a great 'Mother Ship" and are released over our planet in their work as 'Scout Ships'. Many of these smaller craft must replenish their magnetic (light) drive by drawing on the magnetic field of the Earth itself. Naturally they would look for, and find, the areas of greatest magnetic concentration from which to do their 're-fuelling'.

However, these areas of magnetic energy can be *natural* or they can be *artificial. In Other Tongues-Other Flesh* we discussed the possibility of a new science—the science of *cultural magnetism.* In part, we said:

... where meteorites fall there is great civilization or highly civilized peoples .. this is because meteorites are attracted to the anomalies (magnetic anomalies found in various parts of the world), and the anomalies are amplifiers of Universal Knowledge constantly permeating all space as the 'music of the spheres'. Great cultural centers are found over and near such anomalies. The individuals living in such areas are receivers of this Universal Knowledge and it manifests itself in great works of art, music, literature, scientific achievement, architecture, philosophy, etc. Depending on what vibration an individual is operating in, he will create in one of these fields.

A study of the major fault lines of Earth also shows that culture follows these lines because magnetic anomalies are found along them as well as volcanoes. Trace the fault lines of Earth and see where they cross areas of great cultural advancement...

... the anomaly acts as a Universal radio because it amplifies everything coming in from outer space. Highly sensitive individuals have strange experiences when they enter an anomaly area. Their ability at reception is increased to a fantastic degree...

All of the above discussion in *Other Tongues-Other Flesh* was concerned with *natural* areas of magnetic concentration (vortical action). If we study the major fault lines of Earth we find one goes right through the centre of Italy and another one goes through the entire length of Peru. Therefore, we could explain UFOs showing up over magnetic concentration centers in these two countries from the standpoint of *natural magnetic* areas. Also, we know that great cultural advancement has taken place in the past in the Italian area, and this is also true of Peru in the area of the mystery lines and figures. We find the finest weavings in the world at Paracas, and we find beautifully wrought ceramics at Nazca. Again this proves our contention that the development of culture and the effects of magnetism are somehow related.

However, there is one point that may indicate some of the magnetic 're-fuelling' stations of the UFOs or space ships are *artificial.* This is the fact that UFOs show up so frequently over the gigantic monoliths in all parts of the world. Why are these stone carvings found over areas of magnetic concentration? The appearance of UFOs over *natural* magnetic areas is understandable from the 're-fuelling' standpoint, but why are the great stone figures nearly always present also? In the case of the 'Lines of Nazca' there are no giant statues, but there are thousands of directional lines.

It is entirely possible that the areas where we find the great carvings constitute centers where underground are located the still intact cities of the 'El's'. The UFOs could 're-fuel' or draw energy from the ancient 'El' laboratories and complicated magnetic devices. Is that why Cattoi saw a space ship over the great stone head? Is that why the granite images of Marcahuasi emit an odd humming sound?

Maria Reiche says:

... an analysis might lead to the result that the tracings (of Nazca-Palpa) could not have been astronomical at all, although it is difficult to imagine how their existence could be explained otherwise.'

Their existence might be explained by the fact that visitors from interstellar space, coming to our planet millennia ago, traveling the *road in the sky* of innumerable *yesterdays,* needed signal stations in all parts of the world. These served as directional markers to point the way to either natural or artificial areas of magnetic energy for the 're-fuelling' of their reconnaissance ships.

The 'mystery' of the 'Lines of Nazca' is that they were *beacons for the 'gods'.*

TRAVELING THE PATH BACK TO THE ROAD IN THE SKY

THE MARTIAN MINIATURES

AS we travel our highway of *yesterdays,* we come to another area where surely the great *road in the sky,* in some far distant time, swept down to the Earth planet and left traces of its coming.

We don't know the date, but it is many hundreds of years ago; the day is exceedingly warm; there isn't a cloud in the sky and the sun burns fiercely upon us. We have walked a long way and finally see in the distance the form of another human being. As we approach closer we see that this other being is holding a great globe or sphere in one hand, and with the other hand deft fingers seem to be moving rapidly over the rounded surface. As we continue to walk towards the working figure we suddenly realize that this must be a map-maker at work-someone is adding details to a many-colored globe. The pattern is indistinct at such a distance and we pause for a moment in wonder. What sphere is this? What world could it represent? Surely it is not the Earth!

We continue on and move ever closer, and then the stark reality of the scene falls into place and we step into the freshly swept yard in front of a mud and stone house belonging to a Pueblo Indian family of the Great American Southwest. For a time we felt as though we were watching a medieval chart-maker creating some fantastic land surfaces on an even more fantastic planet. But we were in North America, and it was hundreds of years before the advent of Columbus in 1492. Our 'vision' from the past is vivid as we look down at the seated figure of a very old and wrinkled Indian. She sits beside her yucca leaf brushes, her many pigments in shallow receptacles, and a great polished clay vessel that is ready for more decorations. With a start we realize that the 'fantastic sphere or globe' of a few minutes before is really the 'polished clay vessel', a great pottery bowl that the Indian woman had been painting. She picks it up again and begins to apply her colors; her

TRAVELING THE PATH BACK TO THE ROAD IN THE SKY

skill is amazing for she does not sketch her design in advance, nor does she do any measuring. If a pattern of the design is repeated around the entire bowl, it simply comes out right. If we ask her how she manages to do this, she will say: 'Well, it seems as if something is telling me what to do, and I just do it.' The elements of her designs, often complex, are painted with complete accuracy. A curve moves smoothly and its arc is correct, a straight line does not waver and does not vary in its width, yet, her work is swiftly done. Was it just the heat of the burning desert sun that had blurred our vision and made the great painted, polychrome bowl appear to represent some unknown terraqueous globe? Was it the distance that had made all details seem indistinct, or was it the desert haze that had given the entire scene an unearthly, unreal quality? What had caused us to think that our journey backwards in Time had brought us to an old chart-maker's shop or ancient astronomer's observatory—observatory! —that was it!

In the modern 20th Century we had often gone to the hill overlooking Flagstaff, Arizona, and there we visited the Lowell Observatory; we had seen its 24-inch refracting telescope and its odd museum. It was in the museum that we recall seeing the great white globes on which Dr. Percival Lowell had drawn his surface markings of the 'Red Planet' Mars. He had been the foremost observer of the continually changing surface of this planet. In 1894 he had built his observatory and later charted a total of nearly 700 canals on the face of Mars, some as much as 3,000 miles in length. The canals intersected, he said, and at such points existed the 'cities' or oases where the inhabitants of Mars came together to be near the precious and dwindling water supply. From 1894 until 1915, Dr. Lowell and his staff of astronomers studied the 'Red Planet' carefully. 'Mars is inhabited,' said Lowell, 'we have absolute proof!' It was those 'white globes' of Mars with the unique markings indicating surface features that our mind recalled when we had walked in the desert sun towards the quaint old Indian woman of the early Pueblos. But surely we would find no scientific study of the planet Mars in such a setting. Areology couldn't possibly exist among the primitive agricultural people of the American Southwest removed only a millennium from the birth of Christ.

Why had the ceramic designs viewed at a distance reminded me of a global map, and why had I later tied them in with the globes made by Lowell of the planet Mars? We look down again as the deft fingers of the old Indian continue to move rhythmically over the partially painted bowl and we realize suddenly that there is no change, for as we study the designs they no longer appear to be the abstract geometric patterns of vessels, but appear for all the world like Lowell's charts, maps and globes of Mars. We look out over the sandy wastes to see the long straight lines of the irrigation canals, and along their border grow many plants and stunted desert trees that eagerly grasp for the water brought to the fields by the men of the tribe. We realize that these are the canals whose ruins have been excavated by archaeologists in the 20th Century.

When we return from our 'Time Trip' a greater revelation comes to us. What were the potters of an Indian tribe doing when they made their sacred designs painted on pottery so resemble the known surface features of the planet Mars that almost anyone could use these 'ceramic charts' as reliable maps if he were to find himself on the 'Red Planet'? We also wonder if there is any connection between the fact that the Indians of that day lived in an arid country that required the construction of elaborate canal systems and the fact that Lowell said the Martians had built canals because they lived in a dry world and had little water? What do the irrigation canals of a planet millions of miles away in space have to do with an Indian tribe that also constructs canals in the desert and makes strange designs on clay vessels that unmistakably resemble the surface complications of the said planet?

We could call this Indian work 'planetary pottery portraits', for here are representations on a much reduced scale that might have been conceived by a Schiaparelli or a Lowell while observing Mars. These, then, are 'The Martian Miniatures'.

Recently, a friend wrote to me and gave me some ideas which most definitely were connected with the research I was engaged in at that time. Briefly, this is what she had to say:

A number of years ago, while going through some examples of Southwest Indian pottery designs in search of new material for jewelry and fabric designs, I was struck by the resemblance of one of these designs to an area on a map of Mars. This seemed like an interesting 'coincidence', so I copied the design and made a map of the area it resembled. I did this just for the sake of curiosity at the time.

However, because I have almost no faith in 'coincidence', I kept my eyes open, and somewhat later two more fragmentary designs turned up and both bore the same strange resemblance to part of the surface mark-

TRAVELING THE PATH BACK TO THE ROAD IN THE SKY

ings of the planet Mars.

Time passed until last year (1957) when I happened to read the large two-volume Smithsonian Institution reports on the archaeological research undertaken in 1900-1901 in the Little Colorado-Gila River area, This included the sites of Homolobi, Kintiel, Chaves Pass, Chevelon, Four Mile Ruin and others. The illustrations I found were startling. Not only was I able to check up on the fragments I had found previously, but there were other and even better examples showing the same kind of unbelievable correspondence.

By this time, I had a much better and more detailed map of Mars to work with. This was the Mercator Projection Map from : *Astronomy For Everyman.* However, the projection distorts the designs to some extent, although the main elements still appear quite clearly. I obtained a small globe and proceeded to transfer the Mercator Projection Map back to a sphere! When I had finished, I was startled to find that the correspondence stood out even more clearly, and I was greatly impressed by the fact that most of the Indian designs appeared in bowls or on the rounded surfaces of jugs and jars.

Figure 33a

Figue 33b

The Martian surface features as found on ancient Indian bowls were stylized into the nearest geometrical shapes according to the potter's usage of designs and the custom of the day in artistic ceramic expression. However, this does not prevent recognition of the features at once, for every salient detail of the Martian area is retained.

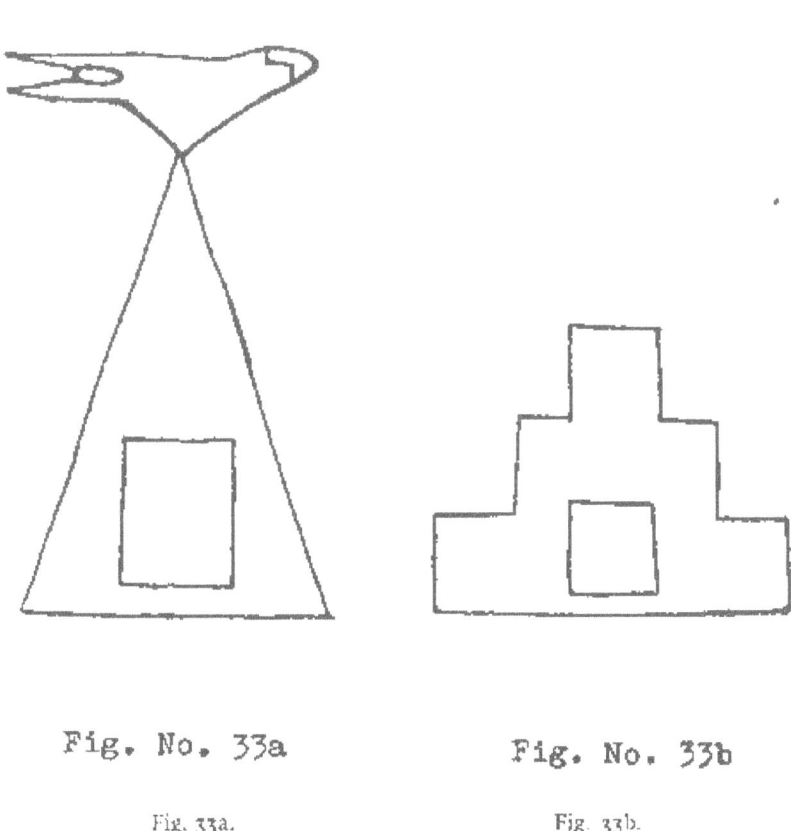

Fig. No. 33a

Fig. No. 33b

Fig. 33a.
One of the ancient designs from Chevelon.

Fig. 33b.
A variation of Fig. 33a.

TRAVELING THE PATH BACK TO THE ROAD IN THE SKY

Anthropologists now give very modern interpretations or meanings to the various shapes and figures. To arrive at these deductions they use 'informants' among the Indians who are now the present inhabitants of the ancient area where the polychrome pottery is found buried in countless ruins. The geometric designs are called : 'rain clouds,' 'arrows,' 'mountains', 'feathers,' 'valleys,' 'eagle,' 'sun,' etc.

Certainly the modern Indians do not really know what those very ancient designs mean, and like the scientists, they have invented names for them-what looks like a'mountain' becomes a'mountain' and so forth. The original meaning is lost in antiquity for contact was broken off with the ancients who at one time apparently had a use for the strange 'ceramic charts'.

In the Smithsonian Institution (Bureau of American Ethnology) reports of 1900-1901, we read:

'A symbol of the rain cloud among the people of the pueblo, now a ruin, at the mouth of Chevelon Fork, was a triangle enclosing a rectangle. These symbols were found on a stone slab excavated from that ruin in 1896, and were figured in reports of the work accomplished in that year.'

This so-called 'rain cloud symbol' is one of the most prominent elements of design found in ancient Indian pottery. The triangle (sometimes it is plain and sometimes it is stepped) stands on its base and generally contains a rectangle within it which is always lighter in color than the triangle.

If you will look at **Fig. No. 33** you will immediately see that one does not have to employ imagination at all to recognize the prominent triangle of the *Syrtis Major* area on Mars with the brighter (and lighter) area of *Hellas* at its base.

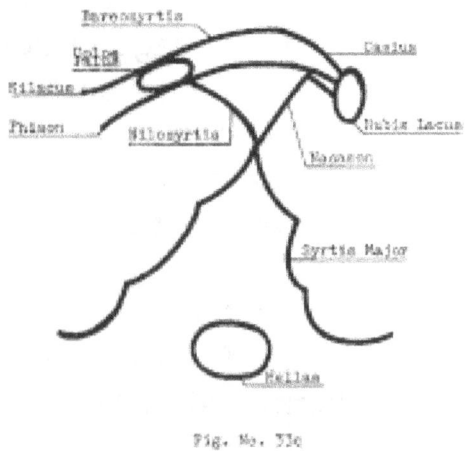

Fig. No. 33c
A map of Martian features

Fig. No. 33a is one of the ancient designs from Chevelon which displays the triangle, the bright area translated into a rectangle for the sake of design, and a birdlike figure surmounting the entire drawing. **Fig. No. 33b** is a variation of 33a which is sometimes found on Indian pottery. Its stepped outline is even more similar to the lines of *Syrtis Major*. **Fig. No. 33c** is a map of the Martian features.

TRAVELING THE PATH BACK TO THE ROAD IN THE SKY

The 'bird-like figure' has some very interesting features. There is a bifurcated 'tail' bearing an oval area within the fork and there is a triangular 'body' with a 'head' that has a peculiar stepped line separating it from the rest of that 'body'.

If we look directly beyond the apex of *Syrtis Major* we can see a triangular area formed by the Martian canals Nilosyrtis and Nasamon. Where Nasamon runs up towards, but not into, Nubis Lacus, we find the angles which are similar to the stepped line of the 'bird head'. Nubis Lacus is in the position of the 'head' and the canals Casius and Bareosyrtis form the 'back' of the bird-like figure. Silacus and Phison form the bifurcated tail, and in the same place where it appears on the ancient Indian design is the oval area of Coloe Palus.

Of course, the entire design, as used by the Indians, has been stylized. But the major elements have been preserved and are in their proper relationship to one another.

Syrtis Major, in common with certain other areas, shows points, or inverted deltas, where Martian canals run out from it into the desert regions of the planet. In some pottery designs these features are preserved and depicted in their exact number! In others, however, the idea of 'steps' is retained but without any apparent attention to the number.

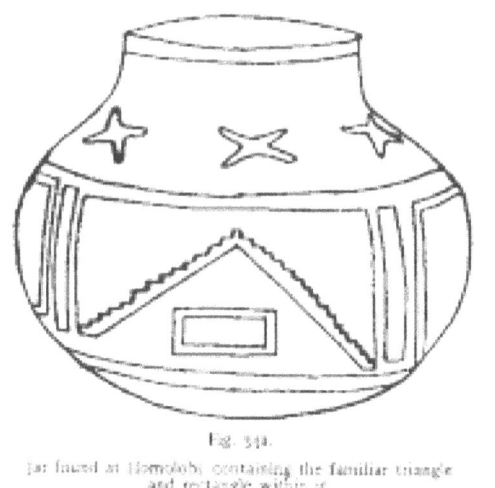

Fig. 34a.
jar found at Homolobi containing the familiar triangle and rectangle within it.

Figure 34a

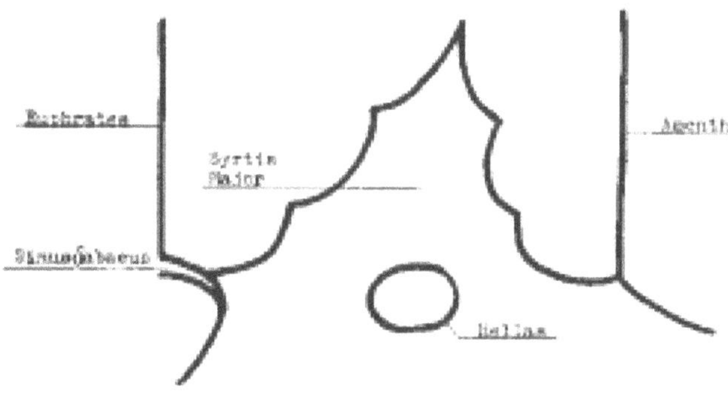

Fig. No. 34b
This shows more details of the *Syrtis Major* area

Figure 34b

TRAVELING THE PATH BACK TO THE ROAD IN THE SKY

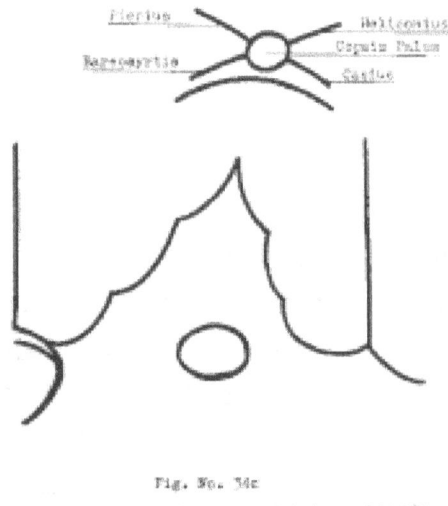

Fig. No. 34c
The two vertical lines are the Martian canals Euphrates and Amenthes.

Figure 34c

If we look at Fig. No. 34, we see yet another example of the features of *Syrtis Major* being employed for ceramic decoration. **Figure No. 34a** is of a jar that was found at Homolobi. It contains the familiar triangle and light rectangle within it. However, in this design strong vertical lines run up either side of the triangle and frame the entire motif. Crosses extend around the shoulder of the vessel well above the apex of the big triangle. **Fig. No. 34b** shows more details of the Syrtis *Major* area, and we can plainly see two heavy vertical 'lines' in the exact position where the Indian artisans painted them on their pottery vessel. These two 'lines' are actually the very wide Martian canals, Euphrates and Amenthes. **Fig. No. 34c** reveals even more Indian ingenuity. We have already seen that the triangular bird-shape is directly above and connected with the apex of Syrtis *Major.* However, let us ignore this connection (as it is ignored on the jar from Homolobi) and leave out the major part of the bird-like design. **In Fig. No. 34c** then, we add that Martian surface feature which is just above the 'back' of the bird-like area. In the map of the area we find Bareosyrtis and Casius again, the same canals we depicted in **Fig. No. 33c.** This time, however, they are shown entering *Copais Palus,* and the canals Pierius and Heliconius go off towards the Martian polar region. Comparing this map **(Fig. No. 34c)** then, with the design elements of the Homolobi jar **(Fig. No. 34a)**, we see that the canals Bareosyrtis, Casius, Pierius and Heliconius actually form the four sections which make up the cross on the shoulder of the jar, and Copais *Palus* forms the very centre of this cross.

TRAVELING THE PATH BACK TO THE ROAD IN THE SKY

Fig. No. 35 concerns a beautiful bowl from Four Mile Ruin and the area of Mars surrounding Nubis Lacus. Fig. No. 35a shows only a part of the complete bowl design. Actually, the complicated design elements omitted here represent other surface features near Nubis Lacus in a startling way, but for matters of simplification they are not considered here. Fig. No. 35b really speaks for itself. If you will compare the elements of the Indian bowl with the Martian canals and features you will discover the amazing similarity. The 'butterfly' wings are formed by canals. The 'head' is represented by Nubis Lacus, and the long 'body' by the formation of Aleyonius. The 'antenna' is beautifully made by Nepenthes and Rhesus. The canal Amenthes becomes part of the line of the spiral effect shown in **Fig. No. 35a,** and *Hellas* (the bright or lighter area) becomes the very centre of the spiral. The dotted lines in **Fig. No. 35b** indicate the position of the lines as added in the Indian decoration of **Fig. No. 35a**. Once again, the Pueblo craftsmen stylized the entire design to conform to the standards of their day.

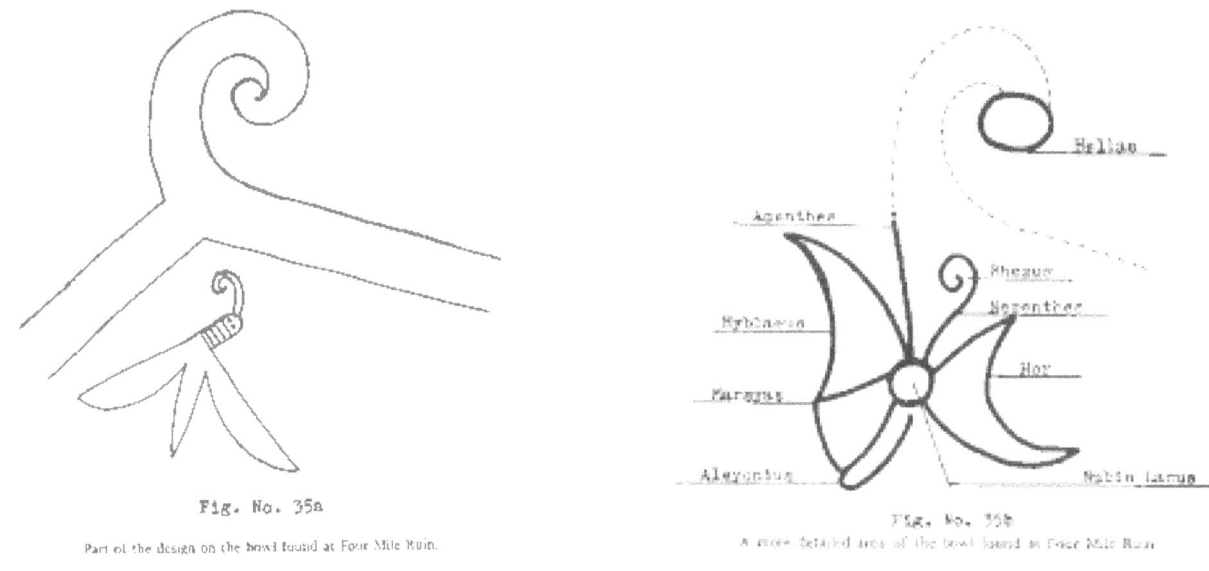

Figure 35a   **Figure 35b**

Fig. No. 36 also shows a highly decorated bowl from Four Mile Ruin. You will notice that the bowl was 'divided in half' by the potter so that each half contains the same identical design. Therefore, when the bow is rotated you will always see the design in the same position as it faces you. **Fig. No. 36a** shows the bowl with 'three arrows', two dark triangular areas, an elongated stepped area and a peculiar little square towards the rim of the bowl (bottom centre). The square is divided by a diagonal line running from one corner to another. Of course, the design has been stylized to make a good

TRAVELING THE PATH BACK TO THE ROAD IN THE SKY

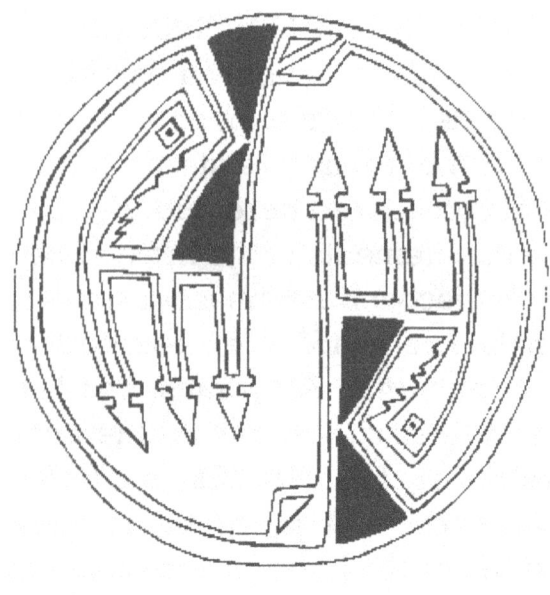

Fig. No. 36a
Portion of another highly decorated bowl from Four Mile Ruin.

balanced pattern, but the Martian area represented here is startling. **Fig. No. 36b** is of the corresponding area of Mars. From Trivium Charontis three great canals branch out. They are Tartarus, Lastrygon, and the double-canal Cerberus. Looking at **Fig. No. 36a** we see all three canals are shown as 'arrows' and represented as double-canals. We wonder if this was done by the Indian designer for symmetrical reasons or if all three canals are actually double-canals like Cerberus? If astronomers some day declare Tartarus and Lastrygon to be double-canals also, we will know that some Indian potter hundreds of years before them knew this fact. Below Trivium Charontis we find a dark triangular area that is almost identical in shape to the area painted dark on the bowl. This area is formed by the canals Hades, Styx, and Boreas. Where Hades and Boreas join at Propontis, another similar dark triangle is indicated formed by the canals Rhyndacus, Choaspes, and Granicus. This area is also painted as a dark triangle on the Indian bowl. The two dark triangular areas on Mars have

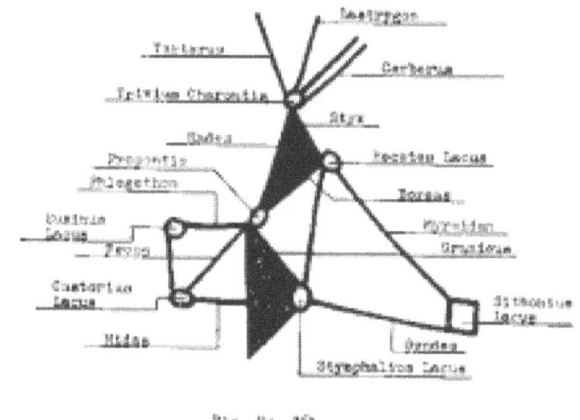

Fig. No. 36b
Corresponding area of Mars as shown on the bowl in Fig. 36a.

shown more indications of vegetation than the other areas immediately surrounding them. Therefore, the artisans depicted them exactly as they are on Mars, on the clay bowl. Where the canal Myrmidan joins Hecates Lacus and the canal Gyndes joins Stymphaliusacus we find another triangular area which is lighter in color. On the bowl we find an almost identical area which is also lighter in color. A distinguishing feature of this lighter triangular area in **Fig. No. 36b** is the odd-shaped and square Sithonius Lacus. In the bowl design we see the same square depicted at the end of the triangular area. Even though the potter made a few changes, these are so slight that the comparison is amazing. In **Fig. No. 36b**, we look to the left of Propontis to find a

TRAVELING THE PATH BACK TO THE ROAD IN THE SKY

square area with a diagonal division. Two corners of the square are Euxinus Lacus and Castorius Lacus, and two sides are formed by the canals Phlegethon and Midas. One side is formed by another canal which is not named on the existing Martian maps. The canal Fevos forms the diagonal line cutting across the square. In the bowl design of **Fig. No. 36a** we find the same square area divided by a diagonal line (and going in the right direction) towards the rim of the bowl (bottom centre).

The many corresponding elements in this design alone make 'coincidence' seem absurd.

The Smithsonian Institution reports of 1900-1901, have this to say about this strange design of **Fig. No. 36:**

'The design shown... is unique among all forms of ornamentation known and its meaning is incomprehensible to the author.'

What we have given above on the correspondences between Martian surface features and the designs on prehistoric Indian pottery vessels is, of course, only a very small example of what really exists. There are countless Indian patterns that duplicate the surface formations of the 'Red Planet' Mars. What is the answer? Here is the great enigma of the Southwestern American desert.

All of this reminds us of another enigma, one of the so-called 'mysteries' of the southern Peruvian desert-the 'Lines of Nazca'. In both the American and Peruvian areas we find that primitive people made polychrome vessels using highly stylized designs. We also find that both the ancient Americans and Peruvians transferred those pottery designs, in the form of birds, spiders, men, etc., and placed gigantic duplicates of them on the ground. (Recently gigantic patterns of such forms were discovered from the air on the North American deserts.) We also find that the Pueblo Indians of America depended on a complicated irrigation system, and so did the Nazca people of Peru. As a final addition to our large list of correspondences, we find that the great canal system of Mars also indicates that a race there has developed an enormous irrigation system covering their entire planet.

Why is it that in three great desert areas (American, Peruvian, and Martian) we find the people of two of those areas (American and Peruvian) have constructed immense patterns on the ground after transferring such patterns from pottery motifs? Who were supposed to view those patterns from the air? Were they built for the people of the third desert area (Mars)

TRAVELING THE PATH BACK TO THE ROAD IN THE SKY

who had irrigation systems like the people of the first two areas (America and Peru)?

And finally, what were the ancient Pueblo Indians of North America doing when they made their sacred designs (which are even now interpreted as symbols of the sky and *its phenomena)* painted on pottery so resemble the strange surface features of a far away planet that men of a future age would recognize the connection after studying 20th Century maps of Mars?

'Ceramic charts'? 'Planetary pottery portraits'? Why were they made; what were they used for? This is the mystery of the *'Martian* Miniatures'.

TRAVELING THE PATH BACK TO THE ROAD IN THE SKY

FOSSILS, FOOTPRINTS, AND FANTASY

YOU may ask the question, and it should be asked, that if there really were 'giants in the earth in those days', has anyone ever found their fossil remains from past ages preserved in that earth? The answer is that many remains have been found in the past which unquestionably belonged to former dwellers on our planet who were gigantic in stature. However, it is impossible here to go into any great detail on this. Actually, this is not necessary anyway, for there are many excellent books devoted entirely to the subject of giant men and women of legends and of actuality. Nevertheless, we are going to list some of the more interesting and important discoveries.

Several years ago in California, miners were working deep within the Earth, when at a depth of about 130 feet, they encountered a human skull. Examination showed that this skull had been buried under lava and was of the Tertiary Period. That would mean that the man who had belonged to this most primitive skull must have lived somewhere between the Eocene Epoch and the Pliocene Epoch of 6 to 60 million years ago!

Also in California another even more fantastic human skull was found. It was of great size and contained *a double row of teeth!* (In the Babylonian *Talmud*, or *Hulin* section of the *Berakthoth*, we find reference to antediluvian giants who also had several rows of teeth.)

In 1895, the *Chicago Record* printed a sensational story of another California discovery. This story said that an unknown type of ancient animal which had a skull bigger than that of an elephant had been found together with the fossil remains of men and women eight and nine feet tall.

In 1877, a fossil human tibia about 36 inches long was discovered many feet beneath the surface of the ground embedded in quartzite, near Eureka, Nevada.

TRAVELING THE PATH BACK TO THE ROAD IN THE SKY

Explorer Paxson Hayes claimed in 1934 that he had discovered the burial ground of a blonde race of giants near unexplored regions of the fabulous Barranca de Cobre in old Mexico. The 'barranca' is a canyon deeper and wider than the well-known Grand Canyon of Arizona. It is located approximately 550 miles south of Nogales, Mexico, and is 20 miles wide and 7,000 feet deep. It contains semi-tropical flora and fauna.

Hayes decided to explore the Barranca de Cobre after listening to Yaqui Indian legends and stories about it. The Indians claimed there were indications of a vast ancient civilization in a great canyon to the south in Mexico. In relating his discovery, Hayes said:

We entered the canyon through the only known opening, a slot in the rock where a river once ran. Close inside the entrance we came onto the ruins of what once must have been a great city consisting of giant buildings. They were constructed of a cement-like masonry that was mixed with bamboo. One of the mosque-topped buildings still contained the stored particles of ancient grain. The grain was later analyzed by Mexican government authorities who said it fell into no classification known today. However, we found no other traces of this lost civilization... there were no burial grounds, and it is in such places that civilizations leave their true histories. I returned to the United States and one night heard a chief of the Yaqui tell of ancient caves that existed about 45 miles north of the 'barranca' where I had discovered the Lost City. The chief said vast burial grounds could be located in the caves. I headed south again with my Yaqui guide, Rafael Garcia, who said he knew the location of the caverns.

We traveled with mules for 90 miles until we reached another deep canyon with sides sloping upwards to a series of mesas. I noticed on the horizon a strange rock formation which resembled a great cathedral in ruins... it seemed symbolic of what we sought. The cave we found began as a tunnel and ended in a chamber about So feet high, 25 feet deep, and 20 feet wide.

We dug down through eight inches of cave deposits until we reached volcanic ash which extended for another twelve inches... beneath all of this we discovered numerous burial wrappings made of woven mats bound with twisted yucca fiber rope. In these ancient wrappings we found 34 mummified remains of men and women... they originally had been between seven and eight feet tall! These giants were blonds, and to complicate the matter,

TRAVELING THE PATH BACK TO THE ROAD IN THE SKY

the last body we discovered was that of a pygmy!

We also found two small, four-legged stools, that had been carved from solid pieces of wood... as yet, the wood is unidentified. Our greatest experience, however, was finding the saffron-colored burial robes that were plain except for a beautiful light blue pattern of intricately woven pyramids and triangles. The latter contain tiny white dots... one to three... which recur throughout the pattern. Portions of our discoveries are now in museums in California and Arizona.

Several years before the discoveries made by Paxson Hayes, Dr. Byron Cummings, well-known anthropologist of the University of Arizona, and Dr. Manuel Santo Domingo, a Mexican scientist, traveled 160 miles from the border of Arizona and Mexico to a site where they discovered giant skeletons of two men and one woman who were eight to nine feet tall. There were also remains of six children and they were all six feet tall. The giants had been covered with fine jewelry and buried with magnificent burial urns. The year was 1929, and the area was controlled by the fierce Yaqui Indians. Before the scientists could really organize their research, these Indians approached them with guns and knives. The men were told to leave at once or else. Dr. Santo Domingo tried to talk the warriors into letting them stay and work, but one of the Yaquis raised his rifle butt and smashed all the giant remains to dust.

In 1938, Senor de Valda, near Tepic, Mexico, discovered seven skeletons of giant men and women who were between eight and nine feet tall. The remains were found under thin slabs of blue stone in burial mounds. Some of the remains were sent to Dr. Cummings at the University of Arizona.

Besides the fossils found in the above areas, we have the traditional or legendary evidence. The Toltecs of ancient Mexico said that in 'the second era, the Sun of the Earth saw the world populated by *giants,* the Quinametzins, who almost disappeared when earthquakes obliterated the earth. The Wind Sun came third and Olmecs and Xicalancas, human tribes, lived on earth. They destroyed the surviving giants...' The legendary evidence was certainly proved a few years ago with the discovery of enormous carved stone heads of giant men at Olmec culture sites in old Mexico.

Another tradition in Mexico speaks of many pyramids having been built by antediluvian giants such as the giant Xelhua, who is said to have emerged from the mountain of Tlaloc. He was known as the 'Sun God of the

TRAVELING THE PATH BACK TO THE ROAD IN THE SKY

Cross'. His title is of great interest for its symbol is our *Circle Cross* that we have already discussed. Again we find giant beings associated with the symbol that is connected with the 'El's'.

Many legends throughout the world speak of giants coming from great mountains and also dwelling on top of such high places. The Masai Tribe of Africa have ancient legends that go back to a time long before they ever saw a white man, and these legends speak of 'White Gods' on Mt. Kilimanjaro in Tanganyika, near the Kenya border. This is the highest mountain in Africa and its highest peak, Kibo, is 19,321 feet about sea level. These 'White Gods' have been seen by the Masai for many generations, and, in fact, they report they are still being seen today! 'Giant Gods', we will remember, were intimately associated with the Marcahuasi Plateau in Peru which is over 12,000 feet above sea level. 'Giants' and 'mountains' or 'gods' and 'high places' always go together.

The Masai also report that 'strange glowing lights' are often seen above Mt. Kilimanjaro, which makes us recall the famous sighting from a commercial airliner several years ago. The plane was flying near the mountain when all of the passengers observed a gigantic silver, needle-like space ship hover directly over Kibo Peak for well over an hour. This large craft belonged to the type referred to as a 'Mother Ship'.

In August and September of 1956 I was in correspondence with a friend of mine who lives in Nairobi, Kenya, East Africa. At that time he said: 'It seems that Saucers (UFOs) are using Mt. Kilimanjaro (near hear) as a centre—it is our highest mountain, you know.' The name Kilimanjaro means 'White Mountain' in Masai.

Two or three hundred years ago the W'Chagga Tribe came to the slopes of Mt. Kilimanjaro where they had been driven by the warriors of the Masai. The W'Chagga were never war-like and considered Kilimanjaro a very sacred place. The name of the town at the foot of the mountain is Moshi, which means 'smoke' in the Masai language. 'Smoke' and 'glowing lights' and 'giant white gods' on Kilimanjaro make us wonder if we are reading about Mt. Olympus, mythical home of the Greek gods or a high mountain in Africa.

A friend of mine who lives almost on the slopes of Kilimanjaro writes:

I had a W'Chagga Ayah (W'Chagga nurse for children) for my children twenty-five years ago and this ayah said that tall people who 'came

TRAVELING THE PATH BACK TO THE ROAD IN THE SKY

from the clouds' walked on the mountain top and lived in the mountain itself.

Kilimanjaro is a lovely mountain... my house faces it. I have seen space ships here three times and one time I observed a 'light' near the snow line of the mountain and this 'light' moved back and forth in that area. Other witnesses have always been with me when I have viewed the objects. One very spectacular sighting here was first observed by a native night guard who saw a very large, bright light come from Kilimanjaro and hover directly over my house. He called to me and I watched it for about an hour. It pulsated and beams of intense white and bright light came from it. The craft was brilliantly silver. Eventually it went straight up and I watched it while it looked like an immense star until it became a small object and the light was faint.

Lake Victoria in Africa is a short distance from Mt. Kilimanjaro, and west of this lake there is a race of giants still living today. These people range in size from seven to nine feet tall. They have been an aristocracy ruling over the ordinary Bantu negroes. They represent a very advanced people and are known throughout the world for their great dancing skill. (You will remember them from the motion picture, King Solomon's Mines.)

We have already mentioned the major fault lines of the Earth and how one runs through the centre of Italy and another one through Peru (and very near Marcahuasi). We also mentioned the fact that great cultural advancement seems to follow the fault lines due to the influences of magnetism on cultural development. Again we, find advanced people in a fault line area in Africa. The living giants west of Lake Victoria have as their main wealth a breed of cattle adorned with gigantic horns. These creatures are exactly like the Egyptian cattle of the most ancient figurations—the great horns in the shape of a lyre are identical. The old customs of the giants have been suppressed, but they formerly ruled as kings and princes with aristocratic ferocity. These people are completely different from others about them and may be related to the races that came to Egypt thousands of years ago, for it is now believed that they came to their present home in Africa as late as the fifteenth century.

These living giants, Lake Victoria and Mt. Kilimanjaro, are all located almost directly over one of the Earth's major fault lines. Here again we find strange correspondences as we did in Italy and Peru. We have Kilimanjaro with its ancient legends of 'white gods' walking on the mountain and present

TRAVELING THE PATH BACK TO THE ROAD IN THE SKY

reports of 'glowing lights' and gigantic space ships over its highest peaks, and we have the stories of the 'tall men' who lived on the mountain ages ago and we have the modern living tribe of 'giants' west of Lake Victoria. There are too many correspondences here to ignore. Giants, fault lines, space ships.

At Mt. Kilimanjaro we have yet another example of UFOs showing up over a centre of magnetic concentration. But is this centre of natural or artificial origin? Remember the words of my friend's W'Chagga Ayah:'tall people lived in the mountain itself.' Beneath the Kilimanjaro area there may still be the 'polished halls' and 'prismatic crystalline levels' of a great 'El' city. The 'Mother Ship' that was seen by the passengers of the airliner some years ago over Kilimanjaro may have been 're-fuelling' in the same manner that the UFO in the photograph of Prof. Cattoi in Italy was 're-fuelling' when he saw it hovering over a great carved stone head.

We also remember the ancient Huanca Indian legend from Peru: 'In the high places of our land, dwelt the Giant Gods in the days of our ancient fathers.' This legend could be transferred to the Kilimanjaro area, for it applies perfectly. Some very strange happenings have taken place on the mountains or in the 'high places' of the world in the past and these happenings are taking place again today. If someone will take the time to look I predict that they will also find at least part of another 'Sacred Forest', where exist great carved monoliths, somewhere in the little-known high places of Mt. Kilimanjaro.

Returning now to our fossil evidence, we find that the New York newspapers carried an article on July 9, 1903, that Prof. S. Farr and a group of students from Princeton University were excavating fossils of a prehistoric race in the Fish Creek country of Montana. It was reported that they had found ruins of a 'stone age' city and that from one burial mound came the skeleton of a man which measured nine feet in length. The skeleton of a woman was found nearby, and it was nearly as big as that of the man. Part of an animal skeleton was found which resembled a dog, except that it must have been as large as a small horse.

At the turn of the century skeletons were found in South Carolina which indicated the men had been anywhere between eight and eleven feet tall. The newspapers at the time said giant bodies had been found which evidently had belonged to a race which could now 'step over a common rail fence'.

TRAVELING THE PATH BACK TO THE ROAD IN THE SKY

A strange order was passed down by the United States government during World War II that threatened court-martial for any serviceman who revealed certain findings to the public. These 'findings' dealt with fossils, and very big fossils at that. In the Cook Inlet area of Alaska and on some of the Aleutian Islands themselves, gigantic skeletons of men nine feet tall had been discovered, by army men, in ancient villages which had been buried under volcanic ash and debris. We find that Alaskan natives of these areas have retained legends that speak about a race of giant men who formerly lived in the same locations. Our question here is: Why didn't the government of the United States want these findings made public? Surely, ancient fossils of giant men couldn't have disturbed the war effort! However, no one revealed anything and no one was court-martialed. But now that World War II and its restrictions is a thing of the past, certain men who were present when some of the fantastic buried villages were found have revealed the discoveries, and I know several of these men and have had long talks with them.

There is an old prospector who lives in the Northwest Coast area of the United States. He says he believes giant men lived on top of Mt. St. Helens in the Spirit Lake country during a time when water covered most of the land. Undoubtedly, he has heard some of the old Indian men of the area recount their ancient legends. Mt. St. Helens is about sixty miles south of Mt. Rainier, Washington. This mountain is directly in the path of one of the Earth's major fault lines which is the middle fault line in a group of three that move up the west coast of the United States and finally converge at Seattle, Washington. Also, let us remember that it was on June 24, 1947, over the same Mt. Rainier in the Cascade mountain range that pilot Kenneth Arnold observed nine shining, 'saucer-like' objects moving at 1,200 miles per hour! Again we have Giants, 'high places', fault lines, and space ships.

If we go south of Mt. Rainier, through the State of Oregon, we come to another intensely interesting area that figures in ancient legends as well as modern stories. Indians of the Mt. Shasta area in northern California claim that their legends refer to strange mystery objects which appeared about 400 years ago near the area of modern San Francisco, California. The legends say that the leaders of the people at that time informed the tribe that the objects were from 'other worlds in the heavens near the stars'. The Indians always observed the objects going in a *south* to *north* direction. One of the fault lines we spoke of above continues south from Washington and goes

TRAVELING THE PATH BACK TO THE ROAD IN THE SKY

directly through the Mt. Shasta area. Evidently the UFOs observed by the Indians 400 years ago were following this great fault line as it continued north towards Mt. Rainier, Canada, Alaska, the Aleutian Islands, etc.

It has been reported by many people in the past few years that a strange race of highly advanced beings live in the highest areas of Mt. Shasta. Also, strange 'glowing lights' have been seen hovering over the mountain for long periods of time, both in the past and today. The Indians of the area are not referring to meteors in their legends for they always differentiate between objects dealing with natural phenomena and those apparently under intelligent control by the 'star people'.

Mt. Rainier in Washington and Mt. Shasta in California along with Mt. Argentario in Italy and the Marcahuasi Plateau of the Andes Mountains in Peru all begin to sound like Mt. Kilimanjaro in Africa. In the Mt. Shasta area we have again: 'strange beings,' 'high places', fault lines and space ships. Along the entire line from the Aleutian Islands to Alaska, through Canada and the west coast of the United States, on through Mexico and down to Peru, and even further south we find references to the discovery of fossil giants, to legendary giants, and references to modern space ships and Indian 'mystery' objects'. We also find the 'high places' or mountains along the entire length of the same line and a great fault line goes from one end to the other.

The aboriginal people of Australia have a legend that speaks of a time long ago when their country in the area of Lake Eyre, South Australia, existed under a green (not a blue) sky. This sky was supported by three great trees. The 'sky dwellers' came down to the Earth via the huge trees and then cut these trees down, so they could not return to heaven. (Another version says the natives cut the trees down to stop the coming of the 'sky dwellers'.)

Recently, archaeologists have discovered prehistoric petroglyphs in little-known parts of Australia which show many native men standing around a disc-shaped object. Apparently the men are being instructed by a man of importance who stands directly in front of the disc. Evidently the *road in the sky* came down into Australia in the dim past also, for we find both legendary or traditional evidence and we find the archaeological evidence.

In Africa, in a desolate part of the Sahara Desert, scientists have located a great stone carving which depicts a whirling disc in the sky and many men on the ground fleeing from it. Recent expeditions into the Sahara have discovered that warriors in chariots crisscrossed the desert for thousands of years and established sizeable centers in the heart of the present desert. Magnificent frescoes have been found that critics say display fantastic skill, coloring and realism. They compare the unknown artists with the greatest man has ever produced. The frescoes date from 8,000 B.C. to the Christian era.

Whirling discs' in African skies remind us of the name the ancient Egyptians gave to UFOs: 'fire circles'. These 'fire circles' caused quite a sensation in the time of the Eighteenth Dynasty Pharaoh Thutmose III (1501-1447 B.C.) and their appearance was recorded by the Scribes on papyrus in the Royal Annals.

UFOs were called 'flying boats' by nearly all the Indian tribes of North America, and the same name prevailed in ancient India. Over 1,000 years ago in Hawaii the UFOs were known as *Akualele,* or 'flying spirits'. The ancient Hebrew word for *hornet* did not mean the large strong wasp we know under that name, but meant 'flying machine'.

Several references to 'flying objects' are to be found in the Old Testament:

'And I will send *hornets* ('flying machines') before thee, which shall drive out the Hivite, the Canaanite, and the Hittite, from before thee.' (Exodus xxiii:28).

'Moreover the Lord thy God will send the *hornet* among them, until they that are left, and hide themselves from thee, be destroyed.' (Deuteronomy vii:20).

'And I sent the *hornet* before you, which drove them out from before you, even the two kings of the Amorites; but not with thy sword, nor with thy bow: (Joshua xxiv:12).

Dr. J. O. Kinnaman, the Bible archaeologist who conducted research in Egypt with Sir Flinders Petrie, has reported that he actually found ancient parts of 'flying machines' or the Hebrew 'hornets'. These parts were discovered along with metallic insignia that the pilots of such 'flying objects' must have worn during the time of the Biblical Joshua.

Ashur, the chief deity of the Assyrian pantheon, was the god of military prowess and empire, a great god of war. He is always depicted standing upon an enormous disc, and this disc is *winged.* This could easily be another 'god' who came in a 'flying machine'.

TRAVELING THE PATH BACK TO THE ROAD IN THE SKY

Besides the Huanca legends of giants in Peru, there are many others. The Quechua Indians say that ancient fortresses overlooking Lago de Titicaca were 'erected by *giants* before the sun shone'. Also, it has been claimed that tombs of giant men have been found in the jungles of Peru.

Quechua legends state that during the reign of an early Inca emperor, giants reached Peru from the sea. The giant men arrived in boats from the Pacific ocean and landed near Point Santa Elena close to Puerto Viejo. The Quechuas say this happened in a very remote day and they only have the traditions from their ancestors. They also told the story to Don Pedro Cieza de Leon, the Spanish soldierpriest, in A.D. 1945. They told him that the giants were so large that from the 'knee down, they were as tall as a tall man, their hair hung from their great heads to their shoulders, they were beardless'.

The same Don Pedro tells us that near Cuzco in A.D. 1560, during the time of the Viceroy Don Antonio de Mendoza, a tomb was discovered that contained large human bones similar to bones that had already been located in Mexico City.

Another Spanish chronicler, Padre Acosta, reported that human bones of 'huge greatness' were found near Manta on the coast of South America in the same year of A.D. 1560. In 1928, at the same location of Manta, Ecuador, similar human giant remains were discovered in a cave behind gigantic stalagmites. These giants measured over eight feet in height.

The famous English explorer, Col. P. H. Fawcett, reported that Tiahuanaco in Bolivia and Sacsayhuaman near Cuzco, Peru, had been built by a race who handled cyclopean boulders and carved them to fit so perfectly that it is impossible to insert a knife-blade between the mortarless stonework. Col. Fawcett said: '... looking at these remains it is not difficult to believe the tradition that they were erected by giants... indeed, skeletons of giants are said to have been discovered in rock tombs in the vicinity of Cuzco.'

Recently in Peru, Senor Augusto Salazar Moreno released news of a great discovery near the hill known as 'El Agustino' which is now the home of native people. An expedition headed by an Italian was attempting to locate buried treasure and came across a human skeleton of extraordinary dimensions. Two members of the expedition, Miguel Rojas and Ernesto Chumpitas, said: 'We made the sensational discovery in a bed of sand at a depth of 50 meters (well over 150 feet). The skeleton measured 4 meters (13 feet) in height. These remains must have belonged to the giant men that figure in our legends. The matter is of such importance that we now await the opinion of the authorities. At a distance of *800* meters from the giant skeleton, we found other remains of human beings; some of them were covered with what appeared to be uniforms...

I rather imagine that the 'opinion of the authorities' changed the picture somewhat and the remains were either destroyed or hurried off to some dark museum storage room where no one could see them. It seems all such finds meet a similar fate. Man is not anxious (and indeed, not ready) to give up his already established theories and ideas. 'Giants' just upset the scientific 'applecart'.

However, very reputable scientists have reported discoveries of giant men. Some may feel that 'giants' are just a part of fantasy, that such creatures only belong in fairy tales and Greek mythology. However, I rather imagine all of you would accept either a religious proof and/or a scientific proof. Remember, your Bible tells you: 'There were *giants* in the earth in those days...' Many of you who cannot accept 'giants' but can accept Genesis had better start reading your Bibles again. And for those of you who demand scientific evidence, let us take a look at the findings of the anthropologist, Dr. Ralph von Koenigswald. In September, 1946, he walked into the New York Museum of Natural History with a priceless collection of fossils he had brought from Java that were the earliest known remains of man.

In von Koenigswald's collection were three of the greatest anthropological finds ever made. In padded boxes were skull fragments of *Pithecanthropus robustus,* a relative of the famous Java man, *Pithecanthropus erectus.* 'Robustus' was so large that he must have been the ancestor of 'erectus' who lived 400,000 years ago. Until the new finds were made the latter was considered the earliest human fossil. Von Koenigswald also brought with him part of a man called Meganthropus, who is considered even more primitive. However, the greatest and most primitive find concerned three gigantic human teeth, all that remained of *Gigantopithecus,* who was a 'giant' living in the caves of Kiangsi Province, China, close to a million years ago.

Von Koenigswald, a German paleontologist-anthropologist, found the teeth in China and did the rest of his work in Java before World War II. He conducted research for the Carnegie Institution and the Dutch government and was a prisoner for three years after the Japanese invaded Java in 1942. To make sure the important discoveries were safe, the scientist hid the teeth in a milk bottle.

When the great molar of *Gigantopithecus* was compared with an equivalent tooth from the skull of modern man, the similarity was obvious. This ancient 'giant' was definitely a human being and not just a great ape. But even more startling is the size of the teeth. 'They are four times the size of our teeth today and the 'giant' must have stood twenty feet in height! If science can accept such gigantic men perhaps we can accept the smaller twelve-foot man of the Marcahuasi Plateau and the seven, eight, nine, or ten-foot men of other discoveries.

A great modern anthropologist, Dr. Franz Weidenreich, author of *Apes, Giants and Man,* said that each type of fossil from *Pithecanthropus erectus* back to *Gigantopithecus is* larger, more massive and more primitive or earlier than the one before it. He believed that man's earliest known ancestor was a huge being much larger than a creature twice the size of a modern gorilla.

If science and religion both say there were 'giants in the earth in those days' why deny it? Is it fantasy or is it fact?

Fossils of men or beings of gigantic proportions have been found throughout the history of Earth, but is it possible some of those creatures are still living in some of the '.high places' or the unexplored areas of Earth, where they have retreated to be safe from their smaller and deadlier relative, modern man? The thought is intriguing, but is it true?

Not long ago the inhabitants of the desolate region of Puna Atacama, Argentina (approximately 200 kilometers west of Salta), which is located in the heights of the Andean cordillera near the Chilean border, declared that there was evidence indicating the presence of strange large beings on the snowy peaks of the mountain Macon (nearly 22,000 feet).

Witnesses said they saw tracks of giant proportions with humanlike characteristics in the frozen ground of the Macon and also in the snow on the pampas where they live. The tracks or footprints appeared over a year ago for the first time and apparently coincided with an explosion on the side of Macon. People of the area believed some aerial object had struck the mountain, but the matter was never investigated officially. However, some people claimed that the strange object which hit the mountain was a kind of giant airship with a peculiar form like a cigar.

Later, 'flying cigars' were seen in the skies over the Salar de Guisare, and local inhabitants near the Macon again saw the unusual tracks and some of the people began to believe that extraterrestrial beings were landing on Earth. Due to the vastness of the snowy, treeless plains (pampas) the area would be ideal for the landing of gigantic airships. The people of the area are firm in their statements that they have seen many strange ships flying over this region and that some of them were calculated to be 300 meters in length.

The National Police supplied newspapers in Argentina with excellent photographs that clearly showed the passage of strange craft in the skies over the Salta area and these were similar to sightings of UFOs from all over the world. Strange beings were also reported at Puna Saltena on Macon mountain. Many informants have declared that they have heard strange cries resounding throughout the mountain area and across the treeless plains during the time of the setting sun; these sounds they have heard with great clarity.

Other people have reported that they have found many condors and eagles dead and their nests ravaged in the mountains. These witnesses say that in all cases where great quantities of birds have been killed they have seen near or around the nests giant humanlike tracks which cannot be attributed to bears as they thought in the beginning.

All witnesses to the strange happenings in Argentina have been careful of reporting the matter for fear of being ridiculed. However, now the well-known geologist, Dr. Spitch, has also reported seeing the strange footprints and therefore the other witnesses are coming forward with their experiences.

The 'cigar-shaped craft' of Macon mountain sounds very much the same as the 'needle-like ship' over Mt. Kilimanjaro in Africa. We must also mention that one of the Earth's major fault lines goes through the area of the Marcahuasi Plateau, then moves south past the 'Lines of Nazca', and continues south past Lago de Titicaca, and eventually goes directly through the Salta area where the strange happenings have been taking place in Argentina.

Other things have been reported from nearby areas. On February 14, 1957, I was in Lima, Peru, when I saw the following article *in La Prensa: Raro*

TRAVELING THE PATH BACK TO THE ROAD IN THE SKY

y Gigantesco Objeto Hallaron en Andes Chilenos. I contacted a friend of mine who is a newspaper man in Peru and I attempted to obtain permission to fly to Chile and investigate the matter, but I found all doors closed, and closed tight ! Evidently the Chilean government did not want anyone investigating the spectacular occurrence and it was all immediately put under wraps.

On the slopes of the volcano Mino, only 45 kilometers from the town of Ollague, Chile and on the border of Chile and Bolivia, a strange apparatus was found. It was reported to the Prefect of Antofagasta who sent a telegram to the Minister of the Interior. The Prefect said that the apparatus consisted of a very thin piece of material which was transparent and more or less 1,000 meters in length. In the interior of the apparatus, a small oval object which was 30 centimeters in circumference weighing 3 kilograms was found. The oval piece appeared to be made of a metal like aluminum and also had a ring made of the same material along with peculiar strips of a plastic-like material each one about 20 to 25 centimeters long. The Prefect reported that he believed the apparatus had at one time 'flown in the sky' but he did not know the nationality or the origin of it. The 1,000 meters were rolled up and put on a train bound for Antofagasta. Later, parts of the apparatus were sent to the Minister of the Interior. After that, the 'doors closed'. A certain newspaper ran a story entitled: *Flying Disc Falls In The North,* and asked the question: 'If it was a "flying disc", where is the crew?' If they had cared to look they may have found the owners or the 'crew' of the apparatus a few kilometers to the south in the vicinity of the strange beings on Macon mountain in Argentina.

The town of Ollague in Chile is also *directly* on the same fault line and there are strange patterns in the area like those of the NazcaPalpa region in Peru. Let us also remember that Lago de Titicaca is not far from any of these areas and the Rio Desaguadero flows from Titicaca into Lago Poopo where we find the 'mystery' of the two hundred thousand cubic feet of water per minute and the underground location of a great 'El' city. Again we have 'strange beings', 'high places', fault lines and space ships.

On September i9, 1956, *El Comercio* in Lima, Peru, printed the story of a spectacular sighting at yet another 'fault line' location. A strange flying object had made incredible maneuvers in the sky for over two hours over the Peruvian Air Force Base 'Capitan Montes', Talara, Peru. Air Force Chaplain R. P. Emiliano Alvarez, First Lieutenant Jose Jaime Guerra, and other officers and personnel at the base had observed the movements of what they called a 'Platillo Volador' ('Flying Saucer') as it moved with great velocity from east to west with a great sweeping motion. The UFO was oval in form and made many abrupt stops as though it were observing the base. Chaplain Alvarez said: "I have never believed in 'Flying Saucers' but now I am convinced. I believe this object was manoeuvring so that we might observe it. After more than two hours of incredible movements the luminous body disappeared towards the west, but it left within the souls of all spectators the firm conviction that they had seen a 'Flying Saucer'."

Strange things not only happened in the past but they are happening today. In fact, they seem to be on the increase. Chehalis, Washington, is on a fault line and very close to Mount Rainier where Kenneth Arnold had his sighting in 1947. A few months later, on January 6, 1948, Mrs. Bernice Zaikowski of Chehalis said she saw a man with wings attached to his back fly over her farm at an altitude of about 200 feet and then disappear to the south. The witness said: "The 'flying man' made a strange sound as he climbed in flight, but his wings neither flapped nor rotated. I could see no motive power such as a propeller either above or in front of him. Several school children were in my yard at the time and witnessed the 'flying man' also." Not only do we have 'Flying Saucers' but we have 'Flying Men'! Charles Fort would have had a heyday.

In 1956, a strange monster appeared at Marshall, Michigan. Two Mexican beet pickers arrived at the Beet Camp earlier than the other workers. The monster came into their cabin. It was very tall and had stiff hair all over it. It picked up one of the frightened men and looked at him with large, glowing red eyes. The fingers of the creature extended to the back of the man's head they were so large. It also picked up the other man, but it didn't hurt either of them; in fact, the men said they felt it didn't have any evil intentions towards them.

Two years before the above happening in 1954, I was in Detroit, Michigan, and I heard the story of the 'frogin' from reliable friends. Apparently a snake-like creature of great size had been observed in several places in Michigan and finally one was caught and taken to the Humane Society. The man who took care of it said that it frightened him and that it had two great eyes that looked like human eyes. He said it displayed great intelligence and would rise up in its cage and its eyes would follow him as he went about his duties in the room. I attempted to investigate the story of the 'frogin' but when I was about to leave for the office of the Humane Society, a telephone

TRAVELING THE PATH BACK TO THE ROAD IN THE SKY

call informed me that the creature had been put to death painlessly and then buried!

During the last part of 1956, while the beet pickers were wrestling with the 'hairy man', the town of Agua Prieta in old Mexico was near panic from the 'green menace'. Acting Chief of Police Enrique Matty reported that people were seeing a frightful sight. Many observers were so shaken by the experience they could provide no description at all. However, most everyone agreed that the 'menace' walked in robes as black as the night and had a hideous green face. As we said before, there are a lot of strange things going on!

On January 2, 1954, Singapore reported security troops were ordered to bring back alive a group of hairy, fanged jungle creatures whose appearance at outlying rubber plantations had left workers screaming in terror. Weird half-ape, half-human creatures with protruding fangs wandered out of the north Malayan jungles and were first seen on Christmas Day, 1953. Some authorities said the creatures might be descendants of a race of hairy beings who, according to ancient legends, once roamed the forests of northern Malaya. Government officials at Kuala Lumpur said the creatures had a very light skin which indicated they had lived for years in the dark, overgrown Malayan jungles where sunlight rarely penetrates. Also, it was reported that the creatures were heard to speak some kind of a language.

The 'hairy beings' of Malaya may, or may not, have something to do with other creatures that are called Mi-Go by the Tibetans and Yeti by the Nepalese. But, if we follow the great *fault line* that goes through the *middle* of Malaya to the north we will reach an area that more than any other place in the world means mystery, adventure, and supernatural power to millions of people everywhere.

When this fault line reaches Tibet, it is surrounded by fabulous places. First of all, there is *Lhasa,* sacred city of the Buddhists and the location of the Potala, Palace of the Dalai Lama. Also, there is *Darjeeling,* the location of the retreat of Master El Morya. And very near Lhasa is *Shigatse,* the location of the Shigatse Palace which is one of the retreats of Master Kuthumi (Koot Hoomi Lal Singh). Finally, almost in the centre of all this, stands a magnificent spectacle known to the Tibetans as *Chomo-lungma,* the highest known mountain in the world on the frontier of Nepal and Tibet. To us, Chomo-lungma is simply Mount Everest, and this great mountain is a part of the Himalaya moun-

TRAVELING THE PATH BACK TO THE ROAD IN THE SKY

tain system which is 1,600 miles long extending between India and Tibet. Many of its peaks are over 25,000 feet above sea level, and Mount Everest itself rises to 29,141 feet.

This area is similar to Lago de Titicaca and the Andes Mountains of South America because it, too, is shrouded in mystery and ancient secrets, and both areas have a great fault line. They have something else in common, for in their 'high places' is to be found the elusive creature of the ice and snow known as the Yeti or Mi-Go, but known to the world as the 'abominable snowman'.

This creature also has the native name of *Metohkangmi,* which means 'the indescribably filthy snowman'. Whether he is myth or fact has been the subject of story and surmise for nearly two centuries. He was considered mostly a legend, however, until Colonel W. A. Waddell of the British Army reported seeing Yeti tracks in the snows of the Himalayas as far back as 1887. In 1921, members of an expedition to Mount Everest actually found some of the footprints at altitudes far above those where human beings could survive. Since that time the footprints of the creature have been photographed numerous times by the members of other expeditions to many of the highest Himalayas.

Tensing Norgay, who with Sir Edmund Hillary conquered Mount Everest, believes that "the Yeti is as substantial as the summit of the Himalayas'. Tensing says his father was once chased by a Snowman and was forced to seek refuge in a mountain cabin. Thereupon, the creature climbed to the top of this cabin and attempted to tear off the roof in order to gain entry. Tensing says the Snowman gave up when his father started a fire inside the cabin and allowed the smoke to go up through the roof.

Although the footprints have been photographed, the Yeti itself has never been photographed nor captured. Henry John Elwes of England was the first westerner to claim that he saw a Snowman. That was in 1906. Since that time other accounts have been reported. In 1925, the Greek explorer A. N. Tombaji saw the creature, as did the two Norwegians, J. Thorberg and B. Frotis, in 1948. During the first part of 1958, the Russian explorer A. G. Pronin encountered a Yeti.

Other well-known men have seen Yeti tracks. Sir John Hunt, leader of the 1953 Everest expedition, reported that he saw great tracks of the Snowman. Jules Detry, the Belgian anthropologist who accompanied the

TRAVELING THE PATH BACK TO THE ROAD IN THE SKY

Swiss expedition to Ganesh Himal in 1954, came across Yeti tracks in the snow. And many members of the French expedition to Makalu viewed gigantic footprints of an unknown creature.

Stories of the existence of the Snowman have circulated for many centuries among the people of the Himalayas. The creature found its way into Himalayan literature and was called 'the man from the wilds', and 'the creature of the rocks'. Some of the 'holy men' of the mountain called him 'last of the great ones'. Many Lamas and Sherpas have seen the Snowman in the snowy reaches of the 'high places'.

The Yeti is supposed to be a creature midway between animal and man. It is anywhere from 7 to 9 feet tall. Long, thick and stiff hair of a reddish brown color covers its entire body. Some reports claim the creature has hair the color of 'ashes' or grey. It has a flat face, something like an ape, but very wrinkled and without hair of any kind. Its head is extremely high and conical and the nails on its long fingers look like the claws of an enormous bear. It has no tail.

The creature feeds on raw meat, roots and fruits and lives in the Himalayas situated between 10,000 and 17,000 feet. However, it travels as high as 21,000 feet in search of food. It walks on two legs like a man and moves about alone. A few reports have been made which indicate it sometimes moves in groups of three or four.

The people of Nepal and neighboring regions say that in the days when the Himalayan forests were denser than they are today, and men seldom ventured very high, the Yeti lived in great numbers and inhabited extensive regions of the upper Himalayan reaches. In those days the Sherpas had to fight to protect their villages and gardens from the creatures. Now, the Yeti population has declined, for there are very few left in the mountains, and they avoid human habitations. However, there are reports of cases where a Snowman has taken a human female as a wife ! The village of Tarke in northern Nepal is supposed to have a family of Sherpas who are descended from a Yeti father and a Sherpa mother. Another family in the village of Melumche is reported to have just the opposite-children born of a Yeti mother and a Sherpa father.

In 1954, the *London Daily Mail* organized a nine-man scientific expedition to locate the Snowman, but it failed in its efforts to see him. However, many members said they saw much evidence of the existence of the Yeti including a scalp of the creature preserved in a Buddhist monastery. Other explorers in the past have seen Yeti scalps which were shown to them by the Lamas. The official report of the expedition said: 'The Yeti is a biped, human-like animal which dwells in the Himalayas and it is definitely not a bear, monkey, ape or langur as suggested by some investigators.'

In 1953, on an expedition to the Himalayas, Navnit Parekh of the Bombay Natural History Society, became friendly with the Lama of Thyangboche Monastery. The Lama showed him the scalp of a Yeti, and Parekh was allowed to take a sample of the hair. When he returned to Bombay, he showed them to Dr. Dillon Ripley of Yale University. Dr. Ripley suggested Parekh send the hair to Dr. Leon A. Hausman, well-known sociologist and ornithologist and also one of the world's leading authorities on hair. Dr. Hausman reached these preliminary conclusions: (1) The hair comes from the shoulder or back of some kind of large unknown mammal. (2) The age of the hair may be very great and is possibly measured in centuries. (3) The animal from which the hair was taken may not be a native of Tibet, and may come from a land hundreds or even thousands of miles away. (4) The hair is definitely not from a bear, an ape or a langur which many scientists believe the Snowman to be, nor is the hair from any close relation to such animals. Dr. Hausman's conclusions are startling, to say the least.

On June 10, 1956, a sensational discovery was announced in Katmandu, Nepal. Himalayan villagers claimed to have found the complete body of a Yeti imbedded in the solid ice of a crevasse at the foot of Mount Makalu, the 27,790 foot peak on the Tibetan-Nepalese border. However, no further reports of this important discovery reached the outside world.

The Sherpas say that the cry of the Snowman resembles the high-pitched howling of a dog. The Englishman, Peter John Webster, says while he was high in the Himalayas he heard a strange whistling sound, which his guides said was the wail of a Snowman. Webster searched the area but could not locate the creature. Remember our discussion of the 'strange cries resounding throughout the mountain area and across the treeless plains during the time of the setting sun' in the vicinity of Macon mountain in Argentina? What does it all mean? Is there a possible clue in the words of Dr. Hausman's conclusion: '... the animal may not be a native of Tibet... and may come from a land... thousands of miles away'?

Peter Byrne, leader of a 1957 American expedition, reported that the

TRAVELING THE PATH BACK TO THE ROAD IN THE SKY

data collected by the expedition offered unmistakable proof of the existence of the 'Abominable Snowman'. They came across footprints 12 inches long and 6 inches wide which could not have belonged to any known animal. They also collected stiff hair which scientists could not identify.

Trappers and Indians in 1938 reported that 'hairy giants' in the unexplored areas of northern British Columbia, Canada, were still living. The Indians call these creatures 'Sasquatch Man' and say the beings are eight feet tall, and covered with short hair except on the face around the eyes. The description fits the Yeti of the Himalayas. A Canadian Indian agent reported at the same time that he believed the modern giants were very shy creatures, descendants of some ancient tribe. Indians say the hairy men meet on top of the mountains and that they have seen these beings on numerous occasions. 'Sasquatch Man' has also been reported at Harrison Hot Springs which is only about 90 miles north-east of Vancouver, B.C., Canada.

It is reliably reported that a 'Snowman' creature lives on the peaks of the mountains on Queen Charlotte Islands off the coast of British Columbia, Canada. Footprints of a giant being have been seen many times by Indians on the shore.

In the Canadian Northwest Territories, Indian legends speak of giant hairy men who live near the snow line of great mountains. In the Mackenzie River area there is a 'Headless Man's Valley' which received its name from the fact that Indians said men were found with their heads torn from their bodies and that a great 'hairy being' was the cause.

On Vancouver Island there is a strange place known as 'Forbidden Plateau'. Many things are said to live there. Red and blue snow has been known to fall on the plateau and a flying creature known as the 'Wendigo' is supposed to emit eerie sounds that call to a person and make him follow it.

It has been reported by the Lamas of Tibet that the Yetis and other 'hairy giants' throughout the world represent a retarded portion of the human race which can only survive in the most secluded and the highest places. Other Lamas refer to the most ancient records where the Snowman is reverently referred to as 'the last of the great ones'. What the Yeti or his relatives in the 'high places' of the world really are, I do not know, but we may soon discover that he is of the species formerly thought extinct which served as the prototype for the great anthropoid apes and also hu-man beings. We may even discover that the Snowman in some ways displays great intelli-

TRAVELING THE PATH BACK TO THE ROAD IN THE SKY

gence.

The mummified remains of giant men who are 12 feet tall have been reported to have been found in South America and also in the subterranean chambers deep underneath the lamaseries of mysterious Tibet. Again, we find too many correspondences to ignore: 'strange beings', 'high places', fault lines and similar traditional evidence. What is the connection between the 'strange giants' and the peculiar airships of the mountains of Argentina and the 'abominable snowman' of the Himalayan peaks? And why do we have identical reports from other 'high places' in the world? And *why* do we also find fault lines in connection with the reports whether they be legendary or modern, or whether they are from Tibet, Canada, or South America?

Why is there a Great Wall in China that is similar to a Great Wall in Peru? Why were such walls built winding their way over miles of mountain territory? Were they constructed by man to keep *something* away from his inhabited centers? And if they were, what was (or is) that *something?* These are difficult questions to answer, for we are only now on the fringes of the matter, but the correspondences we have related above must be taken into consideration before a final conclusion is reached. Such a conclusion may be horrible, or it may be wonderful. Who *were* or who *are* the 'last of the great ones'?

We have given you a bit of *fantasy* for there may be no *'frogins',* and a Mexican 'green menace' may just be imagination. But what of the *fossils* and the *footprints?* Can we ignore them? We may find that the story of 'Jack and the Beanstalk', or 'Jack the Giant Killer' is not far from wrong! When you discover *fossil evidence* in a certain area, and then hear of ancient legends which describe the same thing, and later actually see for yourself the footprints of the same thing living today, in the same area, you have archaeological, traditional, and modern visual proof that cannot be ignored.

What is the connection between fossils, footprints, and fantasy and the *road in the sky* of time immemorial? We do not know, but we do know that some kind of a connection does exist.

Did the psalmist of old have all this in mind when he wrote in Psalm 95:4: 'In his hand are the *deep places* of the earth: the strength of the *hills is* his also.'

TRAVELING THE PATH BACK TO THE ROAD IN THE SKY

EVIDENCE FROM THE SILENT WORLD

'In the days before water covered the Earth, our forefathers spoke with the people of the heavens who came on a shining road in the sky.' (Machiguenga Indian legend of the Peruvian jungles, South America.)

IN the dense tropical rain forest of eastern Peru live several related tribes of primitive Amazon Indians. Their homeland, called the montaña, stretches Eastward from the cloud-covered slopes of the Andes, a region of rugged mountains and swift flowing streams. The great, almost impenetrable, rain forest is called the 'Silent World', for it guards its secrets well so that no intruder may enter and later leave with knowledge that the world is not yet ready for. Many expeditions are carefully planned and the newspapers tell how 'this one surely will succeed'. Then, in high spirits, the members of such an expedition enter the vast unknown. After that, usually the curtain of silence descends.

The Silent World can be one thing to one man and something entirely different to another man. It can be the 'Green Mansions' of literary fame or it can be the 'Green Hell' of infamy. The jungle treats you as you treat it. What are your motives for entering? Do you seek gold, riches, slaves? Do you seek knowledge, ancient records, medicinal plants? Motive! That determines how you will succeed in the Silent World.

During June and July, 1957, I searched for evidence of the *road in the sky* in the little-known jungle areas east of the Peruvian Andes. In Cuzco I heard a legend about a fabulous 'Lost City' in the unexplored portions of the Cadena del Pantiacolla (Pantiacolla mountain range), which is in the treacherous Madre de Dios country north-east of Paucartambo, Peru.

In 1955, an old Piro Indian died near Manu, Peru. He was 90 years old and knew more about the fabled 'Lost City' than any living man. In 1900

TRAVELING THE PATH BACK TO THE ROAD IN THE SKY

when he was a young man, his wife, who belonged to the Machiguenga Tribe, decided to leave him and go back to her people. He followed her into country that was unknown to him near the headwaters of the Rio Pinquen southwest of Manu. He did not locate his wife, but he did come upon a great stone roadway in the jungle. He followed this road for many miles until he came to an enormous ruin of a city that contained a magnificent plaza with stone temples and houses grouped about it. There were also ancient reservoirs and fountains and carved stone entrances. Later, he told his story, but no one would believe him because there are so many 'Lost City' stories in South America that have existed since the days of the Inca Emperors who searched for the remains of the ancient and forgotten 'Paititi'—Land of the Jaguar King, which was supposed to be east of the Andes. The Incas were never successful. The Spanish conquerors looked for 'Paititi' to plunder its great treasure of gold and jewels. They never located it either.

For many years there have also been stories that near the 'Lost City', which was actually discovered by the Piro Indian in 1900, is located a 'Lost Portal or Doorway', sometimes referred to as the 'Lost Rock of the Writings'. This legend intrigued me, for I felt this might indicate that there really was a place in the unexplored jungles where the ancient inhabitants of 'Paititi' might have carved hieroglyphics that would prove there was a written language in South America after all. Science does not accept the fact that there ever was writing in this area at all, for even the Incas had no written language. But 'Paititi' was a great Amazonian Empire in the interior of South America thousands of years before the Incas ever came to Peru. I believe that South America is the *Old World,* not the 'New World'.

Scientists also laugh at the idea of stone ruins in the jungle areas, but, of course, they have never gone into the 'Silent World' to see if the old legends are true or not. I remember a friend of mine who told me that a certain area I was planning on visiting in the montaña of northern Peru contained no evidence whatsoever of ancient stone cities. He said: 'All you will find in that area is the fact that the ancient inhabitants were a naked nomadic people of the most primitive sort who hardly ever built brush houses, let alone worked stone houses.' He was certain of his conclusions although he had never visited the area in question. I was there about two weeks before I discovered the remains of a great stone road and many stone houses not over a stone's throw from the centre of the modern village itself. 'Authorities' and their 'opinions' are oftentimes quite wrong.

TRAVELING THE PATH BACK TO THE ROAD IN THE SKY

I wanted to locate the 'Lost City' of the Piro Indian, and, at the same time, attempt to find the 'Lost Wall of the Writings'. I knew that somewhere in this area someone would some day discover the writing of the ancient Amazonian Empire known as 'Paititi'. I also hoped to discover legendary evidence amongst the present-day natives that would constitute evidence of this empire and the possibility that its leaders were aware of the *road in the sky*. I knew that if the 'City' could be located first, then the 'Wall' would surely be nearby, or vice versa.

In my investigations I found that several 'Rocks of Writing' had been discovered in the past. The Catholic missionary, Padre Vicente de Cenitagoya, was the first white man to locate such a place in the area of the Madre de Dios. At any rate, he was the first one to report his findings and write about them. In 1918, the Dominican Padres from Spain established a small mission on the Rio Palotoa, but it was abandoned in 1925. The missionaries at this little mission also knew of the existence of 'inscriptions and figures engraved on a great rock' which was located some distance from their mission.

For over a quarter of a century nothing came out of the 'Silent World' regarding 'Lost Rocks of Writing'. In 1953-54, Senor Jorge Althaus of Cuzco, Peru, re-discovered the 'Rock' of Hieroglyphics that had been discovered years before by Padre Cenitagoya.

In 1955, a man I will not name, but who calls himself the 'veteran Peruvian explorer', visited the same area after securing information, food, and guides from the Padres at the Dominican Mission San Miguel located near the mouth of the Rio Palotoa where it joins the Rio Alto Madre de Dios. I do not wish to name this man because of several things I was told by the Padres regarding his actions in the jungle. He secured several Indian boys to act as guides and promised to pay them if they would take him up the Palotoa and then return to the mission and go on downstream on the Rio Madre de Dios to the town of Puerto Maldonado. When he finally reached his destination he refused to pay the guides and would not even return money he had borrowed from them on the journey! I mention this only to show the true motive of this man, and not to injure him personally. Therefore, his name is not important to us here. Needless to say, however, his *motive* is not one readily acceptable in the 'Silent World'. The 'veteran explorer' later claimed in Lima that he went to the headwaters of the Rio Palotoa (sometimes called the Rio Pantiacolla after the mountain range of the same name), but according to

TRAVELING THE PATH BACK TO THE ROAD IN THE SKY

the Dominican Padres no white man has ever been to the headwaters of this river. However, he did visit Padre Cenitagoya's 'carved rock of inscriptions' and did take some photographs which were later reproduced in some of the Lima newspapers. I was told that he also asked the native people to remove their clothing so his photographs would have that 'touch of realism necessary in depicting savage Stone Age people'!

In the early part of 1957, Senor Harmut Winkler of Cuzco also visited the Padre Cenitagoya discovery and he took more photographs. However, he was interested in locating 'good land' in the jungle area for future development.

Later in the year of 1957, I left Cuzco with my friend Senor Miguel Acosta, who is from Ayaviri, Peru. He is a real veteran of the jungle, having spent nearly thirty years in wilderness areas all over Peru. However, he had never been to the country we were headed for in the Cadena del Pantiacolla. We journeyed by truck to Paucartambo and finally to the hot little jungle village of Pilcopata where the Peruvian government is building a road that will take many years to complete. This is the last outpost of the area, for from here on you travel narrow jungle trails where they exist, and where they don't exist you either cut your way through the dense jungle growth or you follow the rough stone shoreline of the rapid rivers. During the rainy season the latter route is not possible as all shorelines are flooded.

We walked on the trails with our back packs or we followed the Rio Alto Madre de Dios north until we reached the mouth of the Rio Palotoa. Upstream a short distance we found the mission San Miguel of the Dominican Padres from Spain. We were greeted by the young Padre Miguel Almaraz, and later by the venerable Superior of the mission, Padre Jose Alvarez. Padre Alvarez has spent forty years in the jungle areas of South America.

The humble but adequate mission served as our base camp. Actually, during our research, we located several areas where 'Rocks of Writing' exist. These areas include the country of the Rio Queros, the Rio Sabaluyoc, and the Rio Sinkibenia ('River of Corn').

TRAVELING THE PATH BACK TO THE ROAD IN THE SKY

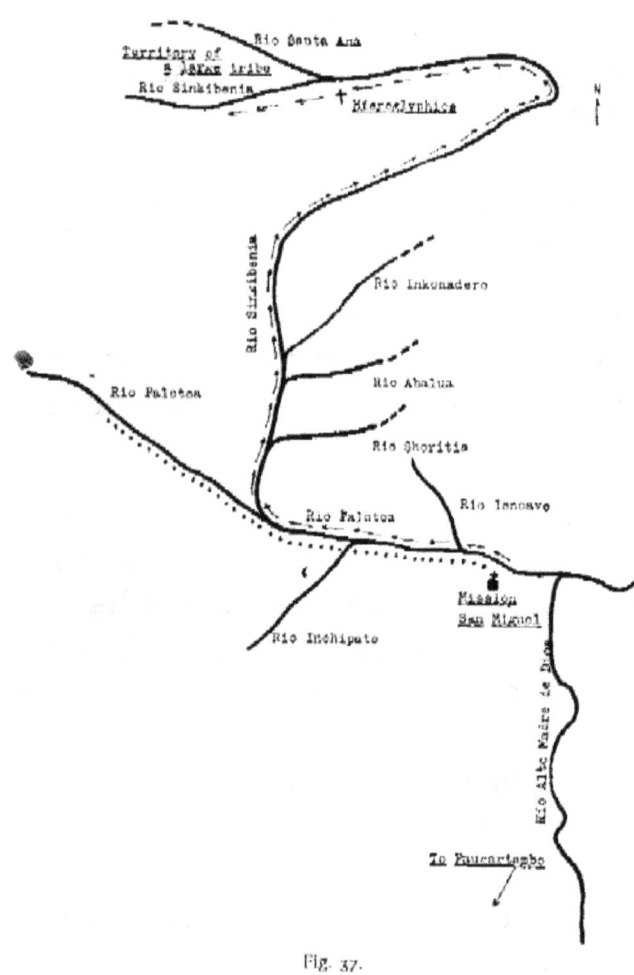

Fig. 37.
A map of the area of the author's 1957 explorations.

Figure 37

Figure No. 37 is a map of the area of our 1957 explorations. We were able to locate and map several new rivers that had never been identified nor charted previously.

The main ones were the Rio Shoritia; Rio Abalua; Rio Inkonadero and the Rio Santa Ana. With two young Machiguenga Indian guides we penetrated the unknown region near the headwaters of the Rio Sinkibenia, but we never reached the source of the river. The line of arrows indicates our route from the mission San Miguel. Where the Rio Santa Ana joins the Rio Sinkibenia, we located a gigantic stone cliff on which were carved thousands of ancient hieroglyphics.

These were photographed in colour and will appear in my book *Land of The Tiger King,* along with a complete account of our discoveries and strange experiences. The 'Rock of the Writing' incident is only briefly mentioned here in order to give a background for the material which I shall present shortly. We reached a point beyond the stone cliff where no white man had ever gone before. We did not locate the legendary 'Lost City' although I feel it is somewhere to the west of our last camp on the Sinkibenia, for carved on the stone cliff in the middle of all the hieroglyphics we found the figure of a helmeted young man with his arm extended and pointing upstream towards the west. Also we discovered the large figure of a jaguar wearing an enormous plumed crown. Here was the 'Jaguar King' himself. Did this mean we were actually near the ancient Empire of 'Paititi'?

The dotted line on the map (**Fig. No. 37**) indicates the route of the 'veteran explorer' on the Palotoa. However, we followed this river for some distance also, and I took photographs of Padre Cenitagoya's 'inscriptions' as others before me had done.

We did not penetrate further upstream on the Sinkibenia because we were in the territory of a large tribe that has never been visited by white or civilized men. We were not ready for such a meeting for we had inadequate equipment and supplies. Padre Alvarez had told us at the mission that he intended to conduct an expedition in order to make friends with this large tribe, and he invited us to join him at some future date. Both Padres warned us, however, that to undertake such a venture without proper planning would mean certain disaster. We remembered these words and decided not to go any further. But I believe that somewhere ahead of our last camp towards the headwaters of the Rio Sinkibenia there is a great and majestic city of forgotten 'Paititi'.

The main point I want to mention here in regard to the hieroglyphic evidence of the Madre de Dios area is that it definitely represents a written language of extreme antiquity. The carved glyphs are not just the crude petroglyphic sketching of some primitive savage, for they constitute a form of writing that has never been studied before. I believe other 'Rocks of Writing' will be discovered in the same area, for surely there must be more than one or two. There are many rivers with many strange rock carvings in their vicinity.

Fig. No. 38 is a photograph I took during our stay at our last camp on the Rio Sinkibenia.

To the left is 'Patiachi', one of our Machiguenga Indian guides, and to the right is my companion Miguel. We had to build our own balsa raft in order to get out of the country and go downstream towards the Rio Palotoa and the mission where we had established our

TRAVELING THE PATH BACK TO THE ROAD IN THE SKY

base camp.

I am now working on a translation of the many glyphs we encountered during our 1957 expeditionary work, but what I want to present here are a few of the native legendary tales that shed light on what caused the fall of the ancient Amazonian Empire, and a startling incident that took place just prior to its destruction.

Fig. No. 39 is a photograph I took of the Dominican Padres in front of the little church at Mission San Miguel. This structure is now gone due to a great flood that forced the Padres to change the location of the mission. The young man to the left, standing up, is a civilized Huachipari Indian. Next to him stands the full-bearded Padre Miguel Almaraz and in his white habit is Padre Jose Alvarez, one of the most godly and one of the finest men it has ever been my honour to know. The other four Indian boys are members of the primitive Masco (Mashco) Indian Tribe that inhabits the area with the more advanced Machiguenga Tribe. These Indians in the photograph are considered to be Christians and civilized.

The Machiguenga legends were of great interest to me. Padre Alvarez told me that when he arrived in the area, the Indians told him that they believed in an angel of great beauty who appeared in white light. They said this angel protected them from evil spirits and from danger. Therefore, Padre Alvarez immediately named the mission San Miguel (Saint Michael) in honour of the Biblical archangel of power and light.

The Machiguenga say they have no particular legend about the 'Rocks of Writing' located in their territory, except that they had nothing to do with the making of such glyphs nor did their ancestors. To them, such places have always been there.

TRAVELING THE PATH BACK TO THE ROAD IN THE SKY

Padre Alvarez has spent many years studying legends of these people and is, undoubtedly, the world's authority on their language and customs, etc. He says that their tales are, in some cases, identical with the stories of the ancient Greeks, Egyptians, Romans, and many of the accounts of the Holy Bible. The Machiguenga and other tribes have tales relating to the 'Garden of Eden' and to the 'Great Deluge'.

Some of the tribes believe that animals came from man, instead of the popular evolutionary concept today that man descended from the animals! They say that men were on the Earth first and there were no animals. Because of evil men working evil spells the animals came about on the Earth. This all sounds like the 'Great Abomination or Adultery' when the 'Sons of God' saw the 'daughters of men'. In other words, the race of Man on the Earth became Human and degenerated to that which was angel/animal and would have to work its way out of an inherited beasthood.

There are many legends that speak of the time before a great flood that covered the Earth. One story tells how many inhabitants of the interior of South America had to flee to a very high mountain in order to escape the water and to find food. While they were attempting to climb the mountain some of them fell in the mouth of a great fish and were swallowed. Others reached the top in safety. In their stories they have preserved the names of some of the heroes of the ancient times in the days of the catastrophe and flood. One name reminds us of the Patriarch Noah from the account in Genesis of the Deluge or Flood. This name is *Noeaha*.

The Masco Tribe says in the time of the great destruction, which destroyed a resplendent and ancient empire that was ruled over by white kings, it took twelve hours to go around a certain giant tree. Some of the people wanted to climb to the top of this tree to escape the catastrophe. But some of them were unsuccessful and fell off the tree into boiling water which covered the Earth.

All tribes of the Madre de Dios area speak of a time when tremendous cataclysms shook the Earth and how in the interior of South America nearly everyone perished.

The Huachipari say that the 'Rocks of Writing' are very ancient and existed before the Spanish, and before the Incas, and even before the Pre-Incas. They, and other tribes, say that those who reached the highest points of mountains were saved in the days of catastrophe, and such represent the

TRAVELING THE PATH BACK TO THE ROAD IN THE SKY

direct descendants of the 'remnant that remained'.

When the catastrophe occurred is not exactly known, but it must have taken place about 12,000 years ago (close to 10,000 B.C.) for there are references to such a period throughout the world. Tremendous earthquakes shook the ground. The sky was filled with fire and blackness. Lightning flashed and it rained and rained and rained. Gigantic meteors streaked through the heavens and thousands struck the Earth sending up dense clouds. Horrid gases rose from the planet and great tidal waves crashed on to the shores and swept inland to cover villages and great cities. The high walled magnificent citadels of the Amazonian Empire did not escape, for most of the splendid temples and plazas and houses were engulfed in great cracks in the Earth's surface. The inhabitants who escaped the destruction of the cities fled to the 'high places' but many succumbed to poisonous gases from the Earth and 'flaming stones' from the sky. One of the greatest civilizations of the world perished in almost a single night. The brief reconstruction above of the scene on the fatal day thousands of years ago in the interior of South America is based on ancient traditional evidence from the modern tribes of the area.

Many other legends exist all over the world that tell of the same catastrophe. In an Aztec codex we read :

'... a rain of fire came following the sun of rain... all was burned... a rain of rocks came and the sky drew near the waters and the earth... darkness covered the earth... men went to the caves but they were sealed in by falling rocks... men climbed trees, but they fell... there was no sun and for five days blackness was everywhere... earthquakes shook the land... flames came from the earth, and flaming stones dropped from the heavens...'

The tribes of the Amazon say: 'On the earth all was dark as night for many moons... hidden for many days was the sun.'

I collected many legends during my stay at the mission San Miguel which proved to me that a great Amazonian Empire had existed thousands of years ago in South America and was destroyed rapidly in a great catastrophe that must have been felt and known over the entire world. However, the most remarkable legend of all is related by the Machiguenga:

'In the days before water covered the Earth, our forefathers spoke with the people of the heavens who came on a shining road in the sky.'

TRAVELING THE PATH BACK TO THE ROAD IN THE SKY

This legend indicates that in the days before the great flood or destruction, the ancestors of the Machiguenga had been in communication with 'people of the heavens' or the 'sky dwellers'. These celestial inhabitants came to the Earth on a 'road in the sky'.

Some researchers may want to interpret 'people of the heavens or sky' as referring to the Incas who lived in their great capital of Cuzco high in the mountains above the jungle tribes like the Machiguenga. Therefore, some may say the native of the tropical rainforest thought of the Inca and his subjects as 'sky dwellers'. However, this interpretation is not possible for several reasons.

First of all, 'people of the heavens or sky' comes from the Machiguenga word *enoqui,* which can only refer to the literal sky. It means 'up in the heavens' (apart from the Earth) and cannot possibly refer to the Incas who lived 'up in the mountains or high places'.

The legend says: 'In the days *before* water covered the Earth...: This indicates that the event took place in very ancient times and could not possibly refer to the Incas who were late arrivals in Peru.

... before water covered the Earth... ' refers to 12,000 years ago, and the Incas arrived on the shores of Peru about 1200 A.D. Also, there was no catastrophe during the reign of the Incas that could be described with such violence as the one above. Unquestionably, the legend refers to a very ancient time and the 'people of the heavens' had nothing whatsoever to do with an earthly people.

Salcamayphua, an ancient chronicler who wrote of the Inca conquests, speaks of an incident that sheds light on the attitude of the jungle people towards the Incas. He tells how tribute payers from the eastern valleys of the rainforest beyond the Andes came to Cuzco. There were three hundred of them and they carried much gold to the Inca Emperor. Their arrival took place during the time of a killing frost that ruined all the crops of the Cuzco area. Because of this bad 'omen' the Incas ordered the three hundred men to the top of a high hill known as Pachatucsa, or Pachatusun, and there they were all buried alive. It is obvious from the study of the legend that whoever the 'people of the heavens' were, the Machiguenga held them in high esteem. The jungle tribes would never revere a nation that murdered three hundred of their men who were bearing gifts.

The Machiguenga legend also states that the communication with the

TRAVELING THE PATH BACK TO THE ROAD IN THE SKY

'sky people' was over a great shining 'road in the sky' which was in the form of a spiral. The communication was cut off immediately after the catastrophe of 12,000 years ago took place. Another version says the communication ended when the people on Earth became 'drunk'. The 'sky people' are said to have been 'good people who never became drunk'.

Did the 'people of the heavens' come to the leaders of the ancient Amazonian Empire to warn them of impending doom? People of other planets would have been aware of cosmic disturbances soon to affect the Earth. Did space ships from other worlds arrive over their 'road in the sky'? Did the occupants of such interplanetary craft land and discuss the coming catastrophe with the enlightened priests and kings of great 'Patititi'? All of this must have taken place for communication did not exist after the time of 'fire, blackness and boiling water'. Do the 'Rocks of Writing' in the Madre de Dios area represent an attempt on the part of the ancient priest-scientists to record for future generations the happenings that destroyed 'Patititi'?

In the same area today, where once the Amazonian Empire flourished, UFOs or space ships are again being sighted and in great numbers. Such craft showed up before to warn the men on Earth that a great disaster was about to engulf them. Why are they now coming to the very same area after thousands of years? Why is the 'communication' being established once more? A study of UFO sightings down through recorded history will show that interplanetary visitors always make an appearance in the affairs of Earth just prior to some great cataclysm or change on this planet.

Since 1955, UFOs have been reported by engineers, explorers, and missionaries working in the little-known jungle areas of South America. The Padres report that they do not know what these strange, unconventional craft are, but they do know they have been seeing them in great numbers, and sometimes singly. The UFOs are always observed heading in the direction of the vast unexplored areas where no white man has ever gone. In other words, they are headed directly for the areas where Colonel Fawcett and others have claimed great stone cities of the ancient South American Empire once ruled the world. Why are they returning to these cities now that these places are in ruins? Do they seek ancient records still buried there? Or is it possible that some of these cities are not in ruins but are still occupied by some of the 'remnant that remained'? And these inhabitants of still living cities of 'Paititi', are they actually in communication with beings from other worlds? What strange and wonderful conclaves we can imagine! In-

TRAVELING THE PATH BACK TO THE ROAD IN THE SKY

terplanetary craft landing in the plazas of forgotten cities that never were abandoned, but continued to live and be occupied by the masters of a great civilization. A magnificent picture forms before our eyes as we see the men of other worlds, who represent the highest in technical and scientific skill and achievement, sit down to confer with the masters of still living 'Paititi' in the majestic and gigantic stone halls of an Empire that ruled the world over 30,000 years ago.

Would all of this account for the fact that for hundreds of years jungle Indians have reported they have occasionally seen 'white masters or teachers in robes' in the unknown areas of the rain forests? These 'white teachers' are not modern missionaries, for the Indians claim they are capable of 'strange powers' and that they come and go as they please and that they live in great cities in parts of the jungle that even they are unfamiliar with. Is this why so many tribes have a great fear of the areas of 'Lost Cities'; is this why they can be used to guide you for a certain distance and to a certain point and then they will not go a step further?

As early as 1948-1949, reports came out of Puerto Maldonado on the Rio Madre de Dios that space ships and strange 'glowing lights' were being seen regularly there. Red, yellow and green objects were reported entering the dense jungle areas. Why are they coming? Some research societies in various South American countries believe that the UFOs are using the unexplored jungle areas for gigantic bases of operation and that they use such areas to insure their *privacy*. Let us remember that there is a lot of 'space' in outer space and the UFOs have been doing a good job of 'hiding' in that space for a very long time. Therefore, do they really need our jungles to hide from us, or are they in those areas for a much more important reason? I believe they have once again established their *road in the sky* and that they are in communication with the master teachers of a dead empire who still guard the ancient wisdom in the high-walled stone citadels of great 'Paititi'. The fact that they have returned to the Earth constitutes a warning for our time that we must heed.

Again we find in a place where legends speak of 'sky dwellers' the same thing happening today, the 'gods' have returned to their former haunts. What does all of this mean to us? Are we facing a world calamity as the ancients did? Let us remember the words of warning from the Ancient Mysteries:

TRAVELING THE PATH BACK TO THE ROAD IN THE SKY

'As above, so below... that which hath been shall return again.'

While I was in the Madre de Dios area in 1957, I heard a story from a friend that comes from a most reliable source. It is reported that an expedition penetrated the area near the unexplored head waters of the Rio Carbon in 1953. One morning they discovered freshly made human footprints all around their camp. Evidently someone had been looking them over closely during the night although they had heard nothing. This in itself would be frightening in an unknown area, but what caused them to abandon their camp at once and head downstream was the fact that those footprints were more than *double the size* of modern man's!

Is it possible that the ancient race of giants mentioned in all the legends did not become extinct? Did some of these great men of old find safety and a new home in the densest parts of the jungle where man today is just beginning to enter? If that is true, some day soon a modern explorer is going to walk right into the middle of a stronghold where he will be dwarfed by men over twice his height.

There is a certain man in Lima who is well-known throughout the Republic of Peru, and who has spent nearly twenty years in search of ancient Inca buried treasure. Several years ago he had an experience which may be connected with the 'freshly made giant footprints' of the Rio Carbon. He says: 'After traveling north from Lima for several hundred kilometers, we (there was one other in his party) found ourselves in a very desolate region of the desert where neither food nor water could be obtained. My companion was frightened at the prospect of spending the night in this place because he said ancient treasures were always guarded. Later in this place we saw in the desert sand the most gigantic imprint of a bare human foot that anyone could possibly imagine.'

Certain legends of Brazil state that in the unexplored Matto Grosso area there are the remains of a forgotten giant race, and that these remains are perfectly preserved in mummified form. Other variations of the same story claim that the giants are not really 'mummified' but are only held in a state of suspended animation. It is even claimed that the descendants of these beings are still alive in the unknown jungle areas of Brazil today. And they are nearly fifteen feet tall. Is there any connection between these 'mummified giants' and those in the subterranean chambers deep underneath the lamaseries of mysterious Tibet? There are many correspondences from ev-

TRAVELING THE PATH BACK TO THE ROAD IN THE SKY

ery age and from every part of our world, but we do not know the answers. I have a strange feeling that we are not going to have to wait long for at least some of those answers.

The *evidence from the 'Silent World'* adds its testimony, brought out of obscurity, to all the other accounts of a fabulous and forgotten *yesterday*.

Since time immemorial the *road in the sky* has spiraled down to Earth. It touched our pristine land one thousand million years ago when the Time-Spanners prepared the Earth for hu-manity. It passed by great monoliths in the Last of the Sacred Forests and it passed over the radiating lines of the desert that served as Beacons for the Gods. It was known to the people of the Pueblos who created 'ceramic charts' painted with the Martian Miniatures. It existed through the time of Fossils, Footprints, and Fantasy upon our strange little globe, and in its wanderings it has left us indisputable proof of its reality in the Evidence From the Silent World.

We have learned something of the eternal *road in the sky* as it was known to the planet Earth during a long and almost forgotten *yesterday*.

TRAVELING THE PATH BACK TO THE ROAD IN THE SKY

PART TWO

Today.

- **The Blessed Meek**
- **The Visitants**

TRAVELING THE PATH BACK TO THE ROAD IN THE SKY

THE BLESSED MEEK

'But the meek shall inherit the earth; and shall delight themselves in the abundance of peace.' (Psalm xxxvii:11).

WE are going to discover that the travelers along the *road in the sky* are interested in other things upon our planet than just that which remains from the dim and ancient *yesterday*. We must remember that they are here *today* and are therefore vitally concerned with the happenings *of* today. The thing that is dearest to the hearts of the extra-terrestrials, and gives them the greatest anxiety at the same time, is the life form that now finds itself 'Lord and Master' of the planet Earth—in other words, man himself. Or, we should say, the members of the hu-man race.

In the early part of 1954 I visited Amish and Mennonite settlements in Ohio and Pennsylvania. I was startled to find that these humble folk had been having some remarkable sightings of UFOs. Due to their simplicity and reluctance for publicity, these observations never reached the newspapers but were discussed within the settlements only, and then only amongst friends.

I soon realized that there was a definite pattern in regard to the interest shown by the UFO intelligences in certain groups and people. I also soon realized that they were primarily concerned with those members of the human race who refused to engage in warfare where they are compelled to kill their fellow men. The Amish and Mennonite people belong to such a group and so do the Hopi Indians of Arizona whom we will be discussing later on.

I remember the words from a contact with the UFO intelligences in 1952 that I was privileged to witness. These words constitute a reference to the Master Teacher we know as Jesus, the Christ. Although His name was not

TRAVELING THE PATH BACK TO THE ROAD IN THE SKY

used during the contact period, it was obvious that the reference was to Him and His stay upon the Earth. We realized that the UFOs were not going to hand over the secrets of the Universe just because we on Earth happened to want such secrets. Why should they? After all, we can't control the 'secrets' we already have, and besides, 'universal secrets' are for true men, actual citizens of that Universe. However, we felt that perhaps the interplanetary visitors would give us something that the United Nations could use to help hu-manity in the present world crisis. And we asked them if they would do this. They answered by saying: 'One came to your Earth world nearly two thousand years ago and gave you all that you need to know to live in peace and in brotherly love upon the planet you know as home. His words have fallen on deaf ears for the most part, although there are a few among you who refuse to kill each other and who show great promise for the future Kingdom of the Creator. He gave you the formula for a Perfect Life. Therefore, why should we now give you that which has already been given ages ago and which has not been followed? Let the so-called United Nations of Earth live that which He gave from the Father, and let the children of Earth prove their intentions by faithful *deeds* and not empty *words.*'

The 'One who came nearly two thousand years ago' is the same One who *'seeing the multitudes, went up into a mountain, and he opened his mouth, and taught them, saying, Blessed are the poor in spirit, Blessed are they that mourn, Blessed are the meek, Blessed are they which do hunger and thirst after righteousness, Blessed are the merciful, Blessed are the pure in heart, Blessed are the peacemakers.'*

This then is the standard that the UFO intelligences would have us live by. What a great contrast with the so-called 'Christian' nations today. They call themselves the followers of the 'One Who came' but they do not live what He taught, for they carry His banner into battle in one hand and destroy their fellow man with a bloody sword in the other hand. I suddenly realized the true situation on Earth-we worship the Infinite Father in vain mutterings and meaningless words, but we do not truly worship with deeds of love commensurate with the Beatitudes. How really simple the formula is.

Jesus, the Christ, calls those *happy* whom the world commonly pities-the discouraged, sorrowful, lowly, spiritually-depressed, merciful, the inwardly pure, the peacefully inclined, and the persecuted. This is the exact opposite of the world's standards. But in each case the blessing is not in the unfortunate condition itself, but in the glorious rewards of the future.

TRAVELING THE PATH BACK TO THE ROAD IN THE SKY

When I studied the words the space intelligences had given us in 1952, I realized that our modern era may see the fulfillment of ancient prophecy, the prophecy which said: 'Blessed are the *meek;* for they shall inherit the earth.' Is it now time for the *meek* to secure their inheritance? If so, who are the *meek* upon the Earth? We don't find them in the 'smoke-filled rooms' of those who attempt to govern us, we don't find them in the places of the lawmakers or the munitions-makers, and they are not to be found amongst those who 'eat and drink with the drunken' nor are they to be found on the countless battlefields of Earth, for the Divine Words still thunder out of Mt. Sinai that ' thou shalt not kill', and it has been prophesied that *murderers* shall not enter through the gates of the Heavenly City.

'Blessed are they that do his commandments, that they ay have right to the tree of life, and may enter in through the gates into the city... for without are dogs, and sorcerers... and murderers..." (Revelation xxii:14-15).

Who are the 'blessed meek'? They must be those 'that do His commandments'. And these 'commandments' are summed up well in the beatitudes. If we look the world over we find few who qualify to be called 'the salt of the earth' or the 'light of the world', but there are some. These few candidates out of millions of people are not perfect and they are the first to admit it ('for there is no man that sinneth not', I Kings viii:46), but they attempt to live that which the emissaries of the Infinite have brought to Earth as His Divine Law for the Perfect Life.

Two different groups of people fall into this category, and they represent two different races of mankind. One group is the Amish/ Mennonite people of evangelical Protestant Christians and the other group are the Hopi Indians of Arizona, who claim they are not Christians, and yet, strangely enough, live that which Jesus, the Christ, taught in a greater way than those who attend a church named after him one day and go out to do battle and destroy their brother the next day. The *meek* are found everywhere on the Earth, but their numbers are small. They are Catholic and Protestant; they are white, black, red and yellow; they are Democrats and Republicans; they are northerners and southerners, they are Gentiles and Jews, they are rich and poor, they are beautiful and talented, they are ugly, sick and despised, they are tall and short, they are fat and slim, they are Americans and they are British, they are Egyptians and they are Russians, they are those who actually *live* the Word of God our Father. In our discussion here, we shall deal with only a portion of the *meek,* the simple Amish/Mennonite people :

TRAVELING THE PATH BACK TO THE ROAD IN THE SKY

is it not written that God 'preserveth the simple'? (Psalm cxvi:6).

In Amish *Life* by John H. Hostetler, the author says :

There exists in Amish communities a generous warmth of brotherhood, mutual respect, and trust.... Their religion forbids participation in warfare. They literally believe : 'Thou shalt not kill'; 'Blessed are the peacemakers'; 'If thine enemy hunger, feed him'; 'Overcome evil with good'; 'Christ also suffered for us, leaving us an example, that ye should follow his steps', and other Bible passages. Nevertheless, they are sensitive to the sufferings of other people and they are generous contributors to foreign relief and rehabilitation, a fact not too well known.

Their mission to America as apostles of peace is td bring healing to a human society and to witness to a higher way of life. They do not entertain any utopian ideas about possessing the whole world, nor converting it.

The fifty settlements of Amish people in North America are small brotherhoods of a kind necessary to national life and well being. The foundations of any civilization depend on the moral quality of the people living in it. Where better can such virtues as neighbourliness, self-control, good will, and co-operation be found than in small communities? A civilization will thrive wherever these qualities are found, and it will break down wherever they cease to exist. Perhaps the modern hurried, worried and fearful world could learn something from the Amish.

After visiting the Amish/Mennonite people, I was well aware of the fact that we could learn something from them, and I told them so. They answered me by saying that they were certainly not perfect and needed much improvement with the help of God. But I told them that they had something, and they do have something.

In order to follow Universal Law we should also literally believe, 'Thou shalt not kill', and we should all be 'apostles of peace to bring healing to a human society and to witness to a higher way of life'. We should not be concerned about the strange Amish costume which is very old and similar to styles once common in Europe during the seventeenth and eighteenth centuries, nor should the beard worn by all adult Amish men cause us undue alarm. These things are all outer appearances only. What counts are the motives of the interior man. As it is written :'by their *fruits* ye shall know them.'

TRAVELING THE PATH BACK TO THE ROAD IN THE SKY

The Amish-Mennonite people believe that it is against Divine Commandant to swear oaths (St. Matthew v:33-48) or hold membership in secret societies.

'And be not conformed to this world : but be ye transformed by the renewing of your mind, that ye may prove what is that good, and acceptable, and perfect, will of God.' (Romans xii:2).

'But I say unto you, That ye resist not evil: but whosoever shall smite thee on thy right cheek, turn to him the other also.' (St. Matthew v:39).

'But I say unto you, Love your enemies, bless them that curse you, do good to them that hate you, and pray for them which despitefully use you, and persecute you; That ye may be the children of your Father which is in heaven...' (St. Matthew v:44-45).

'Be ye therefore perfect, even as your Father which is in heaven is perfect.' (St. Matthew v:48).

'... what fellowship hath righteousness with unrighteousness? and what communion hath light with darkness? ... ye are the temple of the living God; as God hath said, I will dwell in them, an(walk in them; and I will be their God, and they shall be my people Wherefore come out from among them, and be ye separate, saith the Lord... and I will receive you.' (2 Corinthians vi:14-17).

'... he that killeth with the sword must be killed with the sword...' (Revelation xiii:10).

Are the 'glorious rewards of the future' for the meek, the peace makers, the merciful, the pure in heart, etc., now ready to manifest so that such may receive their promised inheritance? Are the UFO intelligences going about in their ships of 'light' like Diogenes o old with his lantern to look for honest men, men who are pure ii heart? If they are doing that, then they would naturally be interested in the Amish/Mennonite people who live by the Bible verses I have given above. Let me state here that I do not belong to this religious group : I am a friend of them all, but a member o none.

The following experiences of Amish/Mennonite people wit] space craft were collected during my stay with them in 1954 and/or were sent to me by my friends in that group.

Mr. and Mrs. John Kauffman of Fredericksburg in Holmes County Ohio,

TRAVELING THE PATH BACK TO THE ROAD IN THE SKY

are respected as reliable and good people. In the summer of 1947 (Kenneth Arnold's sighting was on June 24, 1947) the Kauffman's were sleeping upstairs when they suddenly awoke about midnight to observe a strange luminous disc moving past their bedroom window. The disc was about two feet in diameter, and its outline could be seen clearly. They watched this object as it began to move, over the fence in the yard at the end of the house. It was absolutely silent. Mr. Kauffman went out on the porch downstairs to get ; better look and to be sure it wasn't just a reflection on the glass it the upstairs window. The little disc was still in the yard and was making 90° turns in order to follow the outline of the fence. The disc was observed for about twenty minutes, and finally continuo on its way undisturbed by the witnesses. The Kauffmans went back to bed and never knew what became of the shining object. The: had never heard of 'Flying Saucers' before.

In 1953, at a German settlement near Shelby, Ohio, a small UFO (landed and a man got out of it and went to a nearby stream to get water. Such cases of UFO occupants landing to obtain water have been reported numerous times before. The interplanetary visitor was described as wearing clothing similar to that which the Venusian wore in George Adamski's November 20th encounter in 1952.

During the first part of October, 1953, Aaron Wust of Holmes County, Ohio, was outside the family barn at 12:15 p.m. Looking up he saw a disc-shaped object traveling slowly but high in the sky. It moved with a peculiar up and down fluttering motion that alternated with short bursts of speed. Eighteen-year-old Aaron, who was looking in a north-east direction, said: 'The object was higher than any kite could possibly fly and it was unlike anything I have ever seen before.' The disc would maneuver so that Aaron could see its edge only and then quickly it would turn so he could view it as a perfect round object which displayed dark and light circular spots. The sky was clear and the object stayed in view for fifteen minutes. There was absolutely no sound connected with the disc which gradually disappeared.

At exactly the same time Aaron was viewing the strange disc, his uncle, Dan Unger, observed the same object from half a mile away.

On the same day at 6:00 p.m., Mrs. Mart Unger, Aaron's grandmother, and her daughter Rose, were riding together in a horse and buggy about a mile from where Aaron had seen the disc earlier in the day. They saw an object that apparently was much closer and completely different. However, its motions were similar to what Aaron had described and there was no sound. Instead of one disc, there appeared to be many discs joined together in flight, but retaining a great amount of flexible motion. The object (or objects) was dark grey with lighter circular areas. The women were not fearful although the strange craft came very low to the ground. These witnesses are all well-known in their country neighborhood and are considered very reliable and honest.

Also in 1953, Mrs. Homer Kandel of Berlin, Ohio, was standing at a window in her home watching the progress of a thunderstorm. It was 9:00 p.m. The storm was approaching from the west and suddenly Mrs. Kandel saw a very peculiar circular light traveling at a great speed from west to east. There was no sound and no trail was left by the object. The disc-shaped light was a beautiful bluish-green. It was very close to the ground for it was beneath the low-hanging rain and thunder clouds. The object never veered from its course but moved in a straight path and disappeared in the east. In 1954, her daughter, aged thirteen, was out in the yard when she saw a great 'cigar-shaped' object in the sky. It was also traveling very fast and made no sound. When her mother asked her why she didn't report the incident sooner, the girl replied: 'I was afraid someone would make fun of me!'

On August 15, 1954, Abe J. Hochstetler, an Amish/Mennonite minister, was returning from Sunday church services with his wife at 2:30 p.m. There wasn't a cloud in the sky and the Hochstetlers were headed east in their customary horse-drawn buggy on U.S. Highway No. 62, four miles west of Millersburg, Holmes Co., Ohio.

When the minister and his wife first saw the strange object, they thought it might be a flock of birds in the north-east flying closely together. As they watched, however, they realized it couldn't possibly be birds. It moved in that characteristic up and down fluttering motion with the occasional burst of speed. When it gained momentum, a dark-colored smoke seemed to be ejected from it. There was no sound connected with the disc which displayed a circular view and an edge view. Within its outline, the Hochstetlers could see light and dark areas. The minister said: 'What we saw definitely wasn't a balloon or a kite, and we observed it for nearly twenty minutes.'

The following sighting in 1954 by Mr. and Mrs. Howard Aling and their son Gary, aged 8, is of great importance, for it is similar to others witnessed by Amish/Mennonite people. One night, about midnight, all three members of the family observed a great shining circular light moving over and sometimes behind their neighbor's house. The luminous sphere would change from red to white and would come very low to the ground near the house so that the Aling's could see the hill north of the neighbor's house form a background behind this object. The witnesses were about 800 feet from the light during the sighting. The disc looked almost as large as a 'full moon' and slowly moved up and down with a weird undulation but made no sound.

The important significance of this sighting is the fact that a boy was about to be born to the family living in that neighbor's house. The child was born several hours later at 3:05 a.m. What connection could there be between an interplanetary craft hovering over and circling the yard of a man about to become a father and the child who was soon to enter the world in Holmes County, Ohio?

Mr. and Mrs. Dale Stutzman returned home from Sunday evening services on April 24, 1955. They had attended the local Mennonite church. It was 10.00 p.m. and they usually turned on the radio at this time in order to listen to the Mennonite Hour. However, just before they were able to do this, they heard a loud sound they thought at first must be from an aeroplane. But the sound was extremely unusual and didn't really sound like it was coming from some conventional aircraft. They went outside to see what the cause was. Immediately they saw an odd glowing light in the northwesterly sky; it was very high and appeared to be twice the size of the largest stars. It was very brilliant, but didn't behave like an ordinary star. It moved up and down and from side to side. They watched the object for about fifteen minutes until it left the area at a terrific speed and without any sound.

After the Stutzmans had gone outside, the loud sound stopped. Since the moving light had made no sound they concluded that the sound before the sighting must have been to attract their attention. Mr. and Mrs. Stutzman are both public school teachers and are highly respected in their community. Mr. Stutzman asked his pupils at Holmesville School the next morning if any of them had seen or heard anything out of the ordinary the night before. However, no one was able to give a report. This man and his wife are definitely not 'Flying Saucer' fans. They have no idea what the object may have been. However, both of them stated that there was a definite indication that the object was under intelligent control of some kind.

Mrs. Esther Hostetler was traveling on the highway near Goshen, In-

TRAVELING THE PATH BACK TO THE ROAD IN THE SKY

diana, the home of the Mennonite Goshen College, on June 24, 1955. She noticed something in the sky, which at first looked like it might be an aeroplane. When the object was closer, she realized that its shape was not that of a conventional aircraft. She stopped to observe the object, and when it was directly overhead, it hovered for several minutes, moving in a series of circles. It revealed a perfect disc shape and shone brilliantly with a metallic glare as though it were highly polished. It finally disappeared suddenly with a great burst of speed. At no time did it make a sound.

On September 20, 1955, Mrs. Homer Kandel of Berlin, Ohio, had another sighting. Her five children also witnessed it at 5:00 p.m. The Kandel home is quite secluded in the country situated in a valley which is surrounded on three sides by wooded hills. The sky was clear. The family saw an object coming into view from the northeast at a high altitude which appeared to be an aeroplane. It rapidly came closer and dropped in altitude and finally slowed down until it was just over the nearby tree tops. They could clearly see that the object had no wings and it made no sound whatsoever. Mrs. Kandel remembered her sighting of 1953, and she also knew that certain unidentified objects had been seen recently by many people in the area, so she waved in a friendly manner. Immediately the strange craft began to move, for it had stopped over the trees, and it moved slowly towards the family group. The intelligence behind this object had responded to her friendly gesture!

While this was going on, two conventional type aeroplanes appeared in the sky, and the UFO instantly shot up into the heavens at an incredible speed and angle and disappeared. Mrs. Kandel felt it would not return, so she turned to resume her work. A few minutes later, one of the children came to tell her that the object was coming back again. When they went out into the yard they discovered the UFO was approaching them slowly as before, but immediately the two aeroplanes showed up again and the object left once more in a great burst of speed. This appearing and disappearing act was repeated four times in succession. The family was astonished. Each time, the two planes interfered. Mrs. Kandel knew the planes were interested in the actions of the UFO, but at no time did these planes attempt to chase the craft, for to do so would have been useless.

When the UFO left for the last time, never to return again, many planes were seen in the area for many days following. Mrs. Kandel said at least thirty planes seemed to be investigating the area. One plane with peculiar

TRAVELING THE PATH BACK TO THE ROAD IN THE SKY

markings was seen several times flying low over the Kandel home.

Evidently the UFO was attempting to land and possibly make a contact, but the planes interrupted each time. Since the Kandel home is well secluded, it is an ideal location for such an attempt. The family described the craft as being smaller than a Piper Cub aeroplane. It was somewhat tubular in shape and had a raised blister on top in front and in the rear. It also had a raised blister on the front bottom. It was made of some kind of bright metal and looked like polished aluminium. There were no portholes nor windows. No sound could be heard at any time even though it maneuvered magnificently.

On January 5, 1956, I received a very long letter from Mrs. Kandel, and she told me of an exciting aftermath to the above account. Part of that letter follows :

I just decided to write you this morning. We have been waiting since September 20th last year for another unusual craft to come into our valley. I believe there have been many here, but they come secretly. Why? When that 'Saucer' came that afternoon we waved to it, and it acted as though it might land, but it was chased away.

We have seen other things since that time. I'll bet we became the best sky watchers in Holmes County, Ohio. Just a few days after the September 20th sighting, on September 24th, we were coming home from work at the store about 9:30 p.m. when my daughter Miriam and my son Howard came running out to meet us. They were very excited and said they had watched something strange land in the neighbour's field! They told us it was very odd and even its bright colours were weird and different. We immediately went to look for the object, but evidently it was gone. However, for over a month after that, a star-like object hovered over the neighbour's barn. It didn't come every night, but would appear about twice a week or so.

Five different times I have seen strange objects going over this area from east to west. It looks like the UFOs have a 'mail route' across this area of Ohio! One day I thought I saw two planes over a nearby hill. One was higher than the other one and more brilliant. As I watched I realized that one of the objects was a plane (the shiny one), and it continued on its way out of sight. The other disc-shaped object was dull and had a black spot on it. It finally moved away slowly.

On October 8, 1955, just about two weeks after the Kandel sighting of

TRAVELING THE PATH BACK TO THE ROAD IN THE SKY

September 20th, Robert R. Troyer, another Amish/Mennonite who lives in Millersburg, Holmes County, Ohio, observed a UFO. He was standing on the north side of his farm home at 10:15 p.m. He saw a dull red light in the western sky. As he watched it he became aware of the fact that it was moving closer towards him, and slowly. Finally, he was able to make out the shape of the object. It was spherical but somewhat elongated. There were yellow lights around the sphere which appeared to be as large as a basketball. There was no sound connected with it, and the sky was clear. The object passed over the Troyer farm at a low altitude. Mr. Troyer is described as a man of the 'highest Christian character and reliable judgment'.

The Amish/Mennonite people are not given to fanciful illusions, nor do their imaginations work overtime where unidentified flying objects are concerned. Most of them have never heard of 'Flying Saucers' and are not particularly interested in them when they do hear about them. Because of their simple way of living and their wholesome family life their sighting reports are without question genuine.

Of interest here is the fact that the largest group of Amish/ Mennonite people is not the Lancaster County, Pennsylvania, settlement as is commonly supposed, but the settlement located in Holmes and adjoining counties in east-central Ohio. Therefore, we find a humble and meek people being visited by interplanetary craft in the area where their largest settlement is located. What does it all mean? Does the fact that this area is located *directly* over one of the world's *major fault lines* have any bearing on the matter?

During my stay in Holmes County in 1954 I heard of a very old Amish/ Mennonite woman who had observed a UFO hovering low over a field. Her description of the craft was exactly the same as the description of the Scout Ship in *Flying Saucers Have Landed by* Desmond Leslie and George Adamski. This venerable matriarch had never heard of Leslie and Adamski and their book, let alone Flying Saucers.

I also heard of several cases where UFOs had been observed circling farm houses or hovering over them just prior to a birth in an Amish/Mennonite family. Other sightings occurred during deaths. In my book, *The Saucers Speak!,* an interesting event is mentioned which I believe is connected with the birth-death appearances of UFOs. On page 99, we read :

On October 21St (1952) at 8.10 p.m., a small private plane crashed and burned at Winslow, Arizona. This plane was on a mercy flight to a Phoenix

TRAVELING THE PATH BACK TO THE ROAD IN THE SKY

hospital with a fourteen-month-old polio victim. All four passengers were instantly killed. One of the workers at the Winslow Timber Company was working late, and saw the plane take off and minutes later burst into flames. He told the C.A.A. investigators that immediately after the crash, and before the ambulance and fire truck had arrived, an orange streak sped across the sky and apparently landed by the stricken plane. We know that the 'Saucers' do not harm anyone. Perhaps they knew of the child and tried to help. Of course, we do not know just what did take place.

Why do UFOs appear during the two greatest events any man on Earth can experience his birth or entrance into this world, and his death or exit from it? 'Swing Low, Sweet Chariot' may have a new meaning.

Another possible explanation is to be found in the words of UFO intelligences themselves, where they have stated in various contacts that reincarnation is a fact and that some of their own people have incarnated on the Earth in ages past and today in order to assist humanity here. They say they cannot interfere otherwise, for Universal Law prevents such interference with another world's progress and the progress of its inhabitants. But if they come to Earth and are born as one of us, then they can aid us in whatever manner necessary. What type of group or person would a highly-developed extra-terrestrial pick as his potential family? Undoubtedly, he would pick those who come closest to his standards of perfection. We already know that the UFO intelligences live by a standard which is nearly identical with that given in the Sermon on the Mount. Then would they not look for and choose a group on Earth that attempted to follow those words and succeeded in part in living them? If this is true, the Amish/Mennonite people have all the qualifications.

A group of simple and wholesome people who have a long and exceptional record for living the Christ life going back to a congregation organized in 1525 A.D. in Zurich, Switzerland, may now find itself a chosen group to receive those entities who will one day grow up to adulthood and lead the world into the prophesied New Age where the Christ shall rule. Something is going on in (and above) Holmes County, Ohio, where the largest gathering of people who refuse to kill their fellow man is to be found in the entire world. Here we have fault lines, space ships, and the 'blessed meek'.

We are told today that 'Peace is for the strong', and this motto is de-

TRAVELING THE PATH BACK TO THE ROAD IN THE SKY

clared by those who call themselves 'Christian'. Yet, He who started it all when He walked the shores of the sea of Galilee, said: 'Blessed are the meek: for they shall inherit the earth.'

Peace is not for the 'strong' who build bigger and bigger bombs so that the weak may tremble at the thought of annihilation. The *meek* 'shall delight themselves in the abundance of peace' as it is written.

The travelers on the *road in the sky* that has known no beginning are spiraling to Earth once again. *Yesterday* they roamed the Earth and the heavens above it, and *today* they search out the places of their former visitations, and they follow the great fault lines of Earth to check on possible disaster areas, and they help to neutralize the effects of the deadly radiation released by the scientific militarists/materialists, and they seek out our lost inheritance in the buried repositories of ancient empires whether on land or under seas. They also seek out with a 'lantern of Diogenes' those who are closest to their own kind. Let it be known that the eternal *road in the sky will* also be traveled by those on Earth, but the travelers will be *the blessed meek.*

TRAVELING THE PATH BACK TO THE ROAD IN THE SKY

THE VISITANTS

'Then we upon our globe's last voyage shall go,

And view the ocean leaning on the sky;

From thence our rolling neighbours we shall know,

And on the lunar world securely pry.'

(Old English.)

WEBSTER tells us that a *visitant is* one who, or that which, visits one as if from without one's own sphere. A *visitant* is a visitor, but specifically a migratory bird which appears at intervals for a limited .period. The occupants of the UFOs can certainly be called *visitants,* for they are definitely 'from without our sphere' and they 'appear at intervals for a limited period'. Therefore, we are going to discuss a few of those appearances and periods as they have been reported *today.*

Fifteen years ago, Mabel A. Heury of Whittier, California, was living in Pasadena when she and several hundred other witnesses observed dozens of 'enormous stars moving in majestic circles which were obviously under intelligent control-no one had ever heard of "Flying Saucers" at that time'.

Several months ago, a glowing 'Flying Pole' landed in Ireland in a peat bog behind a farmer's field. He noticed that it didn't touch the ground but hovered a few inches above it. He estimated the weird object was three feet wide and six feet long. The farmer approached it cautiously, and then grabbed it and carried it to a stile. It was amazingly light for its size. He discovered that he couldn't climb over the stile with the object in his arms, so he put it down on the ground. It immediately started to move away so he grabbed it again. It then went straight up with him holding on to it but he

TRAVELING THE PATH BACK TO THE ROAD IN THE SKY

jumped off at a safe altitude and watched it go higher and higher until it disappeared. One wonders what would have happened if he had held on all the way? The Irish farmer's experience reminds us of the 'Flying Telephone Poles' mentioned in my book, *Other Tongues—Other Flesh*. On page 346-347, we read :

The Space Confederation decided to do something about our depleted Earth (the soil) and this is what they have said: 'You have been hearing about strange "Flying Telephone Poles" that are observed to come very close to your Earth. These strike the earth and will take care of a large area. They go into the ground and dissolve in the soil in about one hour. They do not look like shooting stars when they fall, but appear as a blue streak to the naked eye. Your beneficial bacteria are dying and these "flying poles" are sent out by the scientific space laboratories to take care of your Western Hemisphere. In this area of your planet you will find that certain farmers are puzzled as to how the soil became so rich and at times there is evidence of red dust. Many of these "poles" are tube-like, pointed at both ends and usually six feet long by twelve inches in diameter, although they can be much larger. The tubes contain rich, concentrated organic soil material from our own gardens and canals on Mars. They are full of vital, healthy, organic elements that will correct your increasing problem of humus destruction.'

The object in the Irish peat bog came *very close to the ground,* and it was *six feet long,* and it was hovering over a farmer's field. Therefore, it must have been one of the experimental tubes or 'poles' referred to above. If the farmer in Ireland had let the object go about its business undisturbed he might have discovered his future crop of those 'Irish potatoes' to be decidedly more flavorful and abundant thanks to his colleagues on Mars!

There are 'beacons' for UFOs besides the 'Lines of Nazca' and other similar immense patterns to be viewed from the air. A friend of mine was inside an old abandoned mine in Southern California several years ago. She happened to take a photograph from inside the entrance in order to get a picture of the sun shining into the old shaft. When the photograph was developed something appeared in one corner that hadn't been visible in the mine when she exposed the film. I have this photograph and I would like to reproduce it in this book, but my friend has asked me to hold it for a while. However, a small disc-shaped object shows up on the film and it is surrounded by a glow. Out of its top a stream of luminous particles are being emitted. What is it?

TRAVELING THE PATH BACK TO THE ROAD IN THE SKY

Space intelligences have mentioned in the past that in ancient times they placed a driver-mechanism or 'beacon point' in various places close to the surface of Earth, but usually embedded in rock. These 'beacon points' were for automatic triangulation in navigation. Most of these mechanisms are still under the ground and are surrounded by a strange magnetic field which definitely affects certain modem electronic instruments, etc. My friend didn't really photograph the 'beacon' itself, because it was behind several feet of rock in the old mine. But her camera registered the field of energy around the disc and thereby she obtained a picture of its general outline on her film.

TV Channels 10 and 12 were having a great deal of difficulty with interference several years ago in their equipment on top of South Mountain near Phoenix, Arizona. Channel 12 was having the most difficulty. A new Channel (3) began to set up its equipment directly on top of the same mountain. At that moment the UFO intelligences went into action and removed the driver-mechanism or 'beacon' buried a few feet underground that had been giving all the trouble. Even beings from outer space can't seem to stand in the way of our modern TV progress! Before the space mechanism was removed from this mountain there were many sightings of 'glowing lights' and 'strange objects' hovering over South Mountain and the reports filled the Phoenix and other Arizona newspapers. The vortex created by that little disc-shaped mechanism caused all kinds of things to happen to the TV-radio equipment. When three TV stations tried to share the same mountain the UFO intelligences decided it was time to remove their centuries-old navigation aid or 'beacon point'. One wonders what would have happened if those miners in that Southern California mine had dug a little deeper to one side of the shaft? And one also wonders what would have happened if one of the TV stations had decided it wanted a basement?

Near Santa Cruz, California, south of San Francisco, there is an area called a 'mystery spot'. It is similar to other 'mystery spots' throughout the world such as the one in Oregon, called the 'Oregon Vortex'; and the one near St. Augustine, Florida; Guerneville, California, etc.

'Sensitives' who stand over the Santa Cruz 'mystery spot' claim they get the impression that a great space ship crashed there and its driver-mechanism embedded itself in the rock at that exact point. Could all the strange conditions in this area and other 'mystery spots' be caused by the still active magnetic field of the mechanism, or could it be caused by one of

TRAVELING THE PATH BACK TO THE ROAD IN THE SKY

the navigational 'beacon points' we mentioned above? At any rate, there is an anti-gravity effect caused by something.

On February 24, 1955, I interviewed Ted Bennett of the Big Oak Store at East Prairie, Missouri. Ted owns boats and motors which he rents at his camping facilities on the Mississippi River. There is an island in the middle of this great river between the landing at Dorena, Missouri, on one side and the landing at Hickman, Kentucky, on the other side. This island is about one and a quarter miles long and one quarter mile wide, covered with thick saplings. In 1954 I had heard a story from a reliable source that claimed a 'Flying Saucer' landed on this island in the Mississippi and had been abandoned by its crew (where did they go?). The story started because of sightings made by local people and because compasses carried by hunters went 'wild' in the nearby swamps while they were hunting 'coons' (raccoon). Other people had told my reliable source mentioned above that there was something on the island causing magnetic disturbances and that it all had started in 1948 when 'two great white glowing lights' were seen over the Mississippi River and observed by people for twenty miles around. Weird 'fireballs' were also seen about the same time.

I traveled to Dorena, Missouri, in 1955 to find out what I could about the above happenings. Mr. Bennett confirmed what my friend had told me, and said that it was all true. I carried some detection equipment with me and discovered that a maximum signal intensity indicated something unusual south of the landing area. This was in the direction of Reelfoot Lake which was formed in 1812 A.D. by a 'peculiar kind of earthquake'. I did not have the time to take a boat and investigate the island or the lake, but I did learn some interesting things from the local people who are very friendly in this part of the United States.

They all told the same story as related above, and that during 1953-54 large numbers of Air Force planes circled the island at night. As many as fifty or seventy-five planes had been counted at one time. And planes flew above barges going down the river carrying government 'supplies'. Why did the government feel it was necessary to send an escort of planes along with ordinary barges on the Mississippi River, or were they 'ordinary'? Is there some connection between what the barges were carrying and the fact a UFO is somewhere in the vicinity? I didn't find any landed space ships during my visit in Missouri, but something is causing strange emanations that 'make compasses go wild when the men are in the swamps "coon" hunt-

TRAVELING THE PATH BACK TO THE ROAD IN THE SKY

ing.' This entire area is on the same great *fault line* that eventually goes directly through the Holmes County, Ohio settlement of the Amish/Mennonite people.

In 1947, Stanley Elder of Greenville, Michigan, had an unusual experience with a UFO. He was on his farm carrying two buckets of water when he looked up to see three 'stars' headed in his direction. One of these large 'stars' dropped out of formation and hovered a few feet above some trees about 1,000 feet from where Stanley had fallen with his buckets after the surprise of the sighting. The UFO was gigantic, and he estimated it to be about 100 yards long. There were strange 'portholes' around its curved elongated body. Out of these 'portholes' an unearthly brilliant light shone. For many days afterwards Stanley's eyes were affected and gave him much pain. A cow in the barn even had eye trouble for some time after the event. Also, Stanley claimed he could no longer wear a wristwatch due to his body magnetism caused by the encounter with the UFO. A feeling of 'reverence' came over him while he looked at this gigantic craft above the nearby trees, a feeling that stayed with him for a long time. He had a strong compulsion to go to the ship, but he fought it off. The ground seemed to vibrate and a tank beside which Stanley fell was also vibrating. The pulsations seemed to beat rhythmically with his own heart and the bluish-white light of the strange 'portholes' radiated and seemed to extend out to him to bathe him in a scintillation that was unexplainable When the object rose to leave, Stanley saw the bottom of it which was perfectly round, and around the periphery there were about twelve bright lights. This last part of the sighting sounds like the description Robert R. Troyer gave of the UFO he observed on October 8, 1955, in Ohio.

On October 16, 1955, a friend of mine who is employed by Acme Telectronix as an electronic specialist, wrote: 'When I become doubtful (of UFOs), I recall that Mr. L. A. Thompson (K6BDC), our Chief Engineer here, saw a brilliant light streaking at him while he was riding in a jeep with an Air Force officer and two engineers at the Air Force Base in Omaha, Nebraska. This light suddenly veered off and upward at about an 80° angle. The men stopped the jeep and watched it for nearly thirty minutes as it continued on the same course. Even at only 100 m.p.h., that would place the object farther out in space than we have ever gone, and this light was really moving.'

Acme Telectronix of Cleveland, Ohio, maintains a Santa Barbara, California laboratory of which Mr. Thompson is Chief Engineer.

TRAVELING THE PATH BACK TO THE ROAD IN THE SKY

Also in 1955, three West German electronics engineers reported they had heard strange sounds on voice frequency by using the same type of light beams that the Germans used to transmit secret messages during World War II. Consisting of a small microphone, transmitter, and ordinary infrared tungsten lamps, the device not only picked up voice frequency sounds but also bell-like tones approximating code. When this was all slowed down to 1/50 of the reception speed, the similarity to International Morse Code was pronounced, but United States Army cryptographers stationed in West Germany were not able to break the code down into any recognizable language pattern. The West German Interplanetary Society said that they believed the sounds emanated from UFOs outside the Earth's atmosphere. No claim was officially made that communication had been established between the Germans and outer space visitors, but it was a well-known fact at the time that the United States Air Force and also scientists of other countries were lending aid to the experiments.

During August, 1954, a large Canadian family had an experience which is considered authentic. Two of the younger men in the family were a mile or so from the farm house. They were picking peas in a field when all at once their horse began to act in a strange manner. When they went to investigate the trouble they saw, a sphere about nine feet in diameter resting on the ground on one support. It was only about fifty feet away from them. Suddenly they saw a door slide open and a short stairway emerged. As they watched astonished at the sight, a tall man came through the door wearing a tight-fitting suit that looked like rubber. The boys were terrified, and quickly mounted the horse and headed for the farm house. Immediately the sphere rose into the air and followed them to land only a thousand feet behind the house and barn. It remained there for one hour and ten minutes. Several witnesses came to the farm during this time and they too viewed the craft. From a distance it looked as though three men were working around the ship. At one time, a strange spiral encircled the object, starting at the bottom and working around it until the top was reached. This rendered the object invisible for a while. Soon afterwards, the craft left the area.

Three days later, an unknown visitor came to the farm and said he had read about the landing in the local newspapers and wanted to talk to the family about it. However, no article had appeared in the newspapers, although there was some mention made of it several days *after* the visitor's appearance! The man gave a fictitious name and address in Montreal, for later, when a check was made, it was discovered that no such person or address existed there. The man said the object would return that night and that he and one of the young men should go out and meet it. The family was suspicious of this man and they feared the outcome so they placed various people behind fences, the barn, etc., with guns. The object actually appeared in the sky and the unknown visitor ran into the centre of a field waving his handkerchief. However, the craft passed overhead and disappeared. Evidently the space visitors knew about the guns, although I am sure they weren't afraid of them. But who was the 'unknown visitor'? How did he know the ship would return?

On December 24, 1955, Michael W. Kruvant, director of the Flying Saucer Research Association of South Orange, New Jersey, transmitted a message to outer space intelligences via his light beam equipment. Five seconds after the message had gone out, two oval shaped objects passed over his house going in a northern direction. The great confirmation in this sighting is the fact that Mr. Kruvant had specifically asked in his transmitted message that the UFOs go over heading north to let him know his message had been received. A very nice Christmas Eve gift for one Earthman!

A friend of mine in California was listening to his short-wave radio one night during October, 1955, when he heard at 10 p.m. the following message on a band used by the United States Navy: 'Sir, we have tracked the target within ten miles and have it locked into our radar. What are your orders?' A reply came back at once: 'Use extreme caution. Proceed no further until more units arrive to help you.' That was the end of the message, although my friend stayed tuned to the frequency for a long time. I wonder what the 'target' was?

On January 19, 1956, a car was traveling east near Peach Springs, Arizona, on U.S. Highway No. 66 (about 150 miles east of Peach Springs this same highway encounters the area where the *Martian Miniatures* on pottery were discovered). At 2.30 p.m. the people in the car saw what appeared to be a 'flash of lightning'. Then an odd-shaped small object, with a bright metallic glare, dropped close to the ground as if it were about to land. Suddenly, a great cloud of smoke came out of it and it began to dart here and there, turning over and over again. It moved along only a few feet from the ground for a short time and then gained altitude until it reached the side of some hills to the north of the car on the highway. It made strange patterns in the sky, and circled the highway area. It would approach the ground again, only to suddenly move up making incredible angles and turns. There was no sound connected with the object. When smoke came out of the craft it appeared to be emitted from the bottom centre. The witnesses watched the maneuvers for about twenty minutes until the craft disappeared.

During May, 1956, Mrs. Evelyn L. Smith and her family in Indianapolis, Indiana, had strange experiences connected with their TV and radio sets. One day, the Music on a radio programme stopped, and a strange voice said: 'You are masters of the Earth!' After that, the musical programme continued as before. Mrs. Smith, and her twelve-year-old daughter Rita, went outside to see if a UFO was in the vicinity, and when they looked up they saw two strange objects passing over their house. The objects circled the area twice and disappeared to the south-east. Later, in t956, Mrs. Smith's father and mother, who live in the country, observed an enormous object above their house that was tilted on its side displaying a great dome. It suddenly seemed to 'dissolve' and reappeared in the opposite direction. Her father said :'It was as big as the house and the dome seemed to be as big as a court-house dome.' The object was very bright and finally disappeared. Mrs. Smith's sister also witnessed this sighting and was so frightened she ran into the house along with her mother.

The Smiths have a friend in Indianapolis who also heard strange voices and 'code' come over her radio and TV sets during 1956. When the woman went outside she saw UFOs over her house.

On May 15, 1956, while Mrs. Smith was hearing voices on her TV and radio sets in Indianapolis, Indiana, another housewife in Fontana, California, was seeing a UFO from her car as she drove home. At 10:08 a.m. residents of Fontana had felt the shock of a sharp earthquake. Many people became panicky as there was a very loud rumbling sound and a terrific jolt. At 1:00 p.m. the housewife was driving her car near her home. Her son Robert, eight years old, suddenly said: 'Mommy, look what a whirlwind has drawn up into the sky.' The object was directly behind the woman's car traveling from west to east. The street was lined with walnut trees and it was hard for her to view the craft. She continued to drive until she was in an area where she could view what the 'whirlwind had drawn up into the sky'. Then her son said :'Mommy, it's a "Flyring Saucer" ... it's bell-shaped and it has an antenna on it...' The silvery object was only about 1,000 feet off the ground and was traveling slowly. The woman estimated its size at thirty feet in diameter. As she watched the UFO, a small aeroplane passed it in the air without even changing its course. The object was observed for over ten minutes and during that time it changed its shape from that of a bell to an oblong. It made the characteristic fluttering motion until it passed out of sight. Was there some connection between the earthquake and the UFO? UFOs patrol great fault lines to check on possible disaster areas in the event of serious earthquakes. Fontana, California, is on a fault line, and they had an earthquake, and later the same day they had a UFO! Who knows?

On June 22, 1956, a few weeks after the above sightings, an Ohio State University radio astronomer reported that radio signals of a type resembling radio telegraphy in many ways were being received from a source presumed to be the planet Venus. Dr. John D. Kraus, director of the university's Radio Observatory, made no comment on the possible origin of the signals other than to say that 'whatever phenomenon is responsible for the signals must be of a rather complex type'.

Dr. Kraus said the signals accompanied another type of emission from Venus, a crackling signal somewhat resembling static from terrestrial thunderstorms and possibly originating in similar storms on the planet often referred to as Earth's 'twin'. On June 1st, Dr. Kraus had reported the reception of the strong crackling or 'Class I' signals on a wavelength of 11 meters. On June 22nd, the announcement said that, in addition to the static-like signals, Dr. Kraus had been receiving 'Class II' signals of a distinctly different type which presumably also originated on Venus.

Dr. Kraus reported that the second type of radio emission had 'many of the characteristics of signals from a terrestrial radio telegraph transmitting station'. In fact, the astronomer at first suspected interference from this kind of station. Later, however, he noted that the 'Class II' signals were received only when Venus was directly in the antenna beam of the radio telescope and that they commonly accompanied the previously reported 'Class I' signals.

Dr. Kraus said: 'The signals are usually received for only brief periods so that it is difficult to study them. Sufficiently numerous and varied observations of them have been made to make it appear very likely that they do come from Venus. The 'Class II' signals are usually of an intermittent nature but sometimes are observed to recur with a more or less definite periodicity.'

Dr. Kraus did not believe the 'Class II' emissions could have been signals of terrestrial origin reflected from Venus because of the 'tremendous power' necessary for a transmitter on Earth to be heard via reflection from the other planet.

Scientists at the United States Naval Research Laboratory also reported that radio signals were being received from Venus. Three radio astronomers announced that they had been receiving the signals. They were Cornell H. Mayer, Russell M. Sloanaker, and Timothy P. McCullough.

In July, 1956, a 'Flying Saucer' scare came to the simple people of the Fiji Islands in the Pacific Ocean. Three different times scores of people, including many Europeans, observed strange objects in the skies. After two weeks of this, on August 3rd, hundreds of people witnessed a weird sight in the heavens. A brilliant yellow light moved above the islands and was observed from 7:00 p.m. until 3:00 a.m. Other reports said that a spindle-shaped yellow light moved from the east to the north, and pulsated as it moved.

Three days later, on August 6, 1956, hundreds of people watched a 'peculiar red object like a comet' moving in the sky east of Sydney. The object was sighted by witnesses from Bondi to Lane Cove. It was first noticed at 9:00 p.m. and was visible for one hour and a quarter. Groups of people in Bondi stood on street corners watching the object. Mr. H. Warham, Clyde Street, Bondi, said he and his family watched the fiery object for over an hour. He said: 'It was the most astonishing thing I've ever seen. It looked like a rocket with a tail heading for the Earth at terrific speed. It glowed in a fiery red brilliance, then faded almost to a pin point, but seemed to return again. I've seen everything that flies in the sky, but that defies description. Although I don't believe in "Flying Saucers", I find it hard to believe this was anything like a plane. I've never seen anything like it before.'

Mr. W. F. Boyling of Lane Cove said: 'At first, it looked like the light on the top of a television mast. But when it kept rising in the sky I became really interested. At times it was obscured by clouds. But it was quite bright. I've never seen anything like it before.'

An astronomer, Mr. H. Wood, discounted the suggestion that the object was Venus. He said: 'It could have been Mars, but that planet has been in the same position for some time and hasn't drawn much attention from anyone. Cloudy conditions prevented me from observing the object through the Government Observatory telescope.'

On August 11, 1956, a startling message was radioed from Auckland,

TRAVELING THE PATH BACK TO THE ROAD IN THE SKY

New Zealand, to Sydney, Australia : *Flying Saucer Panic! New Zealand Fears Invasions!* 'People are clamoring for government explanations of widespread findings of mystery metals and jelly-like substances. Reliable citizens claim they saw "Flying Saucers", and several experts in responsible positions are talking of early invasions from outer space. Among these are Dr. Bernard Finch and Mr. Harold H. Fulton, chief of the Civilian Saucer Investigation (N.Z.). Mr. Fulton, attached to the Royal New Zealand Air Force engineering section at Whenuapai Base, Auckland, said today recent mass sightings in New Zealand emphasized the imminence of invasion from another planet. Scientists and police, Fulton said, have not explained the mystery. Mass sightings have been reported in the last month and strange jelly-like substances and unknown metals have been found. The experts who predict early invasion of the Earth believe the first landing ground for space ships will be Australia. A big fall of mystery jelly-like substances followed a "Saucer" sighting over Hawkes Bay, N.Z. Government scientists have put the substances through every known test without identifying them. These substances, sometimes like a spider-web, last only twenty-four hours, then disintegrate. The other day there was a sighting over Hamilton, North Island, N.Z., followed by an explosion in the air. Police confiscated a strange cylinder. So far the metal in the cylinder has completely baffled police and scientists. The explosion has not been officially explained, although it is known it was in mid-air. An unknown metal, with burn marks around its edges, has been found in the Auckland, N.Z., suburb of Orange.'

Dr. W. P. Clifford reported at the same time that similar unknown substances had fallen at Glen Innes, north of Sydney, Australia, a few months before. He said: 'When a woman approached these substances they immediately dissolved. We believe they came from "Flying Saucers." '

Well, there was no 'early invasion' from space, in fact, there was no 'invasion' at all, but during several months of 1956, all in all, several thousand people witnessed objects that belonged to the visitants. We might mention, however, that the great *fault line* of the Pacific Ocean passes right by the Fiji Islands, then swings south past New Zealand on its way to the South Pole.

In 1956, a mother in Burbank, California, received a letter from her son who is a pilot with the United States Air Force stationed in Alaska. He wrote that he and five other men had flown four hundred miles out into the ice fields to set down and get into operation a station for instrument studies of cosmic rays. The young officer said he had located a flat surface and landed on it within a few hundred feet of a small hill. All the men got out of the plane and started to walk over towards the hill to see if they couldn't set up their station on top of it. He said they all suddenly heard a strange 'whistle' behind them. This was all they needed to throw themselves face down on the ice. When they looked up, they saw a gigantic black 'Flying Saucer' flying low over the ice field. It had missed them by inches. The men were all very frightened and hurried to their plane and flew back to their base at once. The young officer told his mother the UFO was at least thirty-five feet in diameter, and disappeared over the ice fields never to return. What was the 'black object' doing over those fields? There's a *fault line* there. Fossils of giant men have been found there and Indians say such creatures are still alive in the area. What else could be there?

On May 15, 1957, Dr. J. C. Cooke, at that time professor of applied mathematics at the University of Malaya, announced he believed that 'Flying Saucers' were controlled by intelligent beings from outer space. He said: 'We must not fall into the common tendency of denying the existence of the "Saucers". There is no doubt that the governments of the world are suppressing the truth about such objects because they fear panic and mass hysteria.' Dr. Cooke is now in England with the British Supply Ministry's royal aircraft establishment. He also said : 'The creatures controlling the "Flying Saucers" do not appear to be hostile and might be here to save us from ourselves. Certainly, if we show hostility to them they could easily annihilate us. I personally hope they will intervene if an atomic war starts.' Dr. Cooke is a graduate of Queen's College, Oxford, and the University of London.

During the last three months of 1957, I was in the United States and Canada, completing a 32,000 mile lecture tour on the subject *of The Lost World and the UFOs. I* arrived in Miami, Florida, in October from Peru to begin this tour. Everywhere I went people were talking about the 'Flying Saucers'. Sightings were being made in all parts of North America although very little ever appeared in the newspapers except in small local publications. However, on November 2, 1957, something took place in Texas which made headlines throughout the nation. Three motorists were traveling separately in the vicinity of Levelland, Texas, in the extreme western part of the state. These motorists reported separately to Hockley County Sheriff Weir Clem within a two hour period Saturday night, November 2nd, and early November 3rd, that they had seen a terrifying flying object.

TRAVELING THE PATH BACK TO THE ROAD IN THE SKY

Their reports prompted the sheriff and one of his deputies to take to the highways in an official cruiser. The officers caught a glimpse of bright moving lights that they attributed to the same object. The three motorists reported seeing similar lights on a huge object which they first spotted hovering over the road ahead of them. Two of the three said they caught glimpses of an egg-shaped bulk possibly 200 feet long to which the lights were seemingly attached. All said the object took to the air after a few seconds.

The three motorists reported similar experiences with their automobiles upon reaching the vicinity of the object. They said their lights went out and their motors died. After the object had soared into the air, they said, the lights on their cars came back on and they were able to start the motors.

The sheriff said he and his deputy, Pat McCulloch, saw a 'strip of brightly colored light' cross the highway about 200 feet in front of them but they were unable to distinguish a form. The sheriff said the light was 'like a neon sign' and was 'the color of a setting sun—a brilliant red'. He said he experienced no difficulty with the lights or motor of the car he was driving.

Officers from the Air Force Base at Lubbock, Texas, thirty-two miles east of Levelland, arrived November 3rd to question the sheriff and others concerning the phenomenon. The Air Force announced that it had had no planes in the vicinity during the time of the sightings and had no knowledge of aircraft of any kind in the area.

The first report had come at 11:05 p.m., from Pedro Siado, who was traveling east on Texas Highway No. 116, and was about four miles west of Levelland. Siado said he saw bright colored lights a short distance ahead of him on the highway and heard a roar like a clap of thunder. Then his car lights went out and his motor stopped. He said the lights on the object were blinking on and off every three seconds. Then the object went into the air and he was able to start his car. He was very excited when he arrived in Levelland.

The next report came from Frank B. Williams of Kermit, Texas, who was eight miles north of Levelland on Texas Highway No. 51 when at 12:05 a.m. he reported he saw a huge egg-shaped object squatting on the highway ahead of him. He reported that the lights and motor of his car immediately ceased working and that after about one minute the object, brilliantly illuminated, took to the air.

The third report came from James D. Long, a truck driver, of Waco,

TRAVELING THE PATH BACK TO THE ROAD IN THE SKY

Texas, whose experience with the object took place at 1:15 a.m. on a county highway known as the Oklahoma Flat road three miles north of Levelland. Long said he brought his car to a stop when he saw the object ahead of him in the road and that he was climbing out to investigate when his motor died and his car lights went out. Then the big egg-shaped object shot 200 feet into the air, where its lights vanished.

The sheriff and his deputy decided they had better investigate, and started to drive along the Oklahoma Flat road. When they were five or six miles north-west of Levelland they saw a strip of bright light go across the road from east to west about 200 feet ahead of them. The sheriff said: 'I don't know what it was, but it wasn't a truck or a flash of lightning. I think we saw the same thing the motorists saw.' Two Texas State Highway Patrolmen, following the sheriff in another car, also saw the lights and were mystified.

A. J. Fowler, in charge of the Levelland Police Station during the night of the sightings, said he received at least fifteen telephone calls from local residents and other motorists in the area who also reported they had seen a strange lighted object. Many other residents reported they saw 'flashes of light'.

Representative J. T. Rutherford of Texas, at his Odessa home, called for a statement from the Pentagon on this and other UFO sightings. He said he was dispatching a telegram asking an explanation from Air Force officials in Washington, D.C. Later it was learned that another motorist, Nowell E. Wright, saw an object pass over his car with a 'roar like thunder'. His motor died and his headlights went out, also.

The Ground Observer Corps at Midland, Texas, reported that a woman and her two children saw 'a large object of bluish color flying west and very low' early the night of November 2nd.

Odis Echols, owner of Radio Station KCLV in Clovis, New Mexico, reported he 'saw a streak of light like a great fire ball' moving in a south-easterly direction about 8:00 p.m. on November 2nd. That means it was seen in the neighboring state of New Mexico a few hours before its first appearance to the south-east near Levelland, Texas. Here is confirmation that can't be ignored, and yet it was ignored by official sources. I wonder what Rep. J. T. Rutherford learned-if anything?

Perhaps same of you are a bit tired of hearing about fault lines, but-that's right, you've guessed it! A major fault *line* goes directly through the

TRAVELING THE PATH BACK TO THE ROAD IN THE SKY

Levelland, Texas, area. It may be possible that the UFOs draw energy from such locations. At any rate, a study of UFO sightings will reveal that a great percentage of them take place in the vicinity of, or directly over, major world fault lines.

Texas wasn't the only place where UFOs were being seen during the last part of 1957. Michigan and Ohio reported strange 'red clouds' low over cities and 'glowing lights' and 'disc-shaped objects' were having a heyday.

On November is, 1957, I was lecturing in Cleveland, Ohio, when a report reached me that a UFO had landed on November 6th a few miles northeast of Cleveland. On that date, Olden Moore was driving home from Painesville, Ohio, to Montville, when he saw a blue-green flaming object fly over the highway at midnight. In describing the experience, Mr. Moore said:

In seconds the object loomed up in front of me. It was as large as a house. Then it seemed to split apart. One section disappeared into the sky and the other section settled down in a field near the road. When I first observed the object approaching me, I pulled off the road and turned off the ignition. I watched the craft in the field for about fifteen minutes, then I got out of my car and walked towards it. I heard a ticking sound like that of an electric meter. I stopped before I reached the object and returned to my car and drove home to get my wife so she might be a witness to the landing. When we returned together the object was gone. It was about fifty feet in diameter and shaped like a 'saucer' with an inverted 'saucer' on top of it, There was a cone-shaped dome that came to a point on top. The dome glowed brilliantly.

In the same area on the same day that Olden Moore was having his encounter with the strange craft, a great cigar-shaped object was sighted by many people and also a car windshield was covered with pock marks and found to be radio-active.

On November 8th Olden Moore was interrogated by Lake County Civil Defense Director Kenneth Locke, Geauga County Sheriff Louis A. Robusky, United States Army officials and many newsmen.

However, on November 7th, Mr. Locke covered the field (where Moore had seen the UFO land) with a Geiger counter and discovered that 'the counter registered 150 milliroentgens in the centre of an area So feet in diameter in the field. The reading dropped to 20-30 milliroentgens near the perimeter of that area'.

TRAVELING THE PATH BACK TO THE ROAD IN THE SKY

Robert Seitz, a graduate student at the Case Institute of Technology in Cleveland, said that the normal background count was about 20 milliroentgens. Does this mean that the UFO was radioactive?

Several small, but very deep, round holes were found in the field where the craft had landed. These were arranged in a strange circular pattern. The prints looked as though they had been made by something with 'spikes' on it. The first report said that these were 'footprints'; however, they were actually holes made by a protruding pole or something similar. The holes were very deep, and much force had been used to reach such a depth in the ground. Scientists from the Case Institute took soil samples a few days later but the counter registered a normal count and the ground apparently didn't suffer from the effects of the radiation.

The Geiger counter reading in this case is important, but not because it measured radioactivity. If the element causing the counter to react as it did was radio-active, then its half-life was shorter than that of elements made artificially in atomic accelerators. In other words, we can assume that the reading was due to some other stimulus than radio-activity. Free electrons will actuate a Geiger counter and it is quite possible that the object observed by Olden Moore possessed such a strong magnetic field that it ionized the air and the Geiger count was due to the free electrons.

During my stay in Grand Rapids, Michigan, during the last few weeks of 1957, a 'red cloud' appeared over the city during one of my lectures, and when we went to Radio Station WOOD after the talk for an interview, we discovered the TV and radio newscasts were full of 'Saucer' reports. Sightings were pouring in from all over the state.

'Flying Saucer' reports increased during the end of 1957 in Australia also. On November 8, 1957, a 'mystery object' was sighted from Mount Stromlo Astronomical Observatory and a report was sent to Canberra, New South Wales, Australia. Dr. A. Przybylski and two of his colleagues observed the object at 3:02 a.m. after they had watched the passage of Sputnik II. The scientists described the UFO as a 'pinkish object, brighter than Venus, moving westward on the southern horizon'. It was visible to the naked eye, and was watched for eight minutes.

Dr. Przybylski said the object was completely unlike anything he had ever seen before. It moved far too slowly to be a meteor, and it was not Sputnik I nor Sputnik II, both of which had already passed. The astronomer

TRAVELING THE PATH BACK TO THE ROAD IN THE SKY

had unconfirmed reports that the object had been sighted elsewhere in Australia. He said Dr. H. Gollnow, another astronomer, and an assistant, Mr. G. Oom, had watched the course of the object with him. Mr. Westerlund, a scientist from Sweden's Uppsala University, had seen the mystery object in its last moments and thought it might be an aircraft. A check was made with aviation authorities and this showed there were no aircraft in the sky after 2:00 a.m.

The assistant director of the observatory, Dr. A. S. Hogg, said that it was the first time the observatory had sighted what might be called an unidentified flying object. He said: 'What the object was remains an open question. It is impossible to speculate on the nature of the object on the basis of one sighting. However, rough computations placed the object at not more than 1,600 miles above the Earth.'

If Dr. Przybylski, and Dr. Hogg, and their colleagues really get to work now on some serious UFO investigation they will qualify themselves to be called 'long-haired scientists', or those researchers on the frontiers of new investigation. If they forget the sighting as though they never saw it, then we shall be forced to call them ,short-haired scientists', or those who never reach the new frontiers, but conduct research on everyone else's discoveries. At any rate, a letter I received recently from Australia, tells me that 'an eminent Australian professor of physics who had been lecturing to the effect that "Flying Saucers" were figments of the imagination, has completely changed his opinion since the sighting at Mount Stromlo.'

On February 2, 1958, Senor Jose Valencia D. was driving on the Pan-American Highway from Arequipa to Lima, Peru. In the car with him was his wife, Sra. Maria Teresa Cardenas de Valencia, and his nephew, Manuel Porto Navarro. It was a very dark night, and when a strange 'mushroom-shaped' object appeared in the sky overhead, all of the car lights started to go on and off. Senor Valencia thought he was having difficulty with his car motor, so he stopped the car to make a check. All three witnesses said that the UFO was about fifteen feet in diameter. A luminous red glow surrounded the bottom of the craft and the top contained another red light of a darker shade.

Later in February, 1958, on the same Pan-American Highway, south of Ica, Peru, a man sighted a strange 'glowing globe' in the sky while he was driving. Suddenly, the car radio refused to operate and the motor stopped and the lights went out. The driver described the object as 'bluish-green in color and very large'. This report was given to me by a very prominent Lima physician.

The important point for us to remember here is that Ica is only a few kilometers from the Nazca-Palpa area where we find the *beacons for the gods.* Since the driver was *south of Ica,* he must have been very close to the 'Lines of Nazca'. On February 2nd, Senor Valencia was very near the same area while driving from Arequipa to Lima. Therefore, during the same month, in the same section of the Pan-American Highway, two motorists had similar experiences. One witnessed a 'red mushroom' and the other one saw a 'bluish-green globe'. In the area of the above sightings the Pan-American Highway cuts directly through the immense patterns and delineated lines as we have already seen in Fig. No. 29.

On February 24, 1958, Dr. Carlos Jose da Costa Pereira, prominent lawyer and writer of Brazil, was resting beside the road between the villages of Santo Antonio de Jesus and Coracao de Maria, Brazil. He and two friends had been riding in a jeep that suddenly failed to function. While a check was made of the jeep, and the men were on the side of the road, they saw an object about 9o feet in diameter on the road ahead. The men walked to within 32 yards of it and watched it perform several maneuvers for over half an hour. Before it disappeared into the sky, the witnesses could see the rotating disc-shape.

On April 10, 1958, Millen Cooke Belknap took an unusual photograph of a UFO a little after 12:40 a.m. at Vista, California. (See Fig. No. 40). She took the photograph with her Polaroid Highlander camera and used the new fast film. Dim lights can be seen in the middle of the picture which were from a market about a mile away and below the Belknap house. The two white 'polar' areas on the object were not visible to the naked eye but appeared on the developed film. The larger sphere ejected a single, blinking disc, which appears on the photograph as four separate images due to the speed of the fast film used.

A few hours later, during the morning of April 10th, an Air Force plane appeared over the area where Millen Belknap had observed and photographed the UFO a little after midnight the night before. She observed with her binoculars that the plane was carrying cameras. The next day, helicopters patrolled the same area. Nothing appeared in the newspapers, although the Air Force had reconnoitered the entire location.

TRAVELING THE PATH BACK TO THE ROAD IN THE SKY

On May 4, 1958, radio newscasts carried a startling story that described how a UFO had caused a power failure at an Electric Illuminating Company plant near Cleveland, Ohio. Some investigators thought that a bullet fired from some gun caused the failure, but there were many witnesses to the fact that strange objects were in the sky over the area and that the power failure came about immediately after a blinding flash of light.

As a final gesture in our discussion here of the visitants, I want to mention an intriguing enigma that showed up recently in an exhibition hall in London, England. A magnificent Fourteenth-Century tapestry from Yugoslavia was being admired by exhibition-goers, when suddenly someone noticed one of the ancient designs clearly portrayed a gigantic space ship that contained a man! On the side of the ship there was a curious symbol that exactly duplicates the eight-pointed star with the dot in the centre on the Pre-Inca representation of the *road in the sky* shown in the Frontispiece of this book. What is the connection between a Fourteenth-Century Yugoslavian tapestry and an ancient drawing from Peru, South America?

What we have given here is by no means a complete record of UFO sightings for the last few years. Only some of the sightings are given in order to present some of the varied activities of the visitants-those things that 'appear at intervals for a limited period' and are 'from without our sphere'. These friendly visitors to our world are traveling the *road in the sky* once again; they are here *today!*

Let us all hope that we may be counted among *the blessed meek* so some day we can travel that highway to the stars when

'We upon our globe's last voyage shall go,

And view the ocean leaning on the sky

From thence our rolling neighbours we shall know,

And on the lunar world securely pry.'

PART THREE
Tomorrow.
- **The Peaceful Ones**
- **The Other Side of the Sky**
- **The Unholy Six**
- **Counted, Weighed, and Divided**

TRAVELING THE PATH BACK TO THE ROAD IN THE SKY

THE PEACEFUL ONES

'Some day there will be a road in the sky and a machine will ride this road and drop a gourd of ashes and destroy the people and boil the land.' (Ancient Hopi Indian prophecy, Arizona, U.S.A.)

THE above prophecy comes from a people whose ancestors spoke about the destructive 'ashes from the sky' or the terrible effects of the Atomic Bomb long before the coming of the first white man to America. These people and their civilization are as virile today as they were centuries ago. Why?

These inhabitants of the American Southwest are known as the 'Hopis'—their name literally means 'the peaceful ones'. Many years ago other Indian tribes called them the 'Moquis' which means 'the dead ones'. This name was given to them by the aggressive Indian warriors who thought the Hopis were 'dead ones' because they refused to kill their fellow men in battle. However, the war-like Indian people are now the 'dead ones' and we find that the Hopis have survived all the other North American Indian tribes in the sense that they retain more traditions and old ways of their ancestors.

I like to think of the Hopi Tribe as representing the last great 'camp-fire' of Indian North America. They have survived all the others because their way of life parallels that of *the blessed* meek we discussed before. They believe that '... he that killeth with the sword must be killed with the sword...' While other Indian tribes sought revenge for the acts of the white man when he stole their land, the Hopis continued to follow the Words which had been given to them by the Great Spirit.

John A. Hostetler said of the Amish/Mennonites: 'There exists in Amish communities a generous warmth of brotherhood, mutual respect, and trust. Their religion forbids participation in warfare. They literally believe: "Thou shalt not kill"; "Blessed are the peacemakers"; "If thine enemy hunger, feed

TRAVELING THE PATH BACK TO THE ROAD IN THE SKY

him"; "Overcome evil with good" ...' These identical words fit the Hopi people and their way of life exactly.

The Hopis are not considered Christians although their actions in both word and deed follow the way of Jesus, the Christ, in a much greater way than the actions of many so-called 'Christians' today.

The Amish/Mennonites belong to the White Race and the Hopis belong to the Red or Indian Race. The former are Christians attempting to live the Ten Commandments and to follow the words of the Sermon on the Mount. The latter are called 'pagans' because they are not Christian, Jewish or Mohammedan, yet they put to practice in their daily lives the very Words of one majestic person who was known as the *Messiah* to the Hebrews long before he actually arrived in the world to be named Jesus.

Great doubt is cast on whether the present followers of Jesus, the Christ, are truly 'Christian'. On one hand we find so-called 'pagans' or 'savages' who refuse to kill and who live the Divine Laws set down by the Christian Messiah. They live His Laws, and they have been doing it daily for countless centuries although they never heard of Jesus until missionaries entered their land in recent years. On the other hand we find modern 'Christians' killing each other and advocating 'peace is for the strong' and turning their backs on the very beliefs they profess to be following. One begins to wonder who is 'pagan' and who is 'Christian'?

The great master-teacher of the Hopi people is *Massau*. Notice the astonishing similarity between this word and the Aramic *meshiha,* the Hebrew *mahsiah,* and the Greek *messias*. These words mean : *anointed.* To the Hebrews, the *Messiah* is the expected king and deliverer. To the Christians, the *Messiah is* Jesus, the Christ, son of Mary. And to the Hopis, *Massau* (Massua, Masao) is the deliverer who came before and who will return from the *east* as the 'true white brother'.

In Hebrew, Jesus is: *Yeshua.* Notice the similarity in pronunciation between *Yeshua* and *Massua.*

The Hopis live in villages in the high plateau country of northern Arizona. This area is only a few miles north of the archaeological sites where the 'ceramic charts' we called the *Martian Miniatures* were discovered some years ago. In fact, the Pueblo Indians who made their pottery designs identical in form to the outstanding surface features of the Planet Mars were the ancestors of the present day Hopi Indians!

TRAVELING THE PATH BACK TO THE ROAD IN THE SKY

East of the Grand Canyon of the Colorado River are the villages of the Hopis where they have lived for centuries. They are an extraordinary people and investigators have called them 'amazing men and women whose attainments and manner of life are both absorbingly interesting and significant'. Their way of life is 'significant' indeed, as we shall see presently.

Their land is surrounded by the Navajo Indian reservation, they are like a tiny postage stamp situated in the centre of an enormous envelope. They have felt increasing pressure from the customs and authority of the White Race. Yet, they have maintained their own way of life as directed by Massau. They excel in arts and crafts and are far advanced. They are skilful farmers like their Christian counterparts the Amish/ Mennonites. The Hopi children rank higher in intelligence tests than American white children. As one scientist said:

'Their principles of conduct are soundly conceived and are enforced by traditions which are widely recognized and respected.' Yes, 'recognized and respected' but certainly not *accepted by* the modern world. To the 'Christians' of today, Jesus, the Christ, is also 'recognized and respected' but His Words are hardly *accepted.*

The village of Walpi, high on the summit of First Mesa, is a typical Hopi community. It has occupied its present location for over two hundred and fifty years. The photograph in Fig. No. 41 is from my collection of old and rare pictures of the American Southwest. This photograph was taken in the late 1800's when Walpi was spelled 'Wolpi'. Many stone houses are crowded together on the wind-swept rock where the village is located. Notice the magnificent view below the mesa. The Hopis at Walpi can see for vast distances over the desert of rabbit and sage brush. The view is towards the south and the area of the *Martian Miniatures.*

Remember, we mentioned before that there is a definite pattern in regard to the interest shown by the UFO intelligences in certain groups and people. The Hopi Indians of Arizona are well qualified to be called *the blessed meek.* I have known the Hopi people for many years as my neighbors in my home in Arizona. I have gone to school with them and I have worked with them; I have even danced with them and I have known their joy and sorrow, and I have come to love them and to respect them. I have been a guest in their humble homes on the mesa tops and I have attended their ancient ceremonials. I have been privileged to sit in their sacred meeting chambers, the underground kivas, and to speak with their wise leaders in council. I have sat on the floor and supped with them from a common bowl; my heart has found their heart, and it is a 'good heart'.

I do not intend to present an ethnological report on the Hopi people and their customs, but I do want to introduce you to a remarkable group of fellow beings who are living that which the Creator gave to them, and, after all, there is only one Creator!

There is an ancient Hopi prophecy which says: 'When the people forget to be humble they shall quarrel... then all the world will start to fight. Whoever you are and whatever you do, you must be humble... only then will you be happy.' This prophecy has come true, for we know the condition our world is in today. How similar is the admonition in this Indian prophecy to another warning:

'But he that is greatest among you shall be your servant. And whosoever shall exalt himself shall be abased; and he that shall *humble* himself shall be exalted.' (St. Matthew xxiii:11,12).

The soft-voiced Hopis maintain a society in which the individual has absolute independence and freedom, but is still part of a very closely knit community, and this society is the oldest in North America. The Hopis follow a 'Life Plan' that was given to their ancestors in the dim past by Massau. Each man, woman and child is an independent human being. They choose their own path in life, make their own decisions, and are subject to no orders by any group or person, *yet* every Hopi is also part of a compact community.

The Hopis have retained a legend handed down from father to son for generations about their origin. Briefly, the story says that a long time ago the Hopis lived in the underworld or in a land beneath the surface of our planet. Life in that region was like life on the surface of the earth and the Hopi people were very happy there. But a time came when the crops failed due to a lack of rain and the people became unhappy. When they looked up to the sky they could see a great 'hole' there and this was an indication to them that there may be another land on 'the other side of the sky'. The story goes into detail on how the chief and other Hopi leaders summoned various birds and asked them to fly up towards the sky and go through the 'hole' to see if there was a new land on the other side. Most of the bird messengers failed, but finally a bluebird was successful and he returned to tell the Hopi

TRAVELING THE PATH BACK TO THE ROAD IN THE SKY

people that there was a beautiful country beyond the sky. A medicine man planted a reed, and called on the old men to sing a sacred song with him. The reed started to grow fast and it became very strong quickly. Soon it reached the sky and became a great 'ladder' on which the Hopis could climb to the country on 'the other side of the sky'. The Hopis still believe that they came to the surface of the world by way of the 'ladder'. Almost all of the American Indian tribes have a similar legend of their emergence into the upper world.

We have already mentioned that the Hopi Indians need great amounts of rain every year for their crops for they live in an arid region as did the Nazca of South America. The crude, gigantic figures of the Peruvian southern desert were designed and constructed by a later people who inhabited the area of the more ancient lines and delineated surfaces. And these figures were a reminder to the 'sky gods' who had become 'rain gods' so that they would send rain to the dry fields of the Nazca.

As stated before, the Hopis have a totally different concept of 'rain gods' for their elaborate rituals and ceremonials which constitute prayers for rain take place in the *underground* kivas. The kiva is the ancient and sacred temple or church of the Hopi people. Its location under the surface of the earth symbolizes the underworld which was the original land of the Hopis before they came to their present home on the surface. The tall ladder poles which can be seen standing out against the blue sky in every Hopi village, are used to enter the sub-surface kiva chambers, and *they* represent the 'reed ladder' that was made by the medicine man so their ancestors could reach the land on 'the other side of the sky'. The important point to remember here is that the Nazca people placed their symbols on the *surface of the ground* for 'rain gods' who dwelt in the sky. The Hopi people, on the other hand, conduct their ceremonials and place their symbols in the kivas *under the ground* for 'rain gods' who dwell in the *underworld,* not in the sky. Obviously, the Hopis would not need to attract the attention of such gods by placing elaborate figures on the surface of the immense desert that surrounds them.

However, there is a strange connection between the *underworld* and the sky in Hopi mythology and beliefs which is not always quite clear. For instance, the Hopis say that the Kachinas are happy spirits from the beneficent underworld. These kindly beings are always represented in ceremonies by masked human figures. But as spirits they play an important unseen

TRAVELING THE PATH BACK TO THE ROAD IN THE SKY

role in the life of every Hopi. The Kachinas guard the people and keep them happy, they tell them the ancient traditions and help them train their children. The Kachinas also make supplications to the gods so that the Hopi people may be healthy and have good fortune and have abundant rain for their crops. In this regard, the Kachinas are spiritual intermediaries between the Hopis and the higher gods.

There are also Kachina *giants* who take part in the ceremonies. The *Niman is* a major Hopi ceremony which takes place every year in July. In this ritualistic dance, the Kachinas make their final appearance of the year and then return to their *home in the mountains.* They are supposed to live in the 'high places' of the San Francisco Mountain which rises 12,655 feet high to the southwest of the Hopi villages. The peaks of this mountain (an extinct volcanic cone) are sacred to the Hopi people and many legends and stories from the dim past are woven around them.

If the Kachinas really live in the San Francisco Peaks as the *Niman* ceremony indicates, then why do the Hopi legends also state that they are kindly beings from the *underworld?* How can they live beneath the surface of the earth and in the 'high places' at the same time? Here is part of the strange connection between the *underworld* and the sky in Hopi mythology. We also find that while the Hopi 'rain gods' dwell in the underworld there has to be an intimate connection with the sky, because, after all, the rain for the dry crops eventually comes from that sky!

The Kachinas also appear in ceremonies of other Southwest Indian tribes, and *giant beings* figure prominently in such rituals.

Many legends throughout the world speak of giants coming from great mountains and also dwelling on top of such high places. Remember the legends from Africa that speak of tall people walking on the top of Mount Kilimanjaro in Tanganyika and living in the mountain itself? The Kachinas also are supposed to live *in* the San Francisco Mountain of Arizona. This might partially explain how the Kachinas can live beneath the surface of the earth and in the 'high places' at the same time!

We get a clue as to the possible meaning behind the strange Kachina figures when we study the *Niman* ceremony. Remember, this ritual marks the final appearance of the Kachinas for the year, and their return to their home in the mountains. Like other important ceremonies, the *Niman* begins with very secret rites held in the kiva and these continue for *eight* days fol-

TRAVELING THE PATH BACK TO THE ROAD IN THE SKY

lowed by a ritual lasting one day and held above ground in the village plaza.

The underground kiva can easily be symbolic of the underground home of the Cyclopean Elder Race, and the eight day period for the secret rites can represent the *eighth level* of Thought beyond physical existence-the conquest of Mest. Therefore, the Hopis may be re-enacting in a symbolic way the entry of the Elder Race into the Theta or Thought Universe. On the ninth day the Hopis emerge from the underground kiva into the light of day to perform the final ceremonies on the surface in the plaza. The ladder they use to climb up out of the kiva can be symbolic of the ELevation of the Cyclopeans, and the word *ladder* begins with an 'L'. Our word ladder comes from the Anglo-Saxon *hlaeder*. We have already mentioned that H is the *eighth* letter of the alphabet and its connection with the letter L at the beginning of the old word *hlaeder is* most interesting. The *ninth* day ritual held above ground can signify the fact that after the Elder Race achieved the eighth level of progression and became 'El's' they were free to move into the ninth *level* of the Energy Universe.

Also in the *Niman* ceremony, the final appearance of the Kachinas for the year can be symbolic of the *final appearance* of the 'El's' upon Earth. The return of the Kachinas to their home in the mountains can easily signify the 'El's' reaching their ELevated state. The entire journey of the Kachinas from the underworld to the home in the 'high places' can refer to the Elder Race and the conquest of MEST.

To the Nazca people the ancient 'sky gods' or space visitors became 'rain gods' and the true meaning was lost. This didn't happen with the Hopis as we have already shown. However, there is some evidence that the *visitants* made themselves known to the ancestors of the Hopi people. There is a legend that may allude to such visitations.

A Hopi chief long ago sent his messenger to the home of the People Who Have the Secret of Fire. These 'Fire People' were invited to come and dance at the Hopi villages. The legend tells how these people had miraculous ways of starting fires and how they disappeared in the direction of the San Francisco Peaks. The story says: '... the Fire People disappeared... they were gone so quickly that no one in the village could tell which way they went.' Later in the evening, a glow was noticed in the south-west as though a great 'light' were on top of the San Francisco Peaks. This glow was also noticed the next night and appeared to be much larger. The legend contains

TRAVELING THE PATH BACK TO THE ROAD IN THE SKY

many other elements that are not necessary to speak of here. Something strange happened in the past, but the real meaning is now hidden in the details of the legendary account.

The 'People Who Have the Secret of Fire' could easily have been the *visitants.* This is indicated by the fact that they were able to control fire in a magical way and 'disappeared so quickly that no one could tell which way they went'. After the performance of the vanishing miracle by the 'Fire People' in the direction of the San Francisco Mountain a 'glowing light' was seen by the Hopi people on 'top of the peaks'.

When the Hopis speak of the *underworld,* just what is meant? It is difficult to really know, for the present Indian concept has developed out of a happening or happenings that took place a very long time ago. However, certain questions come to mind as we study the problem.

The Hopi *underworld* has a 'sky' with a 'hole' in it, therefore, the sky of our world (upper world to the Hopis) must also have a 'hole' in it! If the Hopi underworld is beneath the surface of this planet, that is one thing, but if it represents another world or planet altogether, that is something else. It doesn't seem likely that a subterranean world has a sky' in it. We may have evidence in the Hopi origin legend that their ancestors migrated to the Earth from another planet. Remember, it was ancestors of the Hopis who made the Martian Miniatures. Would this explain why prehistoric Indian people were very familiar with the surface features of the planet Mars? Did the forefathers of the Hopis come from Mars in the ancient past?

If we accept the Hopi underworld as being *underground,* we find that the concept is contrary to those of other world cultural groups. Nearly everyone on Earth believes that the heavenly abode of bliss is up in the sky or 'heavens', but the Hopi believe this place of the dead is in the underworld. Other groups believe that 'rain gods' live in the sky, but the Hopis believe such 'gods' live in the underworld.

If we accept the Hopi underworld in a figurative sense instead of a literal one, it could refer to another planetary existence. Then the strange connection between that *underworld* and the sky in Hopi mythology begins to take on exciting new meaning. When the Hopis speak of an 'underworld', are they really speaking of some other happy land in the sky? If they are, then their concepts are not the opposite of those of other cultural groups, but are identical.

TRAVELING THE PATH BACK TO THE ROAD IN THE SKY

Who are the 'gods' that the Kachinas act as intermediaries for? Did the Kachinas originally come from a literal underworld or did they come from the sky? Many interesting questions are brought to mind here and much more study will have to be conducted before even part of the answers are obtained. We must keep in mind that the important point is: What do the Hopis mean by the use of the word 'underworld'? Discover the answer to that one question and you have the key to all the apparent contradictions.

Evidently, the present religious beliefs of the Hopis have been derived from very ancient traditions and these beliefs have taken on new meaning to the Indians themselves who do not know what the original causes were that brought about their present theology. Remember, the Nazca people didn't know the true meaning of the 'sky god' legend and interpreted it to mean 'rain gods' when actually their ancestors were referring to space visitors. In the same fashion, the descendants of the most ancient Hopi people have interpreted the legends and traditional accounts in a way they can understand them. Knowledge of the Elder Race becoming 'El's' and the possible migration of Hopi ancestors to Earth from another planet, and actual space visitors coming to their new home 'beyond the sky' has all been mixed up in the passing of many centuries with 'rain gods' and the great need for water for their crops.

If the ancestors of the Hopis originally came from Mars (how and why we do not know) and communication was somehow later cut off with the home planet, the descendants would forget what really happened as they concerned themselves with growing crops in an arid country. The true past would be lost because the people would be required to place every effort in just keeping alive in a new and strange world. Enough of the true happening would be retained as a racial memory, however, and this knowledge would be incorporated into the religious beliefs, ceremonials and rituals of the descendants.

In the study of the complicated Hopi legends we have that same pattern that is found throughout the world: 'Strange beings', 'high places', fault lines and space ships.

The Kachinas and giants are the 'strange beings', the San Francisco Peaks are the 'high places', the 'Fire People' and the 'glowing light' are related to the space ships, and there is a great *fault line.*

The same fault line that goes through the Levelland, Texas, area pro-

TRAVELING THE PATH BACK TO THE ROAD IN THE SKY

ceeds north-west towards the Grand Canyon of Arizona and goes directly through the centre of an area containing the Hopi villages, the San Francisco Peaks and the Martian Miniatures.

Remember, we said that the Hopis never turn the surface of the surrounding desert into an immense drawing-board? This is because the present Hopis have a totally different concept of 'rain gods' as compared to the Nazca people. The penetration of the 'hole in the sky' by the Hopi ancestors during space flight could not be understood by later generations stranded on a new world. They could only interpret the tradition in terms of the surface of the land they were on. Therefore, the 'hole in the sky' and their former home had to be underground, there was no other place for it to be. The descendants of the original migrating colony knew nothing of other inhabited worlds in space.

The Hopis do not place their symbols on the surface of the desert because they believe the 'rain gods' are in the *underworld.* But I believe they are mistaken in their interpretation of what 'underworld' really means. They are ignorant of their true ancestry. Present Hopis have a totally different concept of 'rain gods', but what about the more ancient Hopis?

We mentioned that recently in the American Southwest designs have been found that are more like the Nazca animal forms than the delineated surfaces and lines. The ancestors of the Hopi people could have easily constructed these figures. Proof of the present misconception concerning the *underworld* is found in the three stages of the degeneration of the original truth. First of all, the first Hopis to arrive on Earth were aware of their Martian origin and background. Second, as time passed, their descendants were unaware of their extra-terrestrial origin, but remembered enough of the truth to feel impelled to construct gigantic figures on the ground to attract the 'sky gods'. They realized they had to attempt communication with something in the heavens. They had to re-establish a communication that had been cut off. They were like a lonely man on a desert island who hopefully puts out a signal so that a passing ship may find him and rescue him. Third, eventually as generations passed, the 'sky gods' that had to be attracted became simply 'rain gods' and the Hopis constructed more immense figures on the American desert exactly in the same way and for the same purpose that the Nazca people made theirs. Their entire past history was lost in their constant fear of not having enough water. The Hopis forgot who the 'sky gods' really were exactly in the same way that the Nazca did. Later,

TRAVELING THE PATH BACK TO THE ROAD IN THE SKY

there must have been some kind of a religious revival where some enlightened priest studied the ancient legends and in order to make the tradition of going to a land on 'the other side of the sky' through a 'hole in the sky' fit present knowledge and beliefs, it was declared that the Hopis had come from the *underworld* and the 'rain gods' dwelt in that location. After this idea was included in and made an integral part of accepted beliefs, the need for constructing the large figures on the surface of the desert was no longer necessary. And, therefore, the Hopis of today do, indeed, have a totally different concept of 'rain gods'. These are the progressive stages in the degeneration of an original truth.

When we discussed the Martian Miniatures we asked the questions:

'Why is it that in three great desert areas (American, Peruvian and Martian) we find the people of two of those areas (American and Peruvian) have constructed immense patterns on the ground after transferring such patterns from pottery motifs? Who were supposed to view those patterns from the air? Were they built for the people of the third desert area (Mars) who had irrigation systems like the people of the first two areas (America and Peru)?'

Let us remember that the desert figures were made by transferring patterns from *pottery* motifs, and the Martian Miniatures were also placed on *pottery* vessels.

For another clue, let us again study the words of the Hopi origin legend:

'A long time ago the Hopis lived in the "underworld"... life in that region was like life on the surface of the earth and the Hopi people were very happy there. But a time came when the crops failed due to a lack of rain and the people became unhappy. When they looked up to the sky they could see a great "hole" there and this was an indication to them that there may be another land on "the other side of the sky".'

This could mean that a long time ago the Hopis lived on another planet ('underworld') and life there was very much like life on the surface of the Earth and the Hopis were very happy there. But something happened. A time came when the *crops failed due to a lack of rain* and the people became unhappy. They studied the heavens and space flight was developed which permitted them to eventually penetrate the 'hole in the sky' and land on a new world (the Earth) on 'the other side of the sky'.

TRAVELING THE PATH BACK TO THE ROAD IN THE SKY

The key in the legend is the fact that the happy life in the former world of the Hopis ended when the crops failed due to a lack of rain. Remember, the planet Mars is known to be covered with desert areas, and Dr. Percival Lowell believed that Mars was a dying planet. He theorized that the Martians were forced to construct their great canal system in order to retard the process of water evaporation and save their civilization. Did the dwindling water supply on Mars force some of her people to migrate in space ships to another world? Did the colonists on their arrival upon Earth pick the deserts of the American Southwest because they only understood the economy of an irrigated area and a desert environment? When the descendants of the original colony later constructed the great figures on the desert to attract the 'rain gods' they must have been impelled by a racial memory that stemmed back to the fear of an insufficient water supply-a fear that constantly overshadowed the lives of their ancestors on 'dying' Mars.

And is it not a strange coincidence that the foremost observer and authority on the planet Mars, Dr. Lowell, built his astronomical observatory in 1894 on a hill appropriately named 'Mars Hill' overlooking Flagstaff, Arizona, which lies at the base of the San Francisco Peaks, the sacred mountain of the Hopis.

In every Hopi kiva and by every Hopi fireside the origin legend is related over and over again. The story also tells how the people thought there might be a land where it *rains* 'beyond the sky' and the crops would grow and everybody would be happy again. This indicates the dwindling water supply on Mars and the need for some of the people to migrate elsewhere since the small supply wouldn't take care of a large population. The legend speaks of the Hopi chief and leaders talking over the situation and deciding to try to find out what 'the other side of the sky' was like. The chief summoned different birds and asked them to fly up towards the sky and attempt to go through the 'hole'. The birds were unable to penetrate this 'hole' and every time a bird was sent it failed in its mission. Every new bird sent was able to go a little further, but the 'hole' was not penetrated.

After each bird would return unsuccessful, the chief and the leaders talked over the situation and always decided to make another attempt. Finally the 'bluebird' was chosen to make the journey. Everyone waited for a long time, and they began to think that the 'bluebird' had been lost and they would never see it again. A long time passed, and at last the people could see a little speck far up in the sky. This speck grew larger and larger and

TRAVELING THE PATH BACK TO THE ROAD IN THE SKY

came nearer and nearer to them. Soon they could hear the 'bluebird' singing, and in a little while it reached the surface of their dry world. All the people crowded around and the 'bluebird' told them: 'Yes, there is a country up there beyond the sky. There is much land that would make good fields, there is much water from flowing springs, and there are many rain clouds.'

The 'chief and the leaders talking over the situation' sounds very much like the scientists of Mars deciding to send out a space expedition to 'find out what "the other side of the sky" was like'. The summoning of the different 'birds' obviously represents the various ships utilizing different propulsion methods that attempted to penetrate the 'hole in the sky'. All the ships failed until the 'bluebird' made a successful expedition. Finally, a craft ('bluebird') was developed that could make the interplanetary journey and return with news of the land with abundant water. It must have taken a long time for the round-trip to be made for the people 'waited for a long time and thought the "bluebird" was lost'. Finally, the people saw a 'little speck far up in the sky'. We can easily reconstruct the scene on the planet Mars as the experimental expeditionary space craft came into view and became larger as it neared the planet. Finally, the people 'could hear the "bluebird" singing', and then it 'reached the surface of the dry world'. The 'singing' stands for the humming sound of the space craft that was heard by the people just before it landed. The people crowding 'around the "bluebird" ' obviously refers to the joyous welcome given to the returning ship by the happy inhabitants of Mars. Then the 'bluebird's' report of 'much land, much water, and rain clouds' refers to the description given the planet Earth by the returning Martian explorers. After all, our planet contains 'much land, much water' and is blanketed with 'rain clouds'.

The legend then tells how the chief had the people prepare food for the journey that would take them to the land 'beyond the sky'. In this so-called inexplicable legend of an Indian people we have a meaning that is startling in its implications. The Hopis came to the Earth world over a great *road in the sky,* and that is why they still speak of their former happy home where the rains ceased, and that is why, without knowing the reason, they continue to pray for the precious rain that is vital to their life, their life on a planet that was colonized by their explorer ancestors when they successfully landed in the American Southwest.

About four hundred years ago the first contact took place between the White Race and the Hopi Indians. The Spanish explorer Coronado arrived

TRAVELING THE PATH BACK TO THE ROAD IN THE SKY

from Mexico and was visiting neighboring pueblos when he sent a small scouting party into the Hopi country. Some years later, another Spaniard, Espejo, visited the Hopi people. After a few years the Hopi villages became part of Spanish territory and allegiance to the King of Spain and to the Church was demanded. The new authorities of Spain attempted to obliterate every phase of Hopi culture for their way of life was declared to be 'heathen' and 'fantastic'.

The Hopis believe in the existence of a spirit world which is vitally concerned and connected with their daily life. To the Hopis, everything is *alive;* every object in the physical world is part of a kingdom of invisible beings, but these beings are as real as anything the Hopis can see or touch. The Hopis believe that the spirit world is eternal and exists everywhere, but they also believe that much of this unseen world does not make itself known to man except at special times.

When a Hopi dies, there are no elaborate rituals or mourning periods. They believe the 'dead' person has completed an important journey in this world and is therefore ready for a graduation to greater things. They do not believe that a tragedy has overtaken the deceased.

To the Hopis, their daily life and their religious life are identical. They believe the white man has a strange custom in his church attendance of one day a week only. They live for the Great Spirit every day.

The Hopis say: 'If you have bad thoughts, you will bring harm to yourself. If you have bad thoughts towards another person, you can harm that person and yourself too.' They believe that 'thoughts are things' and that the life of man is determined by his actions which develop out of his thinking process.

When a Hopi healer attempts to cure a sick patient, he realizes he is not only dealing with a physical condition but also with something unseen which is, nevertheless, as real as the physical condition. He must cure that which is manifested and also that which keeps it company. To do this the healer uses prayer. Perhaps without realizing it the Hopis know the secret behind disease. For it is not the germs that are the real *cause,* but our thinking enters into the picture and other factors that keep company with the manifested physical condition.

An act of Congress in 1924 gave the Hopis the right to citizenship in the United States. Then the Hopis were subject to federal taxation and their young men were subject to compulsory military service. Many Hopi men have died in the white man's wars although their religion strictly forbids participation in such an activity. Even though the Hopis were granted the right to become citizens in 1924, they had to wait until 1948 before the state in which they lived decided they could vote and have other benefits they had been called on to support. The Hopis found that the White Race believed their customs were 'heathen' and therefore had to be completely changed or eliminated.

To the Hopis, the white man is aggressive and does not follow the Words of his own master-teacher, Jesus, the Christ. While the white man calls the Hopi Indian a savage, the opposite may be true, for the Hopis refuse to kill, saying that the Great Spirit forbids it. The Hopis have great respect for the white man's inventive abilities and his scientific achievements, but they cannot accept the white man's interest in material affairs to the exclusion of a spiritual life for the Creator. The Hopis cannot condone the white man's willingness to subjugate other people and to go to war and kill them in the process.

The Hopis do not believe in monster gods who rule through fear or threats. They cannot accept a Great Spirit who is a god of war at the same time. To them God is love and always has been and always will be. Prayer pervades all Hopi life and ceremonies. They pray for health and strength of the physical, mental and spiritual man; they pray for abundant rain and good crops, and they pray constantly that they may have a 'good heart' which to the Hopis means having the right thoughts always. Hopi prayers include every living creature everywhere in this world and the unseen worlds.

The Hopis believe that praying is not just begging the Creator for gifts, nor is it bowing or kneeling. They believe that to pray for something is to definitely will that it shall come to pass. In fact, the Hopi word for prayer is the same word they use for willing and wishing. Prayer to the Hopis must represent absolute and complete desire, for if one wishes and desires anything strongly enough it can be achieved.

Many Hopi school children were given standard tests for observation and mental correlation. It was discovered that they rank 10 to 15 per cent higher than white children in similar white schools. But Hopi children do not wish to be competitors in the white man's struggle for success. The children just want to grow up to become Hopis with good hearts. They do not want

TRAVELING THE PATH BACK TO THE ROAD IN THE SKY

pride and arrogance to set them apart from other Hopis.

Body, mind and will are united in Hopi thought and a Hopi boy must learn to be equally strong in all three. The boy learns to bathe in cold water outdoors on a freezing winter morning without showing that he is uncomfortable. This trains him to be strong in the Hopi sense of the word.

Many missionaries of various creeds have attempted to civilize and Christianize the Hopi people. This is all very ironic, for the missionaries battle amongst themselves and commit acts which certainly wouldn't be considered Christian by their master-teacher. But the Hopis are a kindly and tolerant people-they just watch and wait. Missionaries attending Hopi sacred ceremonials have attempted to drown out the chanting of the rituals by playing loud phonograph records. Is such conduct in accord with the teachings of the gentle Jesus? Who needs to be civilized and who needs to be Christianized? But the Hopi people say: 'The white man has his path and we have ours. There really isn't any difference, we all want to go to the same place.' In such statements, the Hopis display an intelligence that qualifies them to be considered with the world's greatest religious thinkers and philosophers.

An anthropologist once said: 'The Hopis have received great material benefits from the white race, schools, hospitals, better roads, access to markets. These are specific advances. For these the Hopis have not paid too great a price.'

It is rather questionable whether or not the above benefits from the white race are really benefits or represent a plague. Obviously, from what we have just studied, the Hopis had a better school system, and a better understanding of healing. They didn't need modern roads, and they didn't need the white man's markets filled with his commercially poisoned foodstuffs. I think the Hopis have paid a high price, indeed, for the white man's plague!

The Hopis possess sterling qualities and various authorities have claimed that they have achieved more than other groups of people. They have conquered the harsh realities of a desert existence, the pressure of invaders from Spain and foreign religious authority, and the aggressive Navajo Indians who surround them, and a materialistic white civilization. Today they are even stronger in the midst of such negative influences.

A government official said of the Hopis: 'They achieve democracy without any of the forms and procedures which are supposed to be essential to democracy.'

A Hopi is judged by his neighbors according to the quality of his thoughts and the rightness of his actions. He does not believe in the use of intoxicating beverages, for to become drunk is to forfeit respect and confidence of neighbors.

Thoughts have great power according to the Hopi people, and they must be directed towards the good, the constructive, never towards the evil and destructive. They believe that if you think about sickness and misfortune you give power to negative forces and conditions. Therefore, they turn their thoughts towards a happy life, abundant health, strength of body, mind and spirit, and a loving Creator.

The Hopi people have been endowed with a deep sense of beauty and this is evident in all their homes, kivas, and villages. The world could learn much from these people, whose very name means 'the happy, peaceful ones'.

The Life Plan of the Hopis is almost identical with that of the ancient Essenes who were the writers of the famous Dead Sea Scrolls. The Essenes, who had their community centre at Khirbet Qumran, believed in a symbolic washing away of spiritual uncleanliness through repeated purifications. The Hopis believe in the same purifications and bathe in cold spring water every morning in exactly the same manner as the Essenes did at Qumran.

The Essenes practiced simple farming, and grew their crops in the desert country of the Dead Sea area. The Essenes practiced community life, and they maintained storehouses where everyone placed their products to be used later when they were needed by the entire community. The aged were well taken care of and so were the sick and those unable to work. The Essenes believed that all men were equal in the eyes of the One Creator, and they worshipped Him as the One Great Spirit of all mankind. The Essenes sat together at night in a sacred circle and communed with the 'Sons of Light' who watched over them. The Essenes believed there were good and evil spirits and that a man had a choice as to which he would follow during his lifetime. The Essenes also practiced fasting and self-discipline.

The Hopis practice simple farming and till their desert land in the same way as did the Essenes. The Hopis practice community life and maintain common storehouses for the good of all. The Hopis take care of all their old, sick and disabled people. The Hopis worship only the One Great Spirit of all

TRAVELING THE PATH BACK TO THE ROAD IN THE SKY

mankind, *Massau,* and they believe all men are equal. The Hopi chiefs meet in the sacred kivas and commune with the 'good spirits' in the same way that the Essenes communed with the 'Sons of Light'. The Hopi belief in a spirit world parallels that of the Qumran community also, and fasting is a rigid requirement along with other self-denial.

There are many more similarities between the Essenes and the Hopis, but a very important one is that which exists between the records of the Dead Sea Scrolls or the Qumran Manuscripts and the Sacred Hopi Stone Tablets. We will discuss this later.

The Dead Sea Scrolls are far more important than is yet realized. For instance, the Essene document that deals with 'The War of the Children of Light Against the Children of Darkness' is a key to unlock some of the so-called mysteries of world conditions today and even the coming of the UFOs. Many ancient secrets will be revealed in the near future and it all started in our time in the Spring of 1947, when Muhammad Dib was looking for a lost goat and discovered the first of the Dead Sea Scrolls in a dry cave. Across the world, over Mount Rainier, Kenneth Arnold was observing ships not of our world (June 24, 1947) and a new revelation came to the people of Earth.

Remember, we said that prayer to the Hopis represents absolute and complete desire. This reminds us of some words spoken a long time ago: 'And all things, whatsoever ye shall ask in prayer, believing, ye shall receive.' (St. Matthew xxi:22).

Now that we have explained something of the origin, the legends, the way of life, and the beliefs of the Hopi Indians of Arizona, we are going to present some information that is connected with the ancient Hopi prophecy of *a road in the sky,* but a different kind of 'road' than that which the ancestors of the Hopis traveled over on their journey to Earth countless generations ago. While many of the Hopi legends are concerned with *yesterday,* there are others that dramatically portray conditions and life on the Earth in the prophecies for *tomorrow.*

'I wish to assure the members of both the Hopi and Navajo Tribes that their religion and social customs will be fully respected in accordance with this nation's long established laws and tradition.'

The above words of President Harry S. Truman of the United States of America were answered in 1950 by the following letter:

TRAVELING THE PATH BACK TO THE ROAD IN THE SKY

Hopi Indian Sovereign Nation,

Oraibi, Arizona, October 8, 1950.

Harry S. Truman,

President of the United States,

Washington, D.C.

Mr. President:

Today our ancient Hopi religion, culture and traditional way of life is seriously threatened by your nation's war efforts, the Navajo-Hopi Bill, the Indian Land Claims Commission and by the Wheeler-Howard Bill-the so-called Indian Self-Government Bill. These death-dealing policies have been imposed upon us by trickery, fraud, coercion and bribery on the part of the Indian Bureau under the Government of the United States. During all these years, the Hopi Sovereign Nation has never been consulted. Instead, we have been subjected to countless humiliations and inhuman treatment by the Indian Bureau and the Government of the United States. We have been dipped in sheep-dipping vats like a herd of animals. Our young girls and women were shamefully disrobed before the people, and then were either pushed or thrown into the vats filled with sulphur water. Our religious headmen were beaten, kicked and clubbed with rifle butts. They had their hair cut and after being dragged were left bleeding on the ground in their villages.

These immoral acts were done to us by the Government of the United States because we want to be *peaceful* and to live as we please, to worship and make our own livelihood the way the Great Spirit Massau has taught us.

The Hopi Sovereign Nation has been in existence long before any white men set foot upon our soil, and it is still standing and will continue to hold all land in this Western Hemisphere in accordance with our Sacred Stone Tablets for all His people who are with Him here.

But now you have decided without consulting us, you have turned away from us by leading your people down the new road to war. It is a fearful step that you have taken. Now we must part. We, the Hopi leaders, will not go with you. You must go alone. The Hopi must remain within his own homeland. We have no right to be fighting other people in other lands who have caused us no harm. We will continue to keep peace with all men while patiently waiting for our 'true white brother' whose duty it is to purify this land and to punish all men of evil heart. We have never fought your government and never relinquished our rights and authority to any foreign nation and made no treaty with your government whereby our young Hopi men are subject to the military conscription laws of the United States. Therefore, we demand that you, as President of the United States, now and for all time, stop the drafting of our young Hopi men and women, and release immediately all those who are in the armed forces of the United States. And we also demand that a full and complete investigation of the Navajo-Hopi Bill, the so-called Hopi Tribal Council, and the Indian Bureau be made by the President of the United States, the Congress and the good people of the United States. This is your moral obligation to the Red Man, upon whose land you have been living. Time is short, and it is your sacred duty as leader of our people to bring these truths and facts before them. We must set our house in order before it is too late. If the Government of the United States does not begin now to correct many of these wrongs and injustices done to the Red Man, the Hopi Sovereign Nation shall be forced to go before the United Nations with these truths and with these facts.

Sincerely yours, We are, Dan Katchongva, Advisor (Sun Clan) Hotevilla, Arizona. Andrew Hermequaftewa, Advisor (Bluebird Clan), Shungopovi, Arizona.

The above letter was sent to President Truman following the United States involvement in the Korean War. The Hopi Indians have *never* engaged in warfare, and, since they were never conquered by the United States, they have not signed a treaty or agreement with the government that would limit their original sovereignty. They consider themselves a separate and distinct nation, they have retained their own culture, traditional way of life and the ancient Hopi religion. The Hopi way of life is the way of *peace*.

In June, 1953, the Hopis wrote to President Eisenhower asking that all Hopis in the armed services be released. They said: 'Our whole religious order, our culture, and our Hopi way of life are today seriously threatened by your war efforts, and Hopis have gone to prison for refusing to register under the Selective Service Laws.'

TRAVELING THE PATH BACK TO THE ROAD IN THE SKY

In March, 1950, the following letter was sent to Washington, D.C.:

Hopi Indian Sovereign Nation,

Shungopovi, Arizona,

March 2, 1950.

Hon. John R. Nichols,

Commissioner *of Indian Affairs,*

Washington *25, D.C.*

Dear Sir:

You know as well as we do that the whole of mankind is faced with the possibility of annihilation as it was done in the *lower world* because of greed, selfishness, and godlessness. People went after wealth, power and the pleasures of life more than the moral and religious principles. Now we have floods, strikes, civil wars, earthquakes, fires, and the H-Bomb. To the Hopi people these are but 'smoke signals', telling us to set our house in order before our 'true white brother' comes. Who will he punish, the white man or the Indian?

The traditional law of this land cannot be changed because it was planned by the Great Spirit, *Massau.* He has given us these laws and the Sacred Stone Tablets which are still in the hands of the proper leaders of Oraibi and Hotevilla villages. Shungopovi holds all the major altars, being the mother village representing the true Hopi.

We are not children but men, and are able to choose and decide for ourselves what is good and what is bad. We have been able to survive worse droughts and famine in the past. We do not fight such as this with money, but by our humble prayers for more rain and for forgiveness. Our land will bloom again if our souls are right and clean. No, we are not going to sell our birthright for a few 'pieces of silver' such as the $90,000,000. Our land and our resources and our birthright are worth more than all the money the Government of the United States may have.

The white people seem to be at a loss as to what to do now in the face of the terrible H-Bomb. Why don't you come to the most ancient race who know of these things? You can learn what is to be done. We must meet together so that the common man may have his freedom and security. We want

TRAVELING THE PATH BACK TO THE ROAD IN THE SKY

everlasting life, so do you. We are both aware of the fact that we are coming to the same point. To the white man it is a judgment Day or the 'Last Days' and to the Hopis it is a Purification Day—the cleansing of all the wicked forces of the Earth so that the common man may have his day.

Signed:

Hopi Religious Leaders,

Hopi Indian Sovereign Nation,

Arizona, U.S.A.

Only excerpts of the March 2nd letter have been quoted above. The reference to the *lower world* (underworld) is interesting, for it suggests that the Hopi former home was eventually annihilated due to 'greed, selfishness, and godlessness'. Remember, the *underworld* was the other planetary home of the ancestors of the Hopis, and the place where the 'crops failed due to a lack of rain'. The fact that it was later destroyed due to the wrong thinking and actions of the ancient Hopis may indicate that some of the ancestors of the present Hopis originally came from the destroyed planet Maldek and its moon, Malona. [See *Other Tongues—Other Flesh. —Editor.*] This planet and its single satellite are known as Lucifer and Lilith in the Old Testament. They were destroyed by a thermal catastrophe or hydrogen destruction. Therefore, when the present-day Hopis say 'the whole of mankind is faced with the possibility of annihilation' they may be remembering their legends which tell them that the same thing happened before in their former home (underworld or another planet). They say 'time is short, we must set our house in order before it is too late.' The remains of Maldek-Malona or Lucifer-Lilith are today known as the Asteroid Belt between the planets Mars and Jupiter. Since Lucifer-Maldek and Mars were neighbors, it is entirely possible that the ancestors of the Hopis came from both of these planets. The 'underworld' where the 'crops failed due to a lack of rain' can refer to the dry and dying planet Mars, while the 'lower world' (where the 'people went after wealth, power and the pleasures of life') which was destroyed can refer to Lucifer-Maldek. Evidently, the two origin points of the Hopi people have become to them a single location now known as the *underworld* or the *lower world*. That this may be so is found in the words of a Hopi legend:

A long time passed and there were *other worlds* and *other peoples.*

We are now living today as descendants of people who were saved

TRAVELING THE PATH BACK TO THE ROAD IN THE SKY

from the other world (Lucifer?). Now, we call that the Lower World, because there the living stream changed from good into corruption. There were good people and they asked Massau for permission to come live with Him. These peaceful people from that earlier world were permitted to go live with Massau. They became the first Hopis.

Did the 'peaceful people' who were saved from the 'other world' or Lucifer leave their doomed planet before it was destroyed and join with some of the people who were leaving over-populated and dry Mars to become a single migrating colony that arrived on the planet Earth and mingled together to become the common ancestors of the Hopi Indians? The legendary evidence is rather positive in this regard. Because the people migrating from Lucifer and Mars became one people after landing on Earth, it is entirely possible that later generations interpreted the legends as referring to one original home, and the planet where 'the rains ceased' (Mars) and the planet of 'corruption' that was destroyed (Lucifer) became one world, the 'underworld' or the 'lower world'.

The Hopis, therefore, are concerned about the 'smoke signals' or the 'handwriting on the wall' because they know what happened to some of their ancestors on a far-away world a long time ago. They want to 'set their house in order before their 'true white brother' comes. Perhaps they, too, heed the warning from the Ancient Mysteries:

'As above, so below: that which hath been shall return again.'

If hydrogen destruction annihilated some of the ancestors of the Hopi people on Lucifer, they would naturally consider the 'terrible H-Bomb' as an omen or threat of impending calamity and imminent doom for our time.

The $90,000,000 spoken of in the March 2nd letter refers to the United States Government long-range programme opposed by the Hopi people.

On May 19, 1955, the *Washington Post* carried the following :

'Six Hopi Indians, disturbed by an ancient prophecy, came down from the mesa tops of Northern Arizona to Washington last week to seek their tribe's independence from the United States. The *atomic bomb,* together with strangling bureaucratic restrictions will destroy their people, and all North American life... and so, the Hopis want independence.'

The 'ancient prophecy' that disturbed the Hopis says:

TRAVELING THE PATH BACK TO THE ROAD IN THE SKY

'Some day there will be a *road in the sky* and a machine will ride this road and drop a gourd of ashes and destroy the people and boil the land.'

The ashes from the sky could refer to nothing but radio-active fallout, and the machine could be nothing but our planes which carry atomic bombs.

In March, 1951, the following letter was sent to the Capital in Arizona :

Hopi Indian Sovereign Nation,

Oraibi, Arizona,

March 27, 1951.

Hon. Howard Pyle,

Governor of the State of Arizona,

Phoenix, Arizona.

Dear Sir:

The name Hopi means 'peaceful'. We were the first people to inhabit this land for it was given to us by our God *Massau.* He gave us instructions so that we might live pure, clean and spiritual lives. We have held to this tradition even though we have been put in chains, beaten and punished and our land stolen.

We do know that we do not want anything to do with the artificial way of life of the white man. We will get rain if our lives are pure - and if we fast and pray and are humble in seeking forgiveness for our sins. Our God told us centuries ago that great wars would come and a third great war would purify by fire this evil generation. He told us long ago that wagons would run without horses and that men would travel in machines on a *road in the sky*. All this is not new to us. If we remain true to our traditional teachings of prayer, fasting and true living, then we will not be found wanting when the Purification Day comes.

This land that was given to us is held sacred as a peaceful land. We have been told by *Massau* that our oil and minerals must be used for peaceful purposes and not for war. When the desolation of war does come there must be some place of refuge, some place where peaceful people are found who remain true to their sacred teachings. We do not wish to be soldiers in foreign countries to kill people. This is also an evil part of the white man's way of life called 'civilization' and 'progress'. We do not want to have anything to do with war. We have made no agreement or treaty with the government regarding our land or regarding our being soldiers, therefore, it is a violation of all honour and justice to draft our young men to fight in any war. We will not allow our boys to be soldiers.

You have mentioned that there are different groups of people among the Hopis, and you wonder if we represent the majority of our people. We represent the traditional leaders and, if you come to Hopiland, we will have a meeting of young and old, not in a smoke-filled room in secret, but in the open where the sun can witness to the truth in our hearts. In the past, government men have listened only to Hopis who have government jobs and have sought to turn the Hopis away from their true peaceful life.

Sincerely yours, We are,

Dan Katchongva, Advisor (Sun Clan)

Hotevilla, Arizona.

Andrew Hermequaftewa, Advisor (Bluebird Clan),

Shungopovi, Arizona.

This letter came from a people who are so gentle they have been called the Quakers of the American Indians. Many of the ancient Hopi prophecies speak of two destructive world wars that will be followed by an unbelievably terrible third world war that will 'purify by fire this evil generation'. This purification is to take place, say the legends, when the 'true white brother' returns, for it is only by cleansing the land that everlasting life will be possible for those saved. The Hopis say that the good people in all religious groups must follow their own instructions from the Creator so that when the day of Purification comes to the Earth all peaceful men may 'stand with clean hands'. The Hopis believe that our world is now in the critical period spoken of in the prophecies of their forefathers. They also believe that great destruction is soon to come to the entire Earth and that all evil men will be eliminated, leaving the planet cleansed and purified for a New Age made up of only the people of good hearts. And the interesting point is that the Hopis do not say this New Age will be reserved strictly for them or for just Indians. They firmly believe that the evil man, whether he is Hopi, White, Black, Red or Yellow, will be destroyed and that the good man will be saved, no matter to what race he belongs. The Hopis do not picture the coming conflict as a racial war at all, it is simply a battle between the forces of good

TRAVELING THE PATH BACK TO THE ROAD IN THE SKY

and evil, or, as the Essenes at Qumran would say: 'The War of the Children of Light Against the Children of Darkness.'

The Hopis believe that after the land is purified by the 'true white brother' all men will live together in peace as one people. They say: 'If even *one* Hopi holds true to the teachings of the Great Spirit, man on this planet will be saved from total destruction in the coming third world war.'

Representatives of all Indian tribes in the United States were called to a meeting held at Hotevilla, Arizona, on October 19, 1956. At this meeting Dan Katchongva, Chief of the Hopi Sun Clan, said:

I call this meeting to find out if others are following the Life Plan given to them by the Great Spirit. We were instructed to send out a call to all good people when we reached a place where we could go no further. This is to discover the ONE Central Life Plan of the Creator. We must not lose it. By coming together in this way we will find people who are still holding fast to their Life Plan. Through our united discussions we will find a way out of these problems and confusions and then we will walk forward to the Good Life. It is time that white men realize that they have a religion. They must search it out and follow it. We must all work together.

According to our instructions the time has come for the Hopi people to act and work with other tribes as one Indian people using all of the Indian teachings and prophecies and beliefs. We are instructed to start a movement for the benefit of all Indian people as well as all other good people of the Earth. The Hopis believe we are at the end of the traditional Life Plan given to us by the Great Spirit, and in order to preserve human life and be right with Him, we must discover His Plan and work to uphold it. We cannot save ourselves by creating instruments of war ('Peace is for the strong'?). We must work and pray humbly so that we may come closer to our Creator who alone can save us.

The Hopis desire that all Indians look back to their sacred religious instructions and see if they can induce their leaders to gather together as soon as possible.

We will not allow ourselves to be a part of war activities—this great evil force that destroys human life. To take up arms of any kind would be to destroy ourselves. We only pray now that the Great Spirit will bring about this Purification Day as soon as possible, so we will enter everlasting life. Let us now move forward together, uniting tinder this one great Life Plan of

TRAVELING THE PATH BACK TO THE ROAD IN THE SKY

the Great Spirit and lead our people to the day when all mankind will be as *one people,* and will recognize one Supreme Being and will share all wealth and resources. This is our hope and our prayer and our sacred duty in this life.

Are the above words those of savages? The United States Government ignores the letters from the Hopis and disregards their claims even though such claims are legally sound. The small Hopi Nation is like a small centre of light in the midst of a great materialistic country. The words and warnings of the Hopi wise men are considered the babblings of superstitious heathens. However, if we examine the actions of white Christians we find they are to blame and have not lived their own religion. The white man must 'search out his religion and follow it'.

At the October 19th meeting, David Monongye, a Hopi leader from Hotevilla, Arizona, said:

When I remember mistreatment, persecution and hardship, I wonder what the future of the persecutors will be? How can they save themselves from what they have done which is contrary to the Creator's instructions? He created everything for all of us. We know that we and all people are heading for the Purification Day when a few of the faithful will be preserved. We were told that most people will be destroyed—only a few will survive. During the last days before the Purification Day, the numbers of the righteous will dwindle, so we were told, and so it is happening. So now we are looking back to our ancient teaching and searching for those who follow it. Now we are finding each other. We are actually speaking to the Great Spirit, for He is here listening.

The Great Spirit is not only looking on us, but also on the leaders in Washington who claim to be under Him, but who actually disregard Him and worship daily material things—money, wealth, power. They are not trying to follow the Great Spirit's Plan. The day has arrived when the Hopi people must make a call to not only other Indian people but to all righteous people everywhere. We know that many people laugh at us and call us names and mistreat us, it was known that this would be, but we know we will be purified soon and we will stand by His side when that day comes.

The call went out to *the blessed meek,* and many heard that call, for the Hopi people have received letters from all over the world, letters from other people with a good heart. A still small voice cries out from the mesa tops of

TRAVELING THE PATH BACK TO THE ROAD IN THE SKY

the American desert. The Hopi message is an exact duplicate of the prophecies and warnings of the Holy Bible, but few white men will heed them. The Christian message speaks of the day when 'only a few of the faithful will be preserved, that most people will be destroyed, that only a few will survive.' It is also written in Holy Scripture that 'the numbers of the righteous will dwindle'. So have the Christians been told, and so it is happening.

We are reminded of many passages from the New Testament:

'... Come out of her, my people, that ye be not partakers of her sins, and that ye receive not of her plagues. For her sins have reached unto heaven, and God hath remembered her iniquities.' (Revelation xviii:4,5).

Since there is only One Creator, we would expect the instructions and prophecies given to the Hopi people to be identical in meaning. There are so many similarities in the Christian religion and that of the Hopis that it is possible here to give only a few of them. But study the words of your own faith and see if they depart from those of the Hopi Indians. You will not find contradictions, you will only find startling correspondences!

The Hopi people as a part of *the blessed meek* have put out the call to 'Come out of her, my people, that ye be not partakers of her sins...

The answers to David Monongye's question: 'I wonder what the future of the persecutors will be?' might be found in the words of Jesus, the Christ: 'Ye serpents, ye generation of vipers, how can ye escape the damnation of hell?' (St. Matthew xxiii:33). And He also said: 'And these shall go away into everlasting punishment : but the righteous into life eternal.' (St. Matthew xxv:46).

The Hopis say that through the Day of Purification the righteous will achieve everlasting life. Jesus, the Christ called it life eternal.

In connection with the 'mistreatment, persecution and hardship' of the Hopis, we recall the words in St. Mark xiii:13:

'And ye shall be hated of all men for my name's sake : but he that shall endure unto the end, the same shall be saved.'

And the words in St. Luke xxi:12,13:

'... they shall lay their hands on you, and persecute you, delivering you up to the synagogues, and into prisons, being brought before kings and rulers for my name's sake. And it shall turn to you for a testimony.'

TRAVELING THE PATH BACK TO THE ROAD IN THE SKY

The Hopis say 'the numbers of the righteous will dwindle,' and in St. Matthew xxiv:12, we find:

'And because iniquity shall abound, the love of many shall wax cold.'

Another ancient prophecy of the Hopis says:

'The Hopi problem and religion will be heard around the world. The *turtle* rattles and bells in our ceremonies are symbolic of this event.'

This reminds us of the words in the Song of Solomon ii:12:

'... the time of the singing of *birds* is come, and the voice of the *turtle is* heard in our land ...'

This statement is very curious since the turtle has no voice. Could it possibly correspond to the Hopi message (symbolized by the turtle) as their 'voice is heard in our land'?

Another ancient Hopi prophecy says:

'A small group which is influential, will help us in many ways, and there will be signs.'

According to the Hopi religious leaders, the signs point to the fact that this is the time for the small group to appear arid help them.

Remember, according to the Hopi legends, the 'peaceful people' were saved from the 'other world' or Lucifer before it was destroyed and evidently joined with the migrating colony that was leaving dry Mars to become one people and the common ancestors of the Hopi Indians after their arrival in the land 'beyond the sky' or the planet Earth.

When they first came to the new world (the Earth), the ancient legends say the ancestors of the Hopi people agreed to live according to the Life Plan of *Massau.*

The Hopis of today say:

We made a vow that early day and we will never forsake it so long as we are Hopis. We were permitted then to come and live with *Massau*. We were welcome. We were taught the Life Plan of *Massau* and were instructed in His way of good living. After many days with Him, time came for all of the first Hopis to move out over the face of the land. *Massau* gathered us all about Him and gave us instructions as to the obligations He placed upon us. He

TRAVELING THE PATH BACK TO THE ROAD IN THE SKY

provided us with many altars and many emblems which represented the land and the people. These He placed in the hands of our leaders. After a day and night of praying and fasting all the Hopis assembled the next day at dawn to listen to the final message from *Massau.* One clan out of all the group was appointed as the leader-clan in our migration. An emblem was given them which represented the land and the people. *Massau* told the people that their name would be 'Hopi' which meant : 'peaceful and happy'. He told the leaders that He gave them the land and all the people were to be under their care. He gave them an emblem and told them if they would follow it they would be able to lead the people along the path of a good life. *Massau* told the leaders that they would be as fathers to the people and that they should take care of them as if they were their children. He told them to let the people live a long and a good life. He told the leaders to always allow for plenty of rain and for an abundance of food for the children to eat. He told them to lead the people always along the path of a good, clean, and harmonious life so that when time came for them to go beyond this life they would be at peace.

After *Massau's* final speech to the leaders and the people, the Hopis began to move out over the new land. According to the legends, 'they went to different places according to their instructions'. The people carried no weapons of any kind, but the leaders who had been appointed by *Massau* carried the altars with them. Food was carried to feed the children on the way. When the Hopis 'moved out over the new land' they traveled from a place in the *west* and journeyed to the *east.*

On the second day of the migration in the new land, a group was appointed to go ahead of the others and act as scouts. Another group was appointed to follow after the people so that nothing was lost in the journey. This latter group was called the 'Bluebird Clan' in honor of the 'Bluebird' who first penetrated the 'hole in the sky'. Today amongst the Hopis it is still the duty of the 'Bluebird Clan' to follow all others and remind them if they have left anything 'behind' that *Massau* may have instructed them to do. In other words, the 'Bluebird Clan' interprets *Massau's* instructions and reminds the Hopi leaders when they are getting off the true path. This is important today when the Hopis are surrounded by other people who want to change their religion, their way of life and their culture. To stay on *Massau's* path and live His Life Plan they need the 'Bluebird' reminders.

The legends say that the Hopis travelled from one place to another for

TRAVELING THE PATH BACK TO THE ROAD IN THE SKY

many years, and that they never stopped permanently anywhere. They were going to a certain place for *Massau* had given them a 'sign' whereby they would recognize their 'Promised Land'.

After many years in the wilderness and the desert, the Hopis came to a place where they saw the promised sign of *Massau*. They knew then that their wandering was over and that they were to settle down and build their villages and live.

Massau had told the people that when they saw bright fires on the mesa tops and a Great Star hovering over the area, they should stop and build their villages on the mesas where the fires were seen, and the land under the Great Star would be their new country. *Massau* also told the people that when they saw the Great Star this would indicate that He had arrived at His home in the *east*. He told them that some day He would return as the Deliverer and Purifier and would appear in the *east* as the 'true white brother' of all the Hopis.

Two sets of Sacred Stone Tablets were prepared by *Massau* before he left for His home in the *east* and one set was presented to the Hopi leaders and the other set He took with Him. He told the Hopis that they must look after His land while He was gone and they must follow His laws. He also told them that they were to guard the land until He returned from the *east*. The Sacred Stone Tablets contained written commandments and *Massau* 'breathed the Laws into them'.

Remember, we said before, that there are many similarities between the Essenes and the Hopis and a very important one is that which exists between the records of the Dead Sea Scrolls and the Sacred Hopi Stone Tablets. Perhaps by now you have realized that the Hopi legends of their migration and their wandering in the wilderness for many years exactly parallel the Biblical account of the Exodus from Egypt when Moses led the Israelites towards the Promised Land.

Let us examine the legend from its beginning. While there is great similarity between *Massau* (Hopi) and *Mahsiah* (Hebrew), there is also similarity between the other spelling *Massua* (Hopi) and *Yeshua* (Hebrew). Let us consider the similarity existing between all of these with the Egyptian name of the Hebrew prophet Moses. He was called *Meshu* by the royal princess who found him for 'Meshu' means 'drawn or rescued from the water'.

TRAVELING THE PATH BACK TO THE ROAD IN THE SKY

Massau was the anointed deliverer of the Hopi people because He allowed them to come and live with Him when they were saved from the 'other world' (Lucifer).

Mahsiah is the anointed deliverer and expected king of the Hebrews.

Yeshua was Jesus, the Christ, the anointed deliverer or Messiah of the Christians.

Meshu (Moses) was the anointed deliverer of the Israelites for he led them out of bondage in Egypt.

All of the above can be called anointed and deliverers. However, exactly what connection there can be between the Hopi *Massau,* the Hebrew *Mahsiah,* the Christian *Yeshua* (Jesus, the Christ), and *Meshu* (Moses) of the Israelites, is difficult to say. Nevertheless,-there are startling correspondences.

The deliverance of the Hopis out of the 'other world' (Lucifer) which was a 'corrupt world' was similar to the deliverance of the Israelites out of 'corrupt' Egypt. The Hopi 'deliverer and prophet' was *Massau,* while the Israelite 'deliverer and prophet' was *Meshu* (Moses).

Massau provided the Hopi leaders with 'many altars and many emblems', while *Meshu* (Moses) provided the leaders of the various Hebrew tribes with their respective 'emblems'.

The gathering of the Hopi people around *Massau* and the instructions He gave them, corresponds exactly to the Israelites gathering around *Meshu* (Moses) and waiting for their instructions from their 'deliverer and prophet'.

When the Hopis 'moved out over the new land' they traveled from a place in the *west* and journeyed to the *east.* The Israelites did exactly the same thing when they started from Egypt in the *west* and traveled towards the Promised Land in the *east.*

The Hopi legends say that they traveled 'from one place to another for many years, and they never stopped permanently anywhere'. This corresponds to the forty years in the wilderness and the wandering of the Israelites. The Hopis traveled in dry and hot desert country, and so did the people of *Meshu* (Moses).

TRAVELING THE PATH BACK TO THE ROAD IN THE SKY

Massau's sign to the Hopi people was bright fires on the mesa tops. *Meshu* (Moses) received the Decalogue from God on Mount Sinai while the entire mountain was enveloped in smoke and capped at the top with terrifying flames.

'And Mount Sinai was altogether on a smoke, because the Lord descended upon it in fire: and the smoke thereof ascended as the smoke of a furnace...' (Exodus xix:18).

Massu told the Hopis that when they saw the 'Great Star' hovering over them He would have arrived at His home in the *east. Meshu* (Moses) and his people saw the 'pillar of cloud and fire'.

'And the Lord went before them by day in a pillar of a cloud, to lead them the way; and by night in a pillar of fire, to give them light : He took not away the pillar of the cloud by day, nor the pillar of fire by night, from before the people'. (Exodus xiii:21,22).

The Hopis and the Israelites both saw strange phenomena in the heavens, but there is also a similarity between the 'Great Star' that moved above the Hopis indicating *Massau's* home in the *east,* and the happenings that took place at the birth of Jesus, the Christ.

'... Where is he that is born King of the Jews? for we have seen his *star in the east,* and are come to worship him.' (St. Matthew ii : 2).

'... lo, the *star,* which they saw in the *east, went before them,* till it came and stood over where the young child was. When they saw the *star,* they rejoiced with exceeding great joy.' (St. Matthew ii:9,10).

Since we have already shown in *Secret Places of The Lion* that the 'star in the east' was a space craft, and the same one that earlier had led the Israelites out of Egypt, it is altogether possible that the 'Great Star' indicating *Massau's* home in the *east* was also a space craft.

Massau, the 'Deliverer and Purifier' of the Hopis who will appear in the *east* as the 'true white brother', sounds very much like *Yeshua* (Jesus, the Christ), the 'Deliverer and Purifier' of the Christians who will return from the *east.*

'For as the *lightning cometh out of the east,* and shineth even unto the west; so shall the coming of the Son of man be... there will the eagles be gathered together.' (St. Matthew xxiv:27,28).

TRAVELING THE PATH BACK TO THE ROAD IN THE SKY

What is meant by eagles? This may very well be a reference to the *visitants,* or space craft.

It is interesting to note, also, that the Hopi *Massau,* as a 'deliverer and purifier' is a 'white brother', a *true white brother,* and not an Indian.

'*Two sets* of Sacred Stone Tablets were prepared *by Massau',* and they 'contained written *commandments* and *Massau* "breathed the *Laws into them".' Two sets* of Stone Tablets were given by God to *Meshu* (Moses) on' Mount Sinai, and they contained the Ten Commandments which were the *Laws* of God.

'And he gave unto Moses, when he had made an end of communing with him upon Mount Sinai, two tables of testimony, tables of stone, written with the finger of God.' (Exodus xxxi:18).

The first set of Stone Tablets was broken by *Meshu* (Moses) but he received a second set later.

'And the Lord said unto Moses, Hew thee two tables of stone like unto the first : and I will write upon these tables the words that were in the first tables, which thou brakest.' (Exodus xxxiv:1).

Massau was the great *lawgiver* of the Hopis, and *Meshu* (Moses) was the great *lawgiver* of the Hebrews. The Hopis and the Israelites found their 'Promised Land'.

The Israelites and the Hopis both received their Laws and Commandments written on Stone Tablets, and the Hopis say: '*Massau* wrote on them with his finger', just as the Stone Tablets of *Meshu* (Moses) had been 'written with the finger of God'.

Now, the Essenes of Qumran also had 'Laws and Commandments' and these were written on manuscripts and scrolls but they based their teachings on the writings of *Meshu* (Moses) and the Ten Commandments of the Stone Tablets of Mount Sinai. At exactly the same time the Essenes were living at Khirbet Qumran, practicing community life and living a peaceful existence, according to the Laws given by *Meshu* (Moses), the Hopi Indians across the world in Arizona were living the same kind of life and following the Laws of *Massau.*

The Essenes at Qumran lived less than ten miles from the mouth of the Jordan River, and *Meshu* (Moses) was last seen on Nebo, the loftiest peak of

TRAVELING THE PATH BACK TO THE ROAD IN THE SKY

Mount Pisgah, eight miles east of the mouth of the same river. The people who followed *Meshu* (Moses) had seen the 'pillar of cloud and fire', *Massau's* people, the Hopis, saw the 'Great Star', and the Essenes communed with the 'Sons of Light'. Were the 'Sons of Light' who came to Qumran on the Dead Sea, one of the most desolate areas on Earth, space visitors? Such *visitants* had guided the Israelites, and possibly guided the Hopis during the wandering for many years in the desert.

All of these similarities are astounding, to say the least, but there is yet another. We can't be sure when the ancestors of the Hopis arrived on Earth, but the Exodus from Egypt may give us a clue.

In my book, *Secret Places Of The Lion,* I showed how the Final or Greater Exodus had taken place at midnight, on April 6-7, 1233 B.C. This Final Exodus took place amid a great natural upheaval in Egypt, caused by the destruction and abrupt end of the planet Lucifer-Maldek.

According to the Hopi legends, the 'peaceful people' were saved from the 'corrupt world' or the 'other world' (Lucifer) *before* it was destroyed. They then joined the migrating Martians and, after landing on the Earth, became the common ancestors of the modern Hopis. This gives us a key to the time element involved. When Lucifer-Maldek announced its destructive end like an exploding star, the 'peaceful people' who had been saved from the doomed world were in Arizona with the Martian group they had joined. Far away, on the other side of the Earth, *Meshu* (Moses) was leading the Israelites out of Egypt.

Not only do the happenings of the Hopis in their 'wandering in the wilderness for many years' exactly duplicate those of the Israelites seeking the 'Promised Land', but we discover that such happenings to both groups took place at the same time. *Meshu* (Moses) was leading his people out of Egypt, while *Massau* was leading His people into their 'Promised Land' in America.

It seems fantastic, indeed, that there could be any connection between an Indian Tribe of the American Southwest, the Essene community of the Dead Sea area, the fate of an evil planet millions of miles away in outer space, and the Israelites who escaped bondage in ancient Egypt. But we are learning even more fantastic things today about the past, and *tomorrow* holds even more fantasy that to the inheritors of the New World. *The blessed meek will* only be part of history truthfully revealed.

TRAVELING THE PATH BACK TO THE ROAD IN THE SKY

The Stone Tablets of *Meshu* (Moses) were kept for centuries in the Ark, and it is thought that possibly they were destroyed in the Captivity. What if some day they should be found? And if they are found, I wonder how they would compare with the Sacred Stone Tablets of the Hopis which are not lost nor destroyed, but which are today still in the possession of the leaders of Oraibi and Hotevilla villages? These Tablets are said to be made of a strange green stone that is 'like nothing on the Earth'. They are covered with engraved hieroglyphics. The Stone Tablets of Mount Sinai were born out of 'smoke and fire' and the Sacred Stone Tablets of the Hopis are guarded over today by the *Fire Clan,* whose members are the recognized custodians of *Massau's* Laws in stone.

The village of Shungopovi is the mother village representing the true Hopis, and its leaders hold all of the major altars. Remember, the ancient legends say: 'He *(Massau)* provided us with many *altars* and many emblems which represented the land and the people. These He placed in the hands of our leaders... and they carried the altars with them.'

On Mount Sinai, *Meshu* heard this commandment:

'Ye shall not make with me gods of silver, neither shall ye make unto you the gods of gold. An *altar of earth* thou shalt make unto me...' (Exodus xx:23,24).

The Hopi Indians have never made 'gods of silver or gold'. In fact, they do not worship idols at all, but we cannot say the same for some 'Christians'! As *Meshu* (Moses) was commanded to make an 'altar of earth' so the Hopis make their altars of earth, and these follow exactly the pattern as given by *Massau* to the Hopi leaders generations ago.

The Hopi altars are erected on the earth of the underground kivas. These altars and sand paintings are always the focal point of a kiva ceremony. The photograph in Fig. No. 42 is also from my collection of old and rare pictures of the American Southwest. This photograph was taken in 1899 by Dr. J. Miller. It shows the interior of a sacred kiva underground. How Dr. Miller was able to obtain permission to photograph this Sacred Altar I have not been able to find out.

The wealth of details making up the altar in the photograph came down from the dim past when *Massau* provided the Hopi leaders with 'altars and emblems'. We can be certain that there has been no change in them since that remote time. The altar is, of course, deeply symbolic. There are many

TRAVELING THE PATH BACK TO THE ROAD IN THE SKY

prayer feathers in evidence which represent the prayers of the Hopi people as they 'float up' to the Great Spirit carrying their message. They signify the 'breath of life'. The symbol of spiritual food and welfare and the traditional 'staff of life' of the Hopis is corn. Imperfect ears cannot be used on the altar. Yellow, blue, red, and white corn represent the north, west, south, and east, respectively. The sky is represented by purple corn, and the underworld is symbolized by grey corn.

Also, in the altar of the old photograph, you will notice the beautifully made sand painting that is in the central part. This painting depicts clouds and falling rain, symbols that are used by the Hopis in many decorations. Sometimes, the partly concealed face of a Kachina is shown looking out over the billowing clouds. This Kachina face is like the face of some great 'El' being as he surveys the Earth below from his vantage point in Timelessness.

The altar in the photograph actually depicts the ancient *road in the sky* of the ancestors or the Hopis, but today it is symbolic of the coming of rain to the dry earth and the crops of the people. The colors representing the four cardinal directions stand for the 'different places' the ancient Hopis went to 'according to their instructions' from *Massau*. The color representing the sky stands for the 'sky' that contained the 'road' over which they traveled from their former home on the 'corrupt planet' (Lucifer). And the color representing the underworld stands for destroyed Lucifer-Maldek itself.

Falling rain is symbolized by four serpents. If you look closely at Fig. No. 42, you will see that each serpent has a prayer feather behind its head. Here is the fabulous 'Plumed Serpent' that is always associated with water and rain in symbology all over North, Central, and South America. I discovered the same 'Plumed Serpent' on the 'Rock of the Writings' in the deep jungles of eastern Peru.

In the photograph of 1899, we can view the Hopi *road in the sky* of *yesterday* as it has come down to us symbolically. And in the same sky, the ancient Hopi prophecy says:

'... there will be *a road*... and a machine will ride this road...' and atomic bombs will be dropped on the people of Earth.

Another Hopi prophecy says:

'Men on earth will make a *small ball* that shall contain the elements of their earth... and it shall cause a great destruction and a great cloud over all people.'

And yet another says:

'In a future day, there will be seen *houses* in *the sky* and they will have no support from the earth... and some will be joined together.'

The 'small ball' containing the 'elements of the earth' is obviously the atomic bomb. This prophecy has now been fulfilled according to Hopi leaders, because such a destructive device has actually been invented and has caused great damage to the Earth and its people.

The 'houses in the sky' with 'no support' and 'joined together' may stand for the artificial satellites or the proposed space stations that are to orbit above the Earth. Such 'houses' could also refer to UFOs. Other prophecies speak of 'many people dropping out of the sky' in a future time and 'people living on a place up in the sky'.

Another ancient prophecy of the Hopi people says:

'When the Hopis go before the leaders of the world... when they are gathered in one place... then they will obtain justice.'

On March 21, 1958, Sun Chief Dan Katchongva, sent the following words to the Albuquerque Indian Meeting in New Mexico:

'... In order that we do not make the mistake of losing our beloved land and life and religion, I shall continue to work with truth and a determination to see that none of these new ideas of the white man causes us to fall. I shall knock on the door of a 'White House' in Washington, D.C., and if this door is not open to me, then I shall go to the door of the United Nations with all our problems. This is one of the instructions that has been passed down to us by our forefathers.'

Katchongva is referring to the ancient prophecy of Hopis going 'before the leaders of the world' when he speaks of 'instructions from our forefathers' above. But would the Hopi people receive justice from the United Nations? I believe the prophecy refers to another time in the future when the power of the International Bankers has been eliminated from the Earth.

President Theodore Roosevelt once said:

'Certainly the continuance of autocratic rule by a Federal Department

TRAVELING THE PATH BACK TO THE ROAD IN THE SKY

over the lives of more than 200,000... is incompatible with American ideals of Liberty. It is also destructive of the character and self-respect of a Great Race.'

President Roosevelt was, of course, referring to the policy of the United States towards the native American Indians. Today, no one realizes the truth of these words better than Herbert C. Holdridge (Brigadier General, U.S. Army, retired). For ten years this man has been spearheading an intense educational campaign to alert American citizens to chaotic economic and political conditions which have risen up to engulf them. He has given case after case of shocking proof to support his premises and conclusions that *there is no legal, Constitutional government of the United States at this time,* and that we are ruled by political outlaws. Not even his greatest enemies can say Gen. Holdridge is wrong!

The present U.S. Indian policy and administration is another example illustrating the effects of immoral and illegal behavior in high places according to Gen. Holdridge. We should remember that President Abraham Lincoln called the Indian Department 'this accursed system'.

'For we wrestle not against flesh and blood, but against principalities, against powers, against the rulers of the darkness of this world, against *spiritual wickedness in high places.*' (Ephesians vi : 12).

On May 20, 1957, Gen. Holdridge sent the following letter to Washington, D.C.:

Herbert C. Holdridge,

Brig.-Gen., U.S. Army (Ret.),

P.O. Box 186,

Sherman Oaks, California,

May 20, 1957

To : The President of the United States

Hon. James A. Haley, Chairman,

Sub-Committee on Indian Affairs,

House of Representatives,

Hon. James E. Murray,

TRAVELING THE PATH BACK TO THE ROAD IN THE SKY

Chairman, Senate Committee on Internal and Insular Affairs,

Washington, D.C.

Gentlemen :

On Saturday, May 18, 1957, I and two associates, at the express invitation of the Traditional Leaders (the rulers) of the Hopi Nation, attended their council meeting in Shungopovi village. Having been briefed in advance, and after listening to the discussions of these Leaders, we were so shocked and shamed by the attitudes and acts of the U.S. Government and its representatives, that I dispatched a wire to you on Sunday, May 19th, from Flagstaff, Arizona, approved by my associates, as follows:

'I and associates present at meeting Traditional Leaders Hopi Nation May 18 concerning invasion of sovereignty by U.S. Government, particularly Bills S.692 and H.R. 3789 stop As an army officer sworn to defend the Constitution I demand that these bills be killed forthwith as constituting criminal expropriation of resources and destruction of freedom and spiritual values of Hopi people stop These crimes of U.S. Government must, and shall be, exposed to people of U.S. and nations of world stop Letter follows.'

Signed : Herbert C. Holdridge,

Brig.-Gen., U.S. Army (Ret.).

The facts developed in this meeting were, briefly :

The Hopi Nation never made war against the United States and was never conquered. No treaty has ever been signed with them as has been done with other Indian tribes. Hence, their sovereignty has never been impaired, and they exist today as a nation within our borders, more independent, for example, than that of the principality of Monaco within the borders of France, for the sovereignty of Monaco has been impaired by treaty, whereas that of the Hopi Nation has not. Therefore, the U.S. Government has no authority to intervene in the internal affairs of the Hopi Nation unless and until it negotiates a treaty with the historic rulers of the nation, the Traditional Leaders, who constitute a spiritual theocracy governed under the inspiration of the Great Spirit, manifesting a spiritual understanding, motivation and action impossible of comprehension by our materialistic civilization, or our religious orthodoxies.

Notwithstanding this legal bar to intervention within their nation, the

TRAVELING THE PATH BACK TO THE ROAD IN THE SKY

U.S. Government has invaded the sovereignty of this independent nation, has limited its historic land areas, has permitted the invasion of the areas by missionaries of other religions against the will of the people and their rulers, has corrupted their way of life (including the introduction of the sale of alcohol adjacent to their reservation against their will), and has invaded the securities of the people more brutally than the barbarians brutalized Ancient Rome.

Today we find the Hopi Nation as a small spiritual island attempting to survive and maintain its spiritual standards under the impact of the corruptions of modern civilization at the low level manifested in political Washington. Its immediate cause of distress is the imposition 'by command' of the U.S. Government and against the will of the people and their rulers, of a 'puppet government' in the form of an illegal 'Tribal Council', at the head of which they have placed a backsliding, collaborating Hopi, who has been convicted of felony in our Federal Courts and has served sentence; who acts dictatorially even without the approval of his own illegal 'council'; and who collaborates with the forces of exploitation who seem bent upon destroying the Hopi Nation. This technique is in the same pattern as that employed by our government in the establishment of Chiang Kai Chek as their 'puppet' in Formosa to impose their will upon China.

Working lawlessly through this 'puppet' and through the Superintendent of the Hopi Agency, one H. E. O'Hara, our government is now attempting to impose the above mentioned bills upon the Hopi Nation, their fundamental purpose is to expropriate the mineral resources of the Hopi lands for the benefit of conspirators who have drafted the bills. Without discussing the bills in detail, their full effect would be so devastating, and so revolting, as to shock the people of the United States and of the world. Incidentally, this gentleman, O'Hara, present initially at the meeting of the Hopi Leaders, insisted upon our leaving the council chamber before he would speak, notwithstanding the fact he was informed of our presence by their invitation, thus insulting them, showing cynical disregard for the principle of 'open covenants', and of our right to be present to witness matters of public concern; and demonstrated clearly, by his obvious emotional attitude, fear that his machinations would not bear the light of day. After we returned to the meeting it was clear that he had brought heavy psychological pressures upon the Traditional Leaders to force rapid approval of the provisions of the criminal bills mentioned above. For these crimes he should be discharged and indicted before our courts.

The final act of the Traditional Leaders—legal rulers of the Hopi Nation—was to declare null and void all acts by the U.S. Government within its territories; to reassert their legal sovereignty; to dissolve the illegal 'Tribal Council', and to remove the 'puppet'; and to prepare further steps to establish their sovereignty against any further encroachments.

This is an outline of the facts presented to us in such detail that we cannot doubt their truth. Acting as a patriotic citizen, jealous of the honour of our government, I insist that this issue be brought into the open, and that justice be done to this little nation which has won the affection and respect of the thousands who have come into contact with it. My companions agree. We are willing, and anxious, to appear before any official or unofficial body designed to correct the injustices inflicted upon these people.

Very respectfully yours,

Herbert C. Holdridge,

Brigadier General, U.S. Army (Retired).

Copies to:Interested agencies and individuals,The Press.

The 'shocking and shameful acts' Gen. Holdridge speaks of in his letter are not so much the attitudes of the U.S. Government as they are the attitudes of the International Bankers constituting the 'Hidden Empire' who intend to rule the world. Why are such forces of darkness interested in the little Hopi Nation? There are valuable natural resources on Hopi territory that must be obtained for use in the 'Peace is for the strong' campaign and for eventual use on the battlefields of the world, for 'ye shall hear of wars and rumors of wars'.

The Hopi Nation is governed 'under the inspiration of the (one) Great Spirit... impossible of comprehension by our materialistic civilization...' But their way of life of kindness and peace is not 'impossible of comprehension' to *the blessed meek* in all parts of the world who constitute the inheritors of the New Age that the *visitants* from other worlds now herald by their appearance in the skies of Earth.

These powerful words of indictment are made by a man of honor, a General in the United States Army who is sworn to defend the Constitution of the United States!

TRAVELING THE PATH BACK TO THE ROAD IN THE SKY

The Essenes understood this great battle against 'spiritual wickedness in high places' when they wrote their document that deals with 'The war of the Children of Light Against the Children of Darkness'.

As early as 1946, the Hopi message started to 'be heard around the world' as an ancient prophecy foretold. Ward Shepard, in his article 'Our Indigenous Shangri-La', for *The Scientific Monthly,* February, 1946, said:

Western civilization has been darkened by the fog of an unworkable *materialism* which does not nourish the basic needs of the human personality. The Hopis cannot give us the blueprint for a new civilization, but they can instruct us in the nature of society as the nurturing ground of whole men and in the essence of true democracy, in which the eternal and yet infinitely malleable substance of human nature is wrought out to its full beauty... the Hopi community, subjected to an intense and manifold scientific scrutiny, turns out surprisingly to be an 'ideal republic', a pure, achieved democracy, intensely nurturing an ancient spiritual culture. And furthermore the unusual wisdom and the beauty of the Hopi way of life contain a healing message to minds drenched in the terror and pity of world tragedy, oppressed by the spectre of vast and unpredictable change. Even more, the Hopis, having long since mastered the fine art of cultivating the garden of human life, have much to tell us about the essential eternal values required for the sustenance of the human spirit.

Mr. Shepard's article was published by the American Association for the Advancement of Science. About 1946, it all started, and now the Hopi message is being 'heard around the world' as an ancient prophecy out of the dim past said it would be. The Hopi people say they want to be known by everyone in the world as People of Peace, they want all people to hear their voice, they want to share their way of life with all the world, the Hopi people will continue to bring their stand to the attention of the entire world as we all move Forward with increasingly 'faster steps' towards 'Purification Day'.

The Hopis remember well what Massau told them:

'Now live, and never lose faith in what I have given you. If you do lose faith and turn away from this Life Plan I have given you, you will be lost and later bring great trouble upon yourselves. Do not ever lose faith as you go out over this land.'

In his final message, *Massau* also said:

TRAVELING THE PATH BACK TO THE ROAD IN THE SKY

'Never fight against your own people. Never let your people go across the water or into other lands to harm people. You must not kill... stay within this area and uphold this sacred emblem which represents all land and life, until I come again to be your leader.'

This is what *Massu* said to all the forefathers of the Hopis and he continues to speak to the 'good hearts' of the Hopi people today. The Hopis will never forsake their ancient vows made with the Great Spirit.

All of this brings to mind the words of the forefathers of the white men in America:

'... all men are created equal... with certain inalienable rights... Life, Liberty, and the pursuit of happiness ...'

'In order to form a more perfect union, establish justice... and secure the blessings of liberty... do ordain and establish this Constitution...'

An ancient prophecy of the Hopis says that in a future day, shortly before the time of 'Purification', the 'Coyote' will speak for the Hopi people and do all their talking. It is of interest, therefore, that the official interpreter for the Traditional Leaders at this time is Thomas Banyacya, a Hopi who belongs to the 'Coyote Clan'.

In 1957, during my stay at Hotevilla, Arizona, I was told prophecies and legends that the Hopi Leaders had never released before. Some of these appear in this book. Thomas Banyacya told me that it was now time for these ancient warnings and stories to be given to the world. Many of them formerly were known only to the custodians of the most ancient knowledge of the Hopi people. Banyacya also said:

'The Hopi people were warned long ago not to take part in the Three Great Wars, for if they did it would be doubtful if they would survive the "Purification Day". Therefore, the Hopis do not wish to lose their sacred land and be destroyed. We know that the same thing took place in the 'other world' and some of our ancestors escaped from the total destruction of life in that world by asking to follow and live with *Massau*. He gave them permission to come and live with Him as peaceful people. We have vowed to adhere to that life. Many in the world are not living the life the Great Spirit has asked them to live—this is the beginning of destruction. Hopi tradition and teachings are based on a plan for everlasting life which will go into effect when the 'purification' time comes. This time will come when an ancient brother,

TRAVELING THE PATH BACK TO THE ROAD IN THE SKY

known as the "true white brother", who went to the *east* with Sacred Stone Tablets, returns carrying those Tablets with Him. We are now waiting for His return. From His Tablets and from those held by the "Fire Clan" of the Hopi people, the everlasting life plan will be told, and it will be quite different from the human life plan now being lived and nearing its end. In the everlasting life, it is taught that all people will live together in peace and recognize only One Supreme Being, the land will become fertile again, and only those that remain true to the old teachings will live the new life.'

The reference to the 'land becoming fertile again' in the desert country of the Hopis, reminds us of Isaiah xxxv:1,2:

'The wilderness and the solitary place shall be glad for them; and the *desert* shall rejoice, and *blossom as the rose*. It shall blossom abundantly, and rejoice even with joy and singing.'

The Hopis claim that there will be *two* forerunners of the 'true white brother' who will witness for Him. One messenger will carry a Swastika and the other one will carry a Sun-Disc. In this connection, it is interesting to read Revelation xi:3 :

'And I will give power unto my *two witnesses,* and they shall prophesy...'

The Hopis can see the 'handwriting on the wall' for their sacred prophecies outlined the happenings of *today* centuries ago when their ancestors were new in the land 'beyond the sky'. They point to the numerous 'signs' in the heavens as proof of the coming change and the need for the 'Purification Day'.

'And there shall be *signs* in the sun, and in the moon, and in the stars; and upon the earth distress of nations, with perplexity; the sea and the waves roaring; Men's hearts failing them for fear... (St. Luke xxi:25,26).

One of the Hopi prophecies says:

'In the last days *strange lights will* be seen in the sky and they will be watching the Hopi people to see if they are following the Life Plan and these *strange lights* will report to the "true white brother" in the *east* and they will tell Him when it is time for Him to come again.'

The 'strange lights' could be nothing but UFOs or space visitors, and they are being seen today all over the world.

TRAVELING THE PATH BACK TO THE ROAD IN THE SKY

Another prophecy says:

'When the "true white brother" returns, all forms of transportation will be stopped and man will not be able to move about the land... weapons will be useless... a friendly people will come over the land of the Hopis and will rain down from the sky.'

The 'stopping of transportation' sounds very much like the happenings near Levelland, Texas, during 1957, and near Ica, Peru, early in 1958. Ancient prophecies out of a forgotten *yesterday* are pointing a bony finger at the happenings of *today*.

On June 6, 1956, there was a demonstration of UFOs over Hotevilla, Arizona, where the Sacred Stone Tablets are still guarded by the members of the 'Fire Clan'. This took place immediately after a meeting where about thirty-five Traditional Leaders were holding a council.

The Hopi Nation is, indeed, 'a small spiritual island' representing the last great 'Campfire' of Indian North America; if their 'light' they have managed to keep burning and alive goes out in their sacred kivas, the Indian Race is lost forever to Earth. But that 'light' will not go out for the Hopis are holding councils and they are meeting with *the blessed meek* of the world even as you read these words!

One by one, the ancient prophecies out of *yesterday* are being fulfilled *today* as the travelers on the *road in the sky* seek out with a 'lantern of Diogenes' those who are closest to their kind—the *blessed meek* amongst the Amish/Mennonites, *the peaceful ones* amongst the Hopi Indians. But they are not only interested in these two cultural groups of mankind, for they seek those of a 'good heart' wherever they may be on Earth to fulfill the promises of a new *tomorrow*.

They see from their vantage point a 'campfire' burning brightly in Arizona, U.S.A., as 'the voice of the turtle is heard in our land'.

TRAVELING THE PATH BACK TO THE ROAD IN THE SKY

THE OTHER SIDE OF THE SKY

'The Ute and the wandering Crow
Shall know as the white men know,
And fare as the white men fare.
The pale and the red shall be brothers,
One's rights shall be as another's,
Home, school, and house of prayer.'

(J. G. Whittier).

THE message of the Hopi Indians of Arizona is now being heard around the world, and other Indian tribes from Canada to Tierra del Fuego are responding to the call. The last great Indian 'Campfire' represented by the Hopis, is lighting other 'campfires' throughout the world by its spiritual appeal, and there is a rebirth and reawakening of all that is Indian on Earth.

Indians in the United States are searching their ancient prophecies and legends to see what they can learn of their *yesterday,* their *today,* and their *tomorrow.* They are finding that the traditions from the past hold startling implications for the immediate future. We learn this when we study Hopi legends, for we find while some of them refer to the activities of space visitors in the past, others obviously refer to a time in the future when the *visitants* will again appear. For instance, a Hopi 'myth' relates how twin stars in the sky are symbolic of a man and a woman who had strange experiences and eventually journeyed across the sky one following the other. In this so-called 'myth' and many others we may find that certain Indian people in the

TRAVELING THE PATH BACK TO THE ROAD IN THE SKY

past did, indeed, have 'strange experiences' and did actually 'journey across the sky'. The appearance of UFOs in the affairs of ancient people can easily explain such 'myths'.

The Indians who are now attempting to return to their ancient way of community life and religious beliefs as ordained for their ancestors by the One Great Spirit, realize that if they do not follow His way the prophecies of calamity for the future of this world may find them wanting. Countless stories of kindly people who came from lands 'beyond the sky' are to be found in their rich mythologies. No matter where you are in space, there is always *the other side of the sky* to be accounted for. When the Hopis were on another planet ('underworld'), the planet Earth was the land 'beyond the sky', now that they live on Earth all other planets are on 'the other side of the sky'.

In 1950-51 I lived with the Chippewa Indians of Minnesota, U.S.A. These people of the northern forests retain many stories of the 'GinGwin' or 'the objects which shake the earth'. The 'Gin-Gwin' were also called 'the earth rumblers', or 'flying boats'. The venerable old Chippewas still tell of the sacred 'Little People' in a whisper. These highly intelligent little men were supposed to have appeared in ancient times to the people of the Chippewa Nation. While they were with the Indians they taught them better ways of living. When I asked the old Indians why these wise beings are no longer seen (that was 1950), they told me: 'They don't come around much any more since the white man came.'

UFOs exist in the tales of almost all the American Indian tribes from Canada to Tierra del Fuego, and even in the legends of so-called primitive people all over the world. The Paiute and Navajo Indians of the American Southwest speak of the 'Havmusuvs' or the 'Little People' who came to Earth in 'Flying Boats' and carried sun-discs with them that carried some kind of a magic ray. The Sioux, Mandan, and Cherokee Tribes speak of the 'Little Wise People', and the Iroquois and other tribes relate tales of the 'sky dwellers' and the beautiful and wise 'Star People'.

The Machiguenga Indians of the tropical rainforests of eastern Peru speak of the 'people of the heavens who came (to Earth) on a shining *road in the sky*'.

The Quechua Indians of South America speak of the *Illa-Siva* or 'light rings' and the *Rampa-Liviac* or 'litters of electric energies' that were seen in the days of 'Lord Inca'.

TRAVELING THE PATH BACK TO THE ROAD IN THE SKY

We have already mentioned that the 'Plumed Serpent' is known all over North, Central, and South America. In many legends the 'Plumed Serpent' is the 'hissing serpent' that was 'cast to earth' in remote times. His symbol is not only found on Hopi kiva altars but was used by the prehistoric Mound Builders of Ohio and is found in the symbology of virtually every ancient people. It is interesting to note that the Hebrew word for *serpent* means: 'to hiss', or 'bright, fiery one'. There is a wealth of information on extra-terrestrial contact with Earth in the past if we search the legends and 'myths'. Like other stories found throughout the world, the Karens of Burma say that a 'white god' went off in a 'bright ship' and will return again soon. The 'white god' sounds like the Hopi *Massau,* and the 'bright ship' sounds like the 'Great Star'.

To really understand an Indian and his way of life, a white man must follow the words of G. B. Grinnell, in *Indians of Today* :

It is not easy for a white man, unless he has had some special train ing, to place himself on a level with the Indian, and learn how he thinks. Yet this must be done before we can understand him. To fully comprehend him, the investigator must cast aside all that he has been taught, and all that he has absorbed since childhood, must cease to be *artificial* and become *natural.* If one takes part with them in their daily lives, listening to the solemn prayers which they offer when they light the pipe, and joining with eye, ear and voice in the conversation that passes between those who form the circle, he (the white man) will gain an insight into a life and a method of thought that he did not suppose existed.

Ernest Thompson Seton, the world renowned authority on the beliefs and traditions of the American Indian, once said :

'The creed of the American Indian is all-inclusive... their gospel includes and surpasses all others... I am dedicating my life to the perpetuation of this creed.'

The words 'artificial' and 'natural' above, are the key words. All men must learn to be *natural* and live *a natural* life in the coming New Age on the Earth. When civilized man can live simply as the Creator intended, then he will begin to understand the phenomena of nature around him and in the skies above.

Evidently, Ernest Thompson Seton understood this key, for he dedicated his entire life to bringing the beautiful message of the Red man's creed

TRAVELING THE PATH BACK TO THE ROAD IN THE SKY

to all people everywhere. He is directly responsible for much of it being saved. Many of the legends and 'myths' of the Indian people, which are beautiful in the old way, would have been lost to us except for men like Seton and others. If the present trend in Indian affairs is not halted in Washington, D.C., I am afraid that many other phases of the Indian's culture will no longer be permitted to enrich the American way of life.

Recently, in the *Wall Street Journal,* Chief John Big Wind, one of the patriarchs of the Ojibway Tribe in Ontario, Canada, said :

'The white race is doomed to extinction if it does not change its ways! This time is not far *away.* People of the white race apparently hate work, they drink and smoke constantly, and they stay out all night and take each other's women. They kill each other in countless wars and on the highways. What is to become of them if they disobey the Great Spirit's Laws?'

This Indian chief is 94 years old, and was once given a medal by Queen Victoria because she liked his singing.

The famous Indian Chief, White Calf, once said:

'Before our people came in contact with the white people our nation was strong and powerful. They were successful in the hunt, they were healthy and vigorous, they were erect, and could walk straight and steady. They looked up, and not down. Their minds were clear, they could follow a straight line. Now, all is changed. They act like crazy people, they can't run, and they walk crookedly, they are on both sides of a straight line and not following it. They are excited and not calm. They are weak and helpless and fight one another and are destroying themselves. The white man's "firewater" or liquor has done the mischief.'

Lone Wolf, Chief of the Kiowa Nation, in 189i addressed a Christian Council near Anadarko, Oklahoma. He said:

'We shall expect great and good things from you and your teachings. Won't you share your life and sunshine with us? Won't you give us some of your joy?'

The 'great and good things' Chief Lone Wolf spoke of never manifested. The so-called 'Christian' white men answered the chief's request for 'life, sunshine, and joy' with 'death, darkness, and firewater'!

From the beginning of the contact between the White Race and the

TRAVELING THE PATH BACK TO THE ROAD IN THE SKY

Indian Race in North America, the Indian people attempted to learn all they could about the white man's way of life and his religious beliefs. They believed that there was *only* One Great Spirit and that the 'Great Father' of the white man must be the same Infinite Creator. They wanted to know how this Creator had manifested Himself to the White Race for the}, felt that they could thereby learn more of His Wisdom. The white man, on the other hand, always considered the Indian people as 'heathens' and 'savages'. Never once did a white man believe that the Indian's 'Great Spirit' was the same Creator he worshipped as the Father of Jesus, the Christ.

Tragic proof of this is found in the pitiful story of four Nez Perce Indians who traveled from their country in eastern Oregon and Washington in 1832 to St. Louis, Missouri.

The Indians had journeyed a great distance on foot to seek information on the white man's 'Great Father'. They wanted to find a white teacher who would go back with them and bring the 'Book of God' so that they might know what revelations had come to the White Race. One of the Indians, in speaking to General Clarke at St. Louis, said:

'I came to you over a trail of many moons from the setting sun (West). You were the friend of my fathers, who have all gone the long way. I came with one eye partly opened for more light for my people who sit in darkness. I go back with both eyes closed. How can I go back blind to my blind people ? I made my way to you with strong arms, through many enemies and strange lands, that I might carry back much to them. I go back with both arms broken and empty. The two fathers who came with me, the braves of many winters and wars, we leave asleep here by your great water (Mississippi River). They were tired in many moons and their moccasins wore out. My people sent me to get the white man's "Book from heaven". You took me where you allow your women to dance, as we do not ours... and the "Book" was not there. You showed me the images of good spirits, and pictures of the good land beyond... but the "Book" was not among them! When I tell my poor blind people, after one more snow, in the big council, that I did not bring the "Book", no word will be spoken by our old men or by our young braves. One by one they will rise up and go out in silence. My people will die in darkness, and they will go on the long path to the other hunting grounds. No white man will go with them, and no white man's "Book" to make the way plain. I have no more words.'

TRAVELING THE PATH BACK TO THE ROAD IN THE SKY

Not a single 'Book' or Holy Bible could be found in old St. Louis to give to these humble and seeking people. Instead, the Indians saw the white man living in a way that was disgraceful to the Indian Life Plan. They expected 'much' of the White Race and they got it... but it was something entirely different from that which they sought. Their land was stolen and they were deprived of all that was theirs including their very lives! Remember, all Indian tribes and all Indians are not alike. While the Hopis never went to battle and never killed, many tribes were composed of fierce warriors. Today, those tribes have disappeared while the Hopis live on. This is in accordance with the Law:

'... he that killeth with the sword must be killed with the sword...'

George Catlin, the famous traveler and artist, and painter of Indian portraits, came west in the Spring of 1833 to continue his work of preserving for the world the American Indian by means of his art. He joined the annual traders' caravan in which the two Indians mentioned above were returning to their land. Two of the old men had died in St. Louis, and the original Indian delegation of four dwindled to two.

Catlin travelled 2,000 miles with these Indians and liked them very much. One of the Indian men died near the mouth of the Yellowstone River on his way home. He had contracted a disease in 'civilization'. The lone survivor of the great journey across the Rocky Mountains arrived home safely and conveyed to his people the sad news of the death of the three men and the fact no 'Book' was to be found.

Catlin painted the portraits of the two men he knew on the journey and these are still preserved in the Smithsonian Institution, Washington, D.C. But Mr. Catlin did not learn the object of their mission to St. Louis until he returned to Pittsburgh the next Fall. He doubted the report, and so he wrote to his friend, General Clarke, who replied :

'Yes, the story is true; that was the only object of their visit to St. Louis.'

When George Catlin heard this be said. 'Publish this story to the world!'

Although this search for Truth on the part of the Nez Perce people ended in failure and later their lands were taken from them, something did occur shortly after i833 that gives the story a brighter aspect.

A Rev. Lee and a Rev. Spaulding heard about the Indian search and their great journey. In true Christian fashion they answered the call and took

TRAVELING THE PATH BACK TO THE ROAD IN THE SKY

their wives with them as they went by horseback across the wilderness of the Rocky Mountains. George Catlin talked with the Rev. and Mrs. Spaulding in Pittsburgh just before they left on their first missionary tour of the Nez Perce country. Catlin said:

'I believe our religion should be carried directly into the wilderness... beyond the reach and influence of civilization and its vices.'

Catlin saw the missionaries some years later, and they told him:

'The Indians in the native wilds are a kind and friendly people... we have shown the world that the Indians can be civilized and Christianized... we have always been treated with the utmost kindness and respect at all times during our stay with these native people.'

The great Chief Joseph of the Nez Perce Indians said that when his father was a young man, a missionary by the name of Rev. Spaulding who talked 'spirit law' came amongst them. Chief Joseph said that the Indians liked Spaulding very much because he 'told them good things'.

This same Rev. Spaulding met the father of Chief Joseph and learned that the Nez Perce Indians believed this young man had come to them from the 'star' we know as the planet Saturn.

I know of an old Yakima Indian Chief who still tells this story and says that the legends of the Nez Perce and the Yakimas definitely state that the father of Chief Joseph was not a man of Earth but came from Saturn. Little is known of the father, but history has recorded the greatness of the son, for Chief Joseph was one of the greatest men who ever lived, white or Indian.

Wouldn't it be strange indeed if Rev. Spaulding contacted a people who had already encountered intelligences from outer space? And if they had, why did they send a delegation to look for the white man's 'Book'? There is undoubtedly more to this story than we will ever know.

The Hopi Indians of Arizona are surrounded by the aggressive Navajo Tribe. These Indians are in no way similar to their Hopi neighbors, for they are a nomadic people who never live in villages, and their religion, customs, language, dress, rituals, etc., are completely different. There is no more similarity culturally between a man from England and a man from China than there is between a Hopi and a Navajo.

However, like the Hopis, the Navajo people retain a rich mythology

TRAVELING THE PATH BACK TO THE ROAD IN THE SKY

which obviously contains references to extra-terrestrial contact with their tribe in the ancient past.

The Navajos believe they came from the 'underworld' about 3,000 years ago. (This would be close to the time of Moses and the Exodus from Egypt in 1233 B.C.). The Navajos have Four Sacred Mountains: La Platte Mountain, Colorado; Mount Taylor, New Mexico; Navajo Mountain, near the border of Utah-Arizona; and the San Francisco Peaks, near Flagstaff, Arizona.

The first and greatest god of the Navajos is *Hastchazinna.* His name means 'black' or 'dark' and he lives under the Earth in burning pitch and fire. He controls all 'lights' and all heavenly bodies that shine belong to him.

Another great god of the Navajo people is the youthful *Bakochiddy.* This god has light hair, reddish-blond. He is in charge of 'serpents' and 'all flying things'. Like *Hastchazinna,* he is also in charge of all the skies and the stars and rain. This youthful god is very interesting because his activities are very much the same as those of the Christian Messiah. *Bakochiddy* is known as a 'white god'. The Navajos say he now lives in the 'rainbow', and that he 'ascended up into heaven by himself' and now looks down on them.

The initiated medicine men recognize a hidden or secret meaning behind the Navajo gods which is different from that which they give to the members of their tribe.

The Navajos speak of a 'white mountain' that raised up in ancient times and gave 'light' to their ancestors when they were in darkness in the 'underworld'.

Another Navajo god is *Bekitedizza,* or 'the god who had something wrapped around him'. He lives where the 'rainbow' is. He is intimately connected in Indian mythology with the blond god *Bakochiddy,* and the Navajos say he called their leaders together in a meeting long ago and proclaimed an important message to them.

There are legends that speak of the 'six gods' who lived in the 'white mountain' that goes up and down. This home of the gods would emit 'black, dark smoke and flames of fire'.

While the Hopis say they climbed to the country on 'the other side of the sky' on a 'reed ladder', the Navajos say they climbed to the 'upper world' on 'bamboo' that penetrated the 'hole to the Earth'. The Navajos say that

TRAVELING THE PATH BACK TO THE ROAD IN THE SKY

when they first came to the Earth it was covered with water and there were places covered with mud and scattered rocks, and there was darkness on the Earth and the only light the people had was the light from a great 'comet' which was a 'campfire' of a god.

Now the 'white mountain' is supposed to be near La Platte Mountain in Colorado, and the legends say that in the ancient past there was a 'star' with a great 'fire tail' on it in the centre of 'white mountain'.

Several gods are said to have placed 'lightning and the rainbow' over their lodge so that these things 'arched over the lodge'. Gods are also said to have lived inside of great mountains, and a great god who made the Sun, Moon, and stars, placed human life or beings on all celestial bodies so they would be inhabited like the Earth. The Navajos never describe other planets except to say that they are 'points of life'.

The blond god, *Bakochiddy,* told the ancient Navajos:

'The mountains you shall hold sacred. You shall mention them in your prayers and your chants, and, as time goes on, at different periods I shall appear again to you and take note of your doings'.

The Navajos say that the story of *Bakochiddy is* very ancient and has nothing to do with Christian influence. However, this god did go up to heaven, and he has blond hair, white skin, and blue-grey eyes. He is said to have brought white, yellow and black children among the people who came from the 'underworld'. (This sounds like three races of mankind, and the people from the 'underworld' would have been a fourth race, or the 'Red Race'.) The white, yellow and black children grew up to be young men and *Bakochiddy* said they were to teach the ancestors of the Navajos many different things. It is said that *Bakochiddy* could cause the white and yellow children to 'float up in the sky by his breath', but the black child would not go up. The children all lived on a mountain with *Bakochiddy.*

The Navajos speak of great giants called *Yaitso,* who came upon the Earth and of *one-eyed* giants and an 'immense bird with wings' that was called *Tsenahala.* They do not know if the 'bird with wings' was really a bird or not, they only say it was a 'creature with great wings'. Giants were supposed to live near what is now Laguna, New Mexico, in a place called *Tosito.* Laguna is south-east of Mount Taylor, one of the sacred mountains of the Navajo people. The 'immense bird with wings' lived on top of *Tsepitai,* or 'the rock with wings'. This rock is known today as 'Ship Rock' in New Mexico.

TRAVELING THE PATH BACK TO THE ROAD IN THE SKY

As we study this mixture of mythological lore, we begin to see the same old similar pattern. The Navajos say they came from the 'underworld' about 3,000 years ago. This would mean they arrived on Earth about the same time as the Hopis and about the time of the Exodus from Egypt. Did these people also arrive from outer space? One of the four Sacred Mountains of the Navajo people is the San Francisco Mountain (Peaks) of Arizona which is also sacred to the Hopis.

The first and greatest Navajo god, *Hastchazinna,* sounds like a reference to Lucifer-Maldek, who was also 'black' and 'dark' and was enveloped in 'burning pitch and fire'. This god is supposed to control all 'lights' and all heavenly bodies that shine belong to him. This sounds like a reference to Lucifer-Maldek, a 'corrupt planet' that attempted to bring all other 'heavenly bodies that shine' and heavenly 'lights' under its control. This is also mentioned in Isaiah xiv:13,14:

'For thou hast said in thine heart, I will ascend into heaven, I will exalt my throne above the stars of God : I will sit also upon the mount of the congregation, in the sides of the north : I will ascend above the heights of the clouds; I will be like the most High.'

Youthful *Bakochiddy* with the blond hair, the white skin, and the blue-grey eyes, sounds like a *visitant.* The fact he is in charge of 'serpents' (Plumed Serpent?) and 'all flying things' indicates this. Also, he is connected with the sky, the stars and the rain. He is supposed to live in the 'rainbow' and he ascended up to heaven by himself and now looks down on the Navajos. It is said that *Bakochiddy* made all of his travels by the 'light of the rainbow' in a miraculous way. 'Ascending into heaven' and travelling by the 'light of the rainbow' sounds very much like UFO activity and is not unlike the experience of Ezekiel in the Old Testament. *Bakochiddy* caused the children to 'float up in the sky by his breath'. Here is another indication that the blond god had power over things in the air. Remember, this god told the ancient Navajos: '... as time goes on, at different periods, I shall appear again to you and take note of your doings.' This is an obvious reference to a *visitant* who promised to return and help the people when they needed him. *Bakochiddy is* said to have helped the Navajos while they were still in the 'underworld'. The fact that a 'white mountain' raised up and gave them 'light' when they were in the darkness of that 'underworld', may indicate *Bakochiddy* was from another more highly advanced world and came to help the Navajos journey to the 'upper world' or the Earth. Another indication that this may be true is

TRAVELING THE PATH BACK TO THE ROAD IN THE SKY

the fact that the god was 'blond' and of a different race.

I wonder what 'secrets' the medicine men know *today* about the Navajo gods that the tribal members are unaware of?

Bakochiddy's associate is *Bekitedizza,* or 'the god who had something wrapped around him' and he lives where the 'rainbow' is. The 'something wrapped around' the god could refer to the force field of a UFO, and the home in the 'rainbow' could easily refer to the origin point of space craft. The fact that a contact with outer space intelligences outside the sphere of the Navajos was made is indicated by the fact that *Bekitedizza* 'called the Navajo leaders together in a meeting long ago and proclaimed an important message to them'. If the Navajos came from outer space themselves, they were 'visitants' in a sense, also. However, there are many indications that the later Navajo 'gods' had originally been intelligences much more highly advanced than even the ancestors of the Navajos and they arrived on the scene just prior to the destruction of Lucifer-Maldek to assist some of the people in their journey to Earth.

The Navajos are not the only ones who say that when they first came to the Earth it was covered with water, mud and scattered rocks. The Zuni Indians of New Mexico say the same thing, and certain Hopi legends say that there was mud on the Earth when they first arrived. The Navajos may be referring to the period just after the destruction of Lucifer-Maldek when they say there was 'darkness on the Earth' and the only light their ancestors had was the light from a great 'comet' that was supposed to be a 'campfire' of a god. After the planet Lucifer-Maldek exploded a large portion of it, or a great meteoric fragment, headed for the Earth and divided into smaller fragments, which were called 'fiery flying serpents' by the ancients because as they watched them in the heavens approaching the Earth, they did, indeed, look like flaming dragons or snakes. The catastrophe of Lucifer-Maldek could have caused floods which produced the 'mud and scattered rocks' and could have caused the 'darkness on the Earth', and the great 'comet' or 'campfire' of a god could easily refer to the enormous meteoric fragment seen in the skies of Earth. Of course, originally, the ancestors of the Navajos knew perfectly well what was taking place, but later generations did not understand the ancient happenings and the legends now are interpreted in the light of 'gods' and 'rain', and even the *visitant Bakochiddy* became a 'blond god'. However, the very fact that the Navajos say all this took place 3,000 years ago is amazing, for we find that such occurrences were taking place on Earth

TRAVELING THE PATH BACK TO THE ROAD IN THE SKY

in 1233 B.C. that exactly fit the Navajo legendary accounts.

Another indication that the Navajos arrived on Earth during the time of the Exodus and the destruction of Lucifer-Maldek, is the fact that their legends say that *Bakochiddy* traveled to a place known as the 'red earth' which was on the planet Earth; the god noticed the ground was red all around. In *Other Tongues—Other Flesh, I* said: 'One of the first visible signs on Earth of the destruction of Maldek was the *reddening of the Earth's surface by* a fine dust of rusty pigment.'

The 'star' with a great 'fire tail' that was seen by the ancestors of the Navajo people in the centre of 'white mountain' could refer to space craft, but it more likely refers to the 'comet' spoken of above which was a meteoric fragment headed for the Earth. Its position in the heavens might make it appear to be in the 'centre' of 'white mountain'.

Other indications of UFO force fields might be found in the references to the 'lightning and the rainbow' being placed over the lodge of the gods, for they 'arched over' the lodge.

The home of the gods that was a 'white mountain' which went 'up and down' and emitted 'black, dark smoke and flames of fire' sounds like a gigantic space craft.

Bakochiddy told the Navajos that they should hold the mountains sacred and he lived on top of one of the mountains for a while himself. Different gods are said to have lived *inside* the mountains. There is a similarity here with the African legends that speak of 'tall people' living *inside* of Mount Kilimanjaro, and the Hopi legends of the Kachinas who live in the San Francisco Mountain (also a sacred mountain of the Navajos).

Evidently, the Navajos accept the fact that beings like themselves live on other worlds in space. This is clearly indicated by the fact that one of their important gods placed human life or beings on all celestial bodies so they would be inhabited like the Earth. Also, when the Navajos describe other planets by calling them 'points of life' there can be no question that they accept life on other worlds, and life forms like their own.

The reference to the 'white, yellow and black children' who 'grew up to be young men' and were to teach the Navajos 'many different things' may indicate that after the Navajos arrived on the Earth they were instructed by the people of other races.

TRAVELING THE PATH BACK TO THE ROAD IN THE SKY

The *Yaitso,* or giants, sound like the giant men we have already mentioned as existing in different parts of the world in ancient times. The 'one-eyed' giants may have been the 'El's'! Since giants once lived near what is now Laguna, New Mexico, we find that they are somehow connected with Mount Taylor which is only about twenty miles from the legendary home of the giants.

Since the Navajos do not know if *Tsenahala* was really a bird or not, it is possible that this 'creature with great wings' that lived on top of 'Ship Rock' in New Mexico, represents a UFO that landed on this rock in the ancient past. But is that the real explanation? It could be, but what if *Tsenahala* really was an 'immense bird with wings' like some fantastic pterodactyl or flying reptile out of the remote Jurassic Period?

Again we find our old pattern of 'strange beings', 'high places', fault lines, and space ships.

The gods and the giants are the 'strange beings', the Four Sacred Mountains of the Navajos are the 'high places', traveling by the 'light of the rainbow', and *Bakochiddy* of the sky is related to the space ships, and there is the same great *fault line* that goes through the area of the San Francisco Peaks.

The legends of the Navajo people speak of a dim *yesterday* in the same way that the 'myths' of other Indian tribes relate their shadowy beginnings. However, the Navajos like their neighbors, speak of *today* and *tomorrow,* for there have been numerous sightings of UFOs in recent years as these craft hovered over their Four Sacred Mountains. Sightings have been especially frequent over the San Francisco Peaks and Navajo Mountain. One time a large UFO came close to the Earth and many Navajos ran out to greet it, but it started to rise and rapidly disappeared in the sky. The Indians were in no way frightened by this strange craft-on the contrary. When they were questioned about their running out to it, they said : 'We were not afraid of that object, for there are people in those flying "lights", and those are the people our legends tell us we are waiting for'! The *road in the sky* of *yesterday* is active again *today!*

These are just a few of the stories that have been passed down from generation to generation among the native people of North America. I have heard many more. Some I believe I understand, others, I know I do not understand. I have heard them around the campfires and around the Trading Posts of the American Southwest, and I have heard from the lips of my Na-

TRAVELING THE PATH BACK TO THE ROAD IN THE SKY

vajo friends the fact that they are waiting, waiting, waiting, for those friendly people who travel by the 'light of the rainbow'.

The Indian people have really been guilty of only one sin, they had possessions that the white man coveted, and they moved away towards the west and the setting sun to give up their homes to their white brother. But 'as the lightning cometh out of the *east,* and shineth even unto the *west'*, '... The pale and the red shall be brothers, One's rights shall be as another's...' The 'points of life' in interstellar space smile upon the Red Man from *the other side of the sky* and promise him a new life in a brighter *tomorrow.*

TRAVELING THE PATH BACK TO THE ROAD IN THE SKY

THE UNHOLY SIX

"...Believe in Orion. Believe.

In the night, the moon, the crowded Earth.

Believe in Christmas and Birthdays and Easter rabbits.

Believe in all those fugitive

Compounds of nature, all doomed

To waste away and go out.

Always be true to these things."

(Modern School of Poetry).

ONCE upon a time-five hundred thousand years ago!

Again we have a fairyland opening because we are going to tell you another so-called 'unbelievable tale'. This one will be easier for you to accept because the date or age of our story is more in accordance with what 'authorities' and 'experts' consider sane guessing. Prepare yourself for a tale of a dark time in our galaxy, when the 'spawn of night' brought about a fork in the road in the sky causing the timeless highway of the stars to divide into two branches going in opposite directions.

Once upon a time-five hundred thousand years ago there was a planet in space called **Tyrantor**. This planet had been the capital of an old and decadent Empire of the Stars in the Milky Way galaxy. I say had been because half a million years ago it came to an end.

If you will permit, let us go back for a moment to a time about one

TRAVELING THE PATH BACK TO THE ROAD IN THE SKY

million years ago. One of the most notable achievements of the life forms of our galaxy, after the 'El's' achieved their state of Timelessness, was the formation of what has been called the Galactic Administration or the Galactic Pax. In Latin, Pax means 'Peace', and was deified by the Romans. Although the Romans were an aggressive and warlike people, they deified 'Pax' which symbolized the great peaceful amalgamation of numerous solar systems into the Galactic Administration.

About one million years ago, this league of planets reached the apex of its power and beneficent influence. Like the Romans who were to follow them in later times, the people belonging to the many planets of the Administration started to look for the 'easy life'. They were in the exalted position of representing the most advanced beings throughout millions of miles of interstellar space. The inevitable happened, a degeneration of their culture and their way of life began.

The beginning of the end came for the Galactic Pax when a master computer system or mechanical brain was put into operation on a planet called Tyrantor. All the complex problems of co-ordination and organization existing within the Administration were to be solved by the new calculating device that covered many square miles of the surface of Tyrantor.

All went well for a time, but the Administration leaders from all the planets of the league began to place more and more reliance on the computer; there was more 'Play' time for them while the great metal brain solved all matters of governing and even solved matters pertaining to diet, dress, and sex. Day after day, year after year, and century after century, the computer toiled on calculating, calculating, calculating. The Administration was disintegrating quickly, and many of the more serious-minded members of the Galactic Pax realized that something should be done immediately. They formed a delegation and presented their warning to the Tribunal. They suggested that the only solution was to abandon the master computer completely and continue as they had in the days before its existence when they were in the Golden Age of their Administration. They were considered insane by the Tribunal for offering such a suggestion. Can you imagine telling people today to destroy their electric power plants and start living with candles again!

The unsuccessful delegation saw the government of the galaxy crumbling about them, everywhere they saw much evidence of the decay and

TRAVELING THE PATH BACK TO THE ROAD IN THE SKY

death of a great civilization. They wanted to pull away from the Administration, but they didn't know where to go, and besides, they felt they must stay on as long as possible. There was always the faint hope that something could be done and that the Tribunal would realize the master computer system which was to be the crowning achievement of their rule in the galaxy, had become instead, a Frankenstein, a monster that was inflicting the most dreadful retribution upon its creators. The metallic governor of the Administration was destroying its originators.

When the entire way of life was in the worst throes of depression and decadence, a small group of scientists on Tyrantor who were in charge of the functioning of the master computer decided to take over the Galactic Administration through the use of the computer and thereby rule the people of many planets. They would be the real rulers, while the mechanical brain they controlled would be the puppet of the Empire. They knew that the people-most of them anyway-would never question orders coming from the computer, for they had followed such orders for centuries and knew nothing else. They wanted and expected the computer to do all their thinking for them.

Therefore, the insurrection took place quietly without war or strife one day when the master computer began to send out the new order of the day, declaring the birth of the Galactic Empire. At this moment, the 'spawn of night' or the forces behind the downfall of the Administration, caused a fork in the shining road in the sky that had known existence since the time of the 'El's'. Never once had there been a division in this highway of the stars that linked world after world and system after system in a peaceful brotherhood which eventually became the great and good Galactic Pax.

The day the Empire was born, two roads were also created in the heavens, or, we should say, two branches of the same road going in opposite directions. The people were no longer united, for they were opposed by contradiction, a dichotomy was established that still exists in the galaxy today.

The planet Tyrantor became the terminus planet or rainbow's end for the newly created Empire. From the name of this planet we derived our word tyrant which comes to us from the Greek tyrannos, originally meaning 'Lord'. The scientists in charge of the computer became absolute rulers through its use. The mechanical brain that was to enrich the life of the Administration

TRAVELING THE PATH BACK TO THE ROAD IN THE SKY

and bring its people to a state of perpetual bliss, became a cruel despot, a usurper of peaceful sovereignty, a mechanical master.

Tyrantor became the Lord of the Empire and its master computer became the oppressor of the former happy people. Our words tyranny, tyrannical, etc., also come from the name of the terminus planet. Tyr, the war-god of Norse mythology, also obtained his name from the same source. Like all despotic exercise of power, the Empire began in a grand way. The people were constantly looking for new thrills and changes in their life that had grown rather dull under the old and peaceful Administration. The downfall of the Galactic Pax was to them an entertainment, an exciting drama that they enjoyed to the fullest. Therefore, they hailed the new Empire with much enthusiasm and joy. In fact, they celebrated the event for many years, and when they finally woke up they discovered the Empire was brutally exercising absolute power over them and draining their respective worlds of natural resources and manpower to be able to travel its own branch in the road in the sky to new conquests throughout the galaxy.

Tyrantor and its tyrant brain became a terror throughout space. A great military force was assembled, and where justice, peace, brotherhood and love had ruled before, it was replaced by criminal piracy and fear, dread and hate ruled the day. Almost immediately, the Empire began to disintegrate. One by one, hundreds of planets and systems refused to pay tribute to the capital planet, but they continued to be robbed by the space pirates until they joined together with the remnant of the former Galactic Administration that had never become a part of the Empire and represented the other branch of the road in the sky. This remnant became known as the Confederation, and it grew large and strong as many planets joined the rebellion and withdrew from the Empire and the domination of the master computer system.

The rulers on Tyrantor attempted to regain control of their diminishing authority and power by the most terrible space war imaginable. But planet after planet continued to withdraw their allegiance and joined the Confederation. Soon, the pirates of the Empire were greatly outnumbered and were unable to pursue their former activities. The greatest scientist on Tyrantor was the Emperor. The new and powerful Confederation, which was attempting to re-establish the way of life of the Galactic Pax, advised the Emperor and the tyrants of the Empire to abandon the pattern and policies created through the use of the mechanical despot. The advice was refused.

TRAVELING THE PATH BACK TO THE ROAD IN THE SKY

Eventually, the inevitable took place, just as it had in the days of the Administration. The Empire continued to shrink until only six solar systems with their six respective star-suns were still governed by the master computer on Tyrantor. Conditions became dreadful on the capital world and civil war developed between the computer scientists. Finally, the Emperor destroyed himself and the entire planet and its Frankenstein in one fantastic act of tyrannicide. This was the end of Empire.

All of this brings us to: Once upon a time-five hundred thousand years ago.

The rulers of the six solar systems refused to accept the reality that the Empire was dead. They still expected to receive orders from the Emperor and the master computer on Tyrantor although all of these had been destroyed. After finally accepting the fact that the capital planet was gone for ever along with the great computer, they began to place in operation the sub-computers of their own worlds, and they hoped to rebuild the Empire once again with the six solar systems as the centre of operations. However, they never succeeded in obtaining the allegiance of even one other system or planet. The power of the Empire was shattered for ever, and the six systems remaining had to depend on each other for survival. They became known as The Unholy Six.

Half a million years ago the Empire and Tyrantor came to an abrupt end. The power of the master computer was gone, although the sub-computers continued to be used. The six remaining systems of the 'spawn of night' or The Unholy Six are located in the vicinity of the Great Nebula in Orion. This nebula is within our Milky Way Galaxy and is known as a galactic and diffuse nebula. It is vast, gaseous, greenish and of irregular form.

In Other Tongues-Other Flesh, I discussed the Orion systems in The Intruders.

'The negative space intelligences from Orion are not coming directly from the nebula itself, but are coming from planets of star-suns (six) in the vicinity of Orion. The word "Orion" is used by space visitors (Confederation) to indicate the general area from which the evil influences originate.'

Orion is mentioned in the Bible and in countless ancient legends. To the ancient Egyptians, in the V Dynasty, the constellation of Orion was Sahu, hunting through the heavens for gods and men to rip apart and boil for food. This sounds very much like The Unholy Six attempting to obtain the alle-

TRAVELING THE PATH BACK TO THE ROAD IN THE SKY

giance of other systems and planets.

The Hebrews knew Orion as Kesil, the 'Foolish or Self-Confident', or as Gibbor, the Giant, identified with Nimrod and tied to the heavens for impiety.

An ancient Peruvian legend says the constellation of Orion is a criminal held in the heavens by two condors.

The natural resources of The Unholy Six are almost exhausted; they have lived on borrowed time for 500,000 years and their end is near. What started out as a fight to gain control has now turned into a struggle for survival. The situation for The Unholy Six becomes more critical every day, and the rulers are demanding action. They must have resources! These rulers are not tolerant and friendly beings by any means, and they watch the Earth planet, rich in mineral wealth, with greedy eyes.

War rages on the Orion systems now, and they feel that the powerful Space Confederation is encroaching on their domain. However, the encroachment they imagine is really freedom from oppression which narrows down the area of their tyranny.

The descendants of the decadent Empire are found on six solar systems in the vicinity of the Orion Nebula, and the descendants of those in the Galactic Administration who formed the Confederation are today found in the UFOs in our skies. They still belong to what is called the Space Confederation.

The Orion forces comprising The Unholy Six would like to trade with the Earth, but they prefer doing it when there are no inhabitants on our planet with whom to negotiate. In other words, if they could, they would come to Earth and eliminate all life forms on it and then land and use our planet as a great storehouse of natural resources. They would literally take away the animal, vegetable and mineral life of the Earth. The rulers of The Unholy Six want to follow the ancient trail through space that leads to the grandeur of the "El's". They know that under the Earth the crystalline world of the great Time-Spanners still waits to be re-discovered, and they know that the secrets of this subterranean world would give them immortality. Therefore, the Earth planet is a great prize to them and they want to capture it. However, the Space Confederation and its many craft operating around the Earth prevents any outside interference with the Divine Plan now being fulfilled here.

TRAVELING THE PATH BACK TO THE ROAD IN THE SKY

The Confederation has its agents upon the Earth at the present time, and The Unholy Six through its control of the minds of various individuals also has a spy system of a sort. Remember, in Other Tongues-Other Flesh, space intelligences said:

At the present time there is a small group of people on Earth working for Orion. They come among you to disperse all things not in keeping with their own ideas, they prey on the unsuspecting, they astound intellects with their words of magnificence; while their wisdom may have merit, it is materialistic and not of pure aspiration towards the Father. We have our own men of the Confederation who watch over these pirates. Watch out for controlled persons in your midst. The Orion people are The Intruders in your world, they cannot enter your atmosphere usually by space craft, but they can and do reach the Earth world by projecting their intelligence into weak Earthly bodies which they completely control for short periods of time in order to perform their disturbances. Watch for them; their numbers increase as the 'sorrows' of Earth increase; they will persist, but they will not succeed. We will succeed, for our mission is of the Father's authority and His will shall prevail. Worry not about these Orion influences; they cannot harm those who serve the Infinite Father.

While some of the individuals working today to disrupt the plans of the Space Confederation on the Earth are serving the International Bankers, others are agents of The Unholy Six. They are The Intruders. The sub-computers, or the children of the master computer, long since destroyed along with Tyrantor, are still in operation today, and many sensitives on the Earth who claim to be in communication with a certain 'great being of space who commands literally millions of space craft, etc.', are actually receiving information from the sub-computer system. These sensitives mistake a channel of communication used by many beings for a single individual. This is due mainly to the fact that many people on Earth insist upon identification and personification.

It is true that there is much knowledge being relayed by the sub-computers to Earth's sensitives, but remember the words of the Space Confederation: 'They astound intellects with their words of magnificence. While their wisdom may have merit, it is materialistic and not of pure aspiration towards the Father...' Of course, there are also many sensitives who are undoubtedly receiving information and inspiration from the forces of light; that is another matter altogether.

TRAVELING THE PATH BACK TO THE ROAD IN THE SKY

A very sinister part of the operations of The Unholy Six is their use of black crystalline life forms which absorb light, but do not generate or reflect any light themselves. These are used as a prime focus for the projection of their intelligence into weak Earthly bodies. The astounding confirmation of this is the fact that in psychological case studies black and gigantic crystals have been mentioned over and over again by patients. The black crystals are used in connection with the sub-computers.

If we look for the real cause behind the conflict between the Space Confederation and The Unholy Six, we find that the former are Deists and the latter are Ideists. The Deists maintain that there is one single power or Deity of the Omniverse of which all life is a part. The Ideists maintain that the Id or personal creating power of the individual is supreme and that all things are created and put into action by the power of the Individual. They refuse to accept the concept that a Universal power exists. For countless millennia there have been no possibilities of reconciliation between these groups and their beliefs. This brings us to the point where we must introduce a third group.

The dichotomy we spoke of before has been referred to as the Blacks and the Whites. The Blacks represent The Unholy Six forces and the Whites represent the Space Confederation forces.

However, a trichotomy really exists, and the third group is called the Golds. We find that everything in nature appears to be composed of three divisions. For instance, the nature of man is divided into body, soul, and spirit (physical, mental, and spiritual); and there are the animal, vegetable, and mineral kingdoms; and the Holy Trinity.

The Golds are also called the Arbiters. They have the power to decide a dispute and determine the outcome of a certain action on the part of the Blacks and the Whites.

The Wanderers we spoke of in Other Tongues-Other Flesh belong to the Whites since they aid the plan of the Space Confederation. The Intruders belong to the Blacks since they aid the disturbing, but ineffective, plan of The Unholy Six (Orion). The Golds or Arbiters are impartial for they give aid to neither plan nor cause, and they work through what is known as the Bureau. The Arbiters sometimes use the color green—this is when operational action is required of them. Gold is their usual color of passive arbitration and observation. It will be difficult for many people to think of something that does not fit into the black or white dichotomy, but the third group exists as surely as every triangle has an apex.

The Arbiters incarnate on the Earth in the same way as The Wanderers who belong to the Whites. However, while many Wanderers are on the Earth, very few Arbiters or Gold forces have taken up Earth bodies, but there are a few, here and there.

The entire plan now being worked out can be likened to a gigantic chessboard in Time where the Blacks and Whites move alternately, governed by the decisions awarded by the Golds.

The action to take place in the New Age upon this Earth brought about through the work of the Arbiters will settle the desires of the Whites and of the Blacks. Ultimate satisfaction may not be realized by either group, but the major problems and questions will be settled and adjudicated.

Recently, I received a report that is very interesting when we consider the strange case of Karl Hunrath and Wilbur J. Wilkinson who disappeared on November 11, 1953. This famous case is well known in the UFO field, and is related in detail in Other Tongues Other Flesh.

The two men took off in a rented aeroplane from Gardena Airport in November 11th with a three-hour gas supply. Despite widespread search, no trace of the plane or its occupants was seen until a sheriff's posse observed an aeroplane that fitted the description of the missing craft. The men were some distance from the plane when they first saw it, and when they arrived at the location it was gone, although there were indications that some kind of activity had taken place in the area recently.

About December 5, 1953, a mysterious fire swept over the Gardena Airport where Hunrath and Wilkinson had procured their plane. The reports stated that the fire had been started by a mysterious blinding white light. Even more mysterious was the fact that this fire destroyed all the records that dealt with the rental of the plane to Hunrath and Wilkinson.

At this writing, no one knows if the two men are alive or not. Hunrath still has many loyal followers in Los Angeles who believe he is safe and sound on Mars or some other planetary haven. Some people believe the two men are in Mexico, or England, or even in the United States. We showed in Other Tongues-Other Flesh that Karl Hunrath was a brilliant scientist when the forces of The Unholy Six desired to use him for some purpose, and a not too

TRAVELING THE PATH BACK TO THE ROAD IN THE SKY

bright electrician when these forces left him and he became 'himself'. In other words, Hunrath fits The Intruder pattern and was working as an agent for the Blacks of six solar systems of the Orion Nebula.

I wonder what caused that 'mysterious blinding white light' that destroyed the records dealing with the rental of the doomed aeroplane? What black crystalline life form was used on which of the six systems to accomplish that act? We can only guess the answer, but it seems obvious.

While The Unholy Six is having some influence in the world today, it is of little concern in the overall plan, for these forces have had their day under the sun and that day has been 500,000 years of continuing decadence. Their sun is about to set, and their day is done. Their power is momentary now as the Earth prepares for its Graduation Day, its Purification Day.

However, the Blacks or the spawn of night of the old Empire... are the spirits of devils, working miracles, which go forth unto the kings of the earth and of the whole world, to gather them to the battle of that great day of God Almighty.' (Revelation xvi : i4).

The Space Confederation now operating around the Earth contains fifty-one solar systems consisting of six hundred and eight planets controlling some three and a half million space craft. We have little to fear from The Unholy Six. I doubt if they will ever obtain any of the natural resources of Earth. However, these so-called evil worlds have served a great purpose. Those beings who have incarnated on the planets of the six systems have greatly benefited by the experience, and we see in the history of oppression and tyranny eventual good. It has been said: 'Sufficient unto the day is the evil thereof', and for The Unholy Six it has been but a single 'day' lasting for half a million years!

The 'El's' had their day under the sun, but for them the sun didn't set—they lifted themselves above the realm of Suns. They achieved the fundamental steps to divinity.

Hu-manity has had the beginnings of its day under the sun and now that day rapidly draws to a close. The outcome depends on whether or not hu-man beings will successfully take the first steps towards divinity. If the sun does set for the Hu-man Race without that first step being taken, hu-man beings will become simply another past race of potentially intelligent beings and recorded in the Book of Creation as 'a promising child, died in its youth'. And the eternal workers will go on to another day under the sun of

TRAVELING THE PATH BACK TO THE ROAD IN THE SKY

another promising race-child. Sooner or later another major race will make the grade or take the first step to divinity even as the 'El's' did a long time ago. So goes evolution up the stars and ELevation to the spheres of Timelessness.

But we have the promise of the Infinite Father that the Hu-man Race will achieve divinity: so it has been recorded by the scribes in all ages and in all civilizations on Earth.

I don't believe Henry Havelock Ellis would accept the fact that hu-man beings could become divine, for in The Dance of Life, he said:

The sun and the moon and the stars would have disappeared long ago had they happened to be within the reach of predatory human hands.

He is so right. But the predatory hands will not reach out for the crown of divinity. They will fall back into the dust from whence they came. The radiant energy of the Universe will rise like a majestic fountain in the spirit of the remnant that is to inherit the New Age on a New World, the remnant that forgets self in love for all fellow beings everywhere.

Go ahead and Believe in Orion. Believe in the night, the moon, the crowded Earth. Believe in all those fugitive Compounds of nature, all doomed to waste away and go out. Always be true to these things.' But don't forget the eternal road in the sky that soon shall know neither fork nor branch nor division. It will be the one, never-ending pathway to godhood in a golden tomorrow.

TRAVELING THE PATH BACK TO THE ROAD IN THE SKY

COUNTED, WEIGHED, AND DIVIDED

'One God; One Law; One Element; and

One far-off Divine Event to which the whole Creation moves.'

(Inscription, Dome of the Library of Congress, Washington, D.C., U.S.A.)

IN the same hour came forth fingers of a man's hand, and wrote over against the candlestick upon the plaster of the wall of the king's palace: and the king saw the part of the hand that wrote. And this is the writing that was written, MENE, MENE, TEKEL, UPHARSIN. This is the interpretation of the thing: MENE, God hath numbered (counted) thy kingdom, and finished it. TEKEL, Thou art weighed in the balances, and art found wanting. PERES, Thy kingdom is divided, and given to the Medes and Persians. (Daniel v: 5, 25, 26, 27, 28).

The cryptic handwriting on the wall was a message in Aramaic to King Belshazzar of the Neo-Babylonian (Chaldean) Empire. It meant: *Counted, Weighed, and Divided.*

Today, we find that the handwriting of our era is on the wall of Time! The modern kingdom of atheistic materialism has been *counted,* and it is finished, the advocates of godless civilization have been *weighed,* and are found wanting, this kingdom *today* has been *divided,* but to whom shall it be given tomorrow?

'Belshazzar the king made a great feast to a thousand of his lords, and drank wine before the thousand. Then they brought the golden vessels that were taken out of the temple of the house of God which was at Jerusalem; and the king, and his princes, his wives, and his concubines, drank in them.

TRAVELING THE PATH BACK TO THE ROAD IN THE SKY

They drank wine, and praised the gods of gold, and of silver, of brass, of iron, of wood, and of stone.' (Daniel v: 1, 3, 4).

The golden vessels represent the many divine Commandments and Truths of God that have been defiled by the drunkenness of the modern princes who enslave man on the Earth and are leading him down the pathway of physical, mental, and spiritual destruction.

The night the handwriting on the wall appeared in the palace of the king, ominous sounds were heard by the drunken nobles, ominous sounds coming from the great *road* that led into mighty and voluptuous Babylon, city of captivity. The handwriting from God served as an omen of impending calamity, and the sounds from the *road* heralded imminent doom, for the marching Persian host was nearing the gates of Babylon and 'In that night was Belshazzar the king of the Chaldeans slain'.

Today, as in the time of the fall of Babylon, men of the world are drinking wine and are praising gods of gold, and of silver. The modern handwriting on the wall should be sufficient to warn them, but it has been truly said that the signs of God are for those who discern them. It might also be said that such signs are for those who *deserve* them. Remember, Belshazzar could not interpret the meaning of the writing nor could his wise men, only Daniel knew the interpretation for the spirit of god was in him.

The blessed meek, the peaceful ones, they have the spirit of god within them, and they see the handwriting on the wall of today that foreshadows the end of our kingdom. Not only do they *see* worldly conditions that are omens of impending calamity, but they *hear* the sounds from the *road in the sky* that now leads to the very gates of modern Babylon, sounds that once again herald imminent doom for the drunken and freedom for the captives.

The Persian host freed the exiles and the captives of Daniel's time and sent them home to Palestine. Now, a different kind of host presses on towards the gates of tyranny and oppression. Modern Babylon will fall and the captives of *today* will be free to move on towards their own Promised Land. They are the remnant that is to remain and the inheritors of the New World now dawning.

Today, the trumpets announce another conquering army, an army that is greater and more powerful than the army of the Persians. Its chariots are swifter and its weapons are quicker. Can you hear the sounding trumpets along the *road in the sky?* Can you see the handwriting on the wall? Will you

TRAVELING THE PATH BACK TO THE ROAD IN THE SKY

be a part of the kingdom of *tomorrow?*

It is not necessary to discuss the handwriting on the wall of our era: it has become more obvious in recent years and will become even more so in the years ahead. Thousands of people know that the handwriting exists, but only a very few can read what it has to say. There have been the prophesied wars and rumors of wars, nation has risen against nation, there have been famines, and pestilences, and earthquakes in divers places, but all these are the beginning of sorrows.

On March 20, *1954, The Saturday Evening Post* carried an article entitled: *The Day the Earth Exploded,* by Werner Knop.

The biggest and strangest earthquake of our time struck the Himalaya mountain system with the force of 3,000,000 Atomic Bombs on August 15, 1950. *10,000* square miles were turned into a wilderness of desolation. Yet it took nearly four years before the story was released to the public. Like the Atomic Bomb before it, and the UFOs, the cataclysm was one of the most closely guarded secrets of all time. The Assam-Tibet earthquake became known as the Great Lost Earthquake.

The energy released in the upheaval reached two and a half octillion ergs! *The Saturday Evening Post* reported:

It was exactly thirty-nine minutes and twenty-three seconds after seven p.m. Indian time when all hell broke loose in a circle roughly eighty miles in diameter. Its epicentre, at latitude 28.6 N. and longitude 96.5 E., lay just inside Tibet, beyond Assam's north-east frontier. From this circle, one fifty-mile-long finger reached south-west towards the Brahmaputra River. Another pointed north into Eastern Tibet. Here then was the *ne plus ultra* in earthquakes: Intensity XII, or, in the terse language of the Wood-Neuman scale, 'Damage total'. Beyond stretched a vast area of lesser destruction, characterized by a Briton who experienced the quake in Zone X as 'hell minus ten degrees Fahrenheit'. And still farther, the quake was of such power as to alarm the inhabitants of Lhasa (320 miles west), Calcutta (700 miles south-west), and Chungking (600 miles east). The performance of doom could not have been staged in a stranger setting, nor a more elusive one. In its southern Indian half, in mountains largely unexplored, unadministered and utterly innocent of modern civilization, live the Mishmis, Abors and Miris. In the northern half lies medieval Tibet.

We have already mentioned the fact that Lhasa, sacred city of the

TRAVELING THE PATH BACK TO THE ROAD IN THE SKY

Buddhist's and location of the Palace of the Dalai Lama, is very close to the great *fault line* that goes through the middle of Malaya and then proceeds north towards Mount Everest and the Himalaya mountain system. Lhasa is actually situated between two of the world's major fault *lines*. To the west is the fault line that comes from the south (towards Malaya), to the east is the great fault line that was the cause of the disaster on August 15, 1950.

In *1954,* a report said: '...the far larger numbers of dead from the main areas (of the earthquake) will never be known. They may be anywhere between 20,000 and 30,000.' However, reliable sources secretly reported that several million people perished the day the Earth exploded. The *1954* report mentioning a possible 30,000 was designed to keep the public from being too shocked and too interested in this bit of handwriting on the wall!

History repeated itself on December 4, 1957, in a remote part of Mongolia (the area of another great fault line). Near the centre of another earthquake, a fissure appeared more than 155 miles long and up to *70* feet wide. While the Assam-Tibet earthquake was of force XII, this new disaster was of force XI. Prof. Florentson, a member of the Russian scientific team that went to study the effects of the earthquake, said:

'Dense clouds of dust billowing above the mountains to a height of 4.500 feet could be seen as far as 40 miles away. Some peaks cracked and half crumbled, and scars formed, with a sheer drop of hundreds of yards. Rivers died, and rivers were born.'

The 'earthquakes in divers places' have made themselves known, but remember, 'all these are the beginning of sorrows'.

On July 9, 1956, earthquakes and repeated tidal waves struck the Aegean Islands off southern Greece. Many people were killed and eleven islands suffered widespread damage. On the Island of Patmos, a great tidal wave damaged the historic monastery where St. John the Beloved was exiled in 95 A.D. How prophetic were the happenings in July, 1956! The same island where St. John received his visions of the destructions to come in a future age was struck by earthquakes and tidal waves. Later, St. John recorded these visions in the Book of Revelation. The Island of Patmos is almost directly on a great *fault line.* Are not the modern waves angrily striking the shore of Patmos an indication of the handwriting on the wall?

In *UFOs Confidential,* I said:

TRAVELING THE PATH BACK TO THE ROAD IN THE SKY

...for some time, I have been aware that there is a much bigger and even greater purpose behind it all that the UFOs have not yet revealed in any contacts. Although they show great love towards us, why have they decided to put on a mass appearance at this time? What are they educating us for? If we are progressing in our own classroom why should they disturb us at all? What great cosmic *change* or knowledge of it has prompted them to come now?

In 1952, our research group in northern Arizona was in radio communication with the occupants of the UFOs, and at that time we received information that indicated what this cosmic change might be.

During the reception of the radio-telegraphic messages, which were received in International Morse Code, the UFO communicators mentioned the fact that very soon scientists on Earth would discover our planet was being bombarded with cosmic rays, and with an intensity never before known. I realized immediately that here was a fact that could be checked in the future. If such a happening actually was reported in the future, then the statements of the intelligences in the space ships could be verified or declared void. I knew that here was something scientifically provable.

In 1952 we were told that our planet and our entire Solar System was entering the outer fringes of a great cosmic cloud or area of intense cosmic-ray activity. As we entered the fringes of this field of energy, we began to experience the first effects in the form of strange weather, melting polar ice caps, earthquakes, the increase in cosmic-ray bombardment and the effects on radio broadcasting. The governments of the world were deeply concerned over these changes and special projects were set up to study radiation and its effect on organic life, and so on.

A few months after the UFO prophecies of 1952 regarding the future cosmic ray increase, Dr. Kurt Sitte of Syracuse University was conducting studies at latitudes of $10,000^{to}$ 14,000 feet in Colorado. (Summer, 1953.) Through these studies he came to startling conclusions that proved the statements made by the space visitors in 1952 during radio contacts. Dr. Sitte said:

Too many electrons are showering down on us. At least, there are too many of these tiny units of electrical charge to be explained by present theories, which hold that electrons are produced by cosmic rays smashing into the atmosphere high above the Earth. Unknown particles or processes must

TRAVELING THE PATH BACK TO THE ROAD IN THE SKY

be involved.

Dr. Sitte wanted to discover what processes or particles were producing the electrons that could not be accounted for by present theories. He became a visiting professor at the University of Sao Paulo, Brazil, and worked 18,000 feet above sea level at Chacaltaya. In Brazil he reached the same conclusion–'too many electrons are showering down on us'.

Because of the intense cosmic ray bombardment the world's humus supply began to shrink, and this fact was announced by Prof. Vaino Auer of Finland's Helsinki University, one of the world's leading geographers, shortly after Dr. Sitte's announcement in a small scientific publication. Prof. Auer said that there have been six cosmic eruptions since 12,000 b.c., and that they take place at two-thousand year intervals and are marked by drastic changes in plant and animal life, long periods of drought, the rising of the sea level, and the receding of forests, supplanted by desert shrub. In 1953 (and today) we were experiencing all of these phenomena.

Other leading scientists took interest in the problem, and although much research was conducted very little notice of it ever appeared for the public's information. One or two small newspaper articles appeared and then the information was swallowed up by officialdom!

Dr. Marcel Schein of the University of Chicago, said: "... part, if not all, of the cosmic radiation continuously bombarding the Earth comes from *outside* of the Solar System." Dr. Armin J. Deutsch of Mount Wilson and Palomar Astronomical Observatories said that he believed that the cosmic rays coming to Earth may be material thrown off from rotating stars with strong magnetic fields. His findings tended to prove that many (if not all) of these rays are extra-solar in origin.

The fact that 'too many electrons are showering down on us' and present theories won't account for them added to the fact that certain cosmic rays bombard the Earth from *outside* our own Solar System tends to support the idea that our entire Solar System is entering a new possibility area of the Universe. Every phase of our life will be changed—Economics, Religion, Education, Politics, Science, Social life, Medicine, Eating habits, etc. Virtually everything will be influenced, and for the better.

In 1952, the UFO communicators stated that the increase in cosmic rays would be caused by the new area of the Universe that our entire Solar System was rapidly moving into. But this new area of space was not the real

TRAVELING THE PATH BACK TO THE ROAD IN THE SKY

cause behind the electron increase, for every moment our Solar System enters a new area of space. Therefore, I wanted to know why the bombardment was going to increase and what was behind it and what it meant for the people of Earth.

1947-57 has been called the Haunted Decade. And, indeed, it was 'haunted'. Even those individuals who do not believe in UFOs will have to admit that there were startling and significant happenings and changes on Earth during those ten years. Therefore, many will say that outer space intelligences are here now because this is the psychological time for their arrival. Man on Earth is now almost ready to go out on the great interstellar sea of space and if there are other beings in that space it is logical that they would now attempt to communicate with us. However, the *visitants* have come for a much more important reason than just to present a calling card.

In 1952, during the Arizona radio contacts of W7oJQ, our group asked the question: 'Is disaster really coming to the Earth?'

The answer came back: 'Well, we are here, aren't we?' In other words, the UFO intelligences would never have come to the Earth to draw our attention to the skies if a certain amount of catastrophe was not certain.

The UFO occupants also stated, however, that the world was not going to end. There would be great terrain changes and destruction in all parts of the world, but there was to be no literal end of Earth. The statement was also made that the Earth had to be brought quickly into the Interplanetary Brotherhood from which it fell long ago.

I wondered what was meant by this since the same communicators had told us that we had an eternity to complete our lessons on Earth. If this were so, I thought, then why are they rushing us into this Interplanetary Brotherhood, why are they interfering in our way of life on this planet if we have for ever to accomplish our lessons ourselves? Somehow this seemed contradictory.

Then I realized something else. Whenever a so-called superior culture comes in unto a so-called inferior culture it always destroys the lesser group. It doesn't matter what the motives of the superior group may happen to be. Actually, a more advanced cultural group may feel they have to invade and conquer a people in order to give them the benefits of civilization, to improve their health and sanitation and to make their life longer and happier. However, even when the motives are beneficent, the inferior group is

TRAVELING THE PATH BACK TO THE ROAD IN THE SKY

destroyed socially, politically, religiously, and economically.

As an anthropologist I realized this truth, and I also realized that since the UFO intelligences were superior to us (after all they must be since they can go through space in mechanical devices and we cannot), they wouldn't want to come among us knowing that they would destroy our way of life completely. It is a great blow to our pride to accept space visitors as our superiors, but they are, whether we like it or not.

I knew that the visitants were not here to give us paradise on a silver platter or to hand over their secrets of propulsion, etc. They couldn't hope to educate us quickly in order to bring us up to their level of development or cultural or technical achievement. Then why are they here? It must be for an emergency reason only. Our old way of life must be about to be changed or destroyed anyway, and they have come to assist the remnant that remains in the establishment of a New Age upon a New Earth.

If we know what the great cosmic change is that has prompted the visitants coming now, we find that it answers the question of why the cosmic-ray bombardment has increased. UFOs have always appeared in the past just before a world cataclysm. What is going to happen in our time? Remember, in the days before the great flood or destruction, the ancestors of the Machiguenga people in Peru were in communication with people of the heavens or the sky dwellers—celestial inhabitants who came to Earth on a 'road in the sky'.

The coming of the UFOs to Earth and the increase in cosmic rays constitutes a key that unlocks the secrets of our immediate future.

During the last few years, sunspot activity has increased tremendously. Newspapers all over the world have carried such announcements as:

VIOLENT SOLAR EXPLOSION TO BLAST RADIO

Entire World To Feel Impact Quickly

Capri, Italy, July 3 (Reuter)

Radio communications upset all this week by solar activity, today were threatened with further trouble by one of the biggest explosions ever spotted on the surface of the sun. The new blasts only add to the great mystery of the violent explosions on the sun's face.

The explosion today was spotted by a Swedish observation post on

TRAVELING THE PATH BACK TO THE ROAD IN THE SKY

this Mediterranean vacation island at 3:22 this afternoon (Chicago time). A warning was flashed to the Italian geophysical year centre in Rome and to scientists over the world.

A spokesman at the Rome centre said the explosion, a giant geyser of solar particles and radiation, would produce intense ionospheric disturbances in the earth's atmosphere within 20 hours.

Three hours after it was sighted, the colossal eruptive explosion, on the scale of 'three-plus', the maximum measurement, was still in progress.

On June 28 and 30, explosions on the sun caused an almost complete interruption of short wave radio communication, just as scientists prepared for the international geophysical year, the world-wide programme of research into natural phenomena, which opened Monday.

During the phenomenon, a huge tongue of flame leapt from the sun's surface thousands of miles into space producing a volume of white glowing gases which would dwarf the earth in size. Mysterious emissions of radiation particles reach the earth after the blasts and upset .The electrically-charged layer of rarified atmosphere enveloping the earth between the altitudes of about 50 miles and 250 miles.

This layer, the ionosphere, is vital for long distance radio transmission. [t also produces the Aurora Borealis. Both are affected by ionospheric disturbances, known as magnetic storms.

Yngve Ohman, leader of the Swedish team, said the explosion 'was in the same sunspot group as the less brilliant flares on June 28 and 30. We expect magnetic storms and increased cosmic radiation as a result.'

On April 7, 1956, Science *News Letter* reported:

VIOLENT SOLAR EXPLOSION

Sun erupted with violence of 100,000,000 hydrogen bombs in February, astronomer reports to American Astronomical Society. Outbursts interrupted short-wave radio.

The sun exploded with the violence of 100,000,000 hydrogen bombs on February 10, hurling a flaming gas bubble at least 200,000 miles above its surface.

The giant tongue of gas, 1,000,000,000 tons of the sun's substance, was

TRAVELING THE PATH BACK TO THE ROAD IN THE SKY

roughly 20,000 miles in diameter. In a two-minute period, it speeded up from a velocity of 60 miles per second to 700 miles per second, thought to be the record for visual prominences.

The solar outbursts affected short-wave radio communications and caused blasts of radio static, Robert Lawrence of the National Bureau of Standards laboratory at Boulder. Colorado, reported ...

Sunspot Disturbances and Solar Explosions are increasing. The flaming prominences of the star we call our Sun are the solar handwriting on the wall. The Sun which is so vital to all life in the Solar System is the type of star which has the rather nasty habit of blowing up-in other words, exploding and creating a nova. The *visitants* are concerned about this. After all, to some of them, our Sun is their Sun, too.

Scientists have known for many years that during periods of high sunspot activity great emotional disturbances manifest on the Earth. Murder, robbery, crime of all kinds, and a period of general depression always accompanies solar disturbance. This is a mystery that has never been explained. It seems to indicate that there is a definite magnetic connection of some kind between mankind on Earth and his Sun. Not only do the sunspots disturb radio communication and cause magnetic storms, but they also create a state of morbidity in the human population on our planet. At least, that is what some scientists claim. They know what happens, but they do not have the answer. Actually, the reverse is true. The sunspots do not affect us, we affect the sunspots!

Man has more power of creative thought than he realizes. He has far more to fear from the elements in revolt against him than he has from other men. He need not worry about *The Unholy Six,* for such forces constitute a far lesser threat than the natural, forces of Creation that will turn on man causing his destruction if his *thoughts* are not in accord with Universal Law.

The evil thoughts of hu-manity on Earth caused ferocious beasts and creatures of destruction to appear in the most ancient times; such evil thoughts of modern hu-manity are causing disturbances upon the Sun. Between this Sun and the Earth there exists a constant 'feedback' situation. Actually, man's thoughts could destroy the Sun!

In the New Age upon the Earth those of the evil thoughts will be gone. This is spoken of in Isaiah xi: 6, 7, 8, 9:

TRAVELING THE PATH BACK TO THE ROAD IN THE SKY

The wolf also shall dwell with the lamb, and the leopard shall lie down with the kid; and the calf and the young lion and the fatling together; and a little child shall lead them. And the cow and the bear shall feed; their young ones shall lie down together: and the lion shall eat straw like the ox. And the suckling child shall play on the hole of the asp, and the weaned child shall put his hand on the cockatrice' den. They shall not hurt nor destroy in all my holy mountain: for the earth shall be full of the knowledge of the Lord, as the waters cover the sea.

As Daniel in the den of lions came to no harm because the 'spirit of god' was in him, so shall the inheritors of the Earth be able to mingle with the wolf, the lion, and the asp, for 'they shall not hurt nor destroy in all my holy mountain'. The Earth having gone through the Purification Day will 'be full of the knowledge of the Lord'. The Hopi people say this will be the cleansing of all the wicked forces of the Earth so that the common man may have his day.

While the combined thoughts of mankind can and do affect the Sun, and create the environment man finds himself in, there is something else which is the *cause* behind the coming of the UFOs from Outer Space, as well as the *cause* behind the increase in cosmic rays, and solar disturbances.

A recent major discovery of great importance was made when the United States satellites in space registered an intense radiation unknown previously. About 60o miles above the Earth a radiation, assumed to come from the Sun, was found to be one thousand times the intensity scientists had anticipated before.

Dr. Jason J. Nassau, director of the Warner-Swasey Observatory, Cleveland, Ohio, attended the International Science Symposium held recently in Rome, Italy. On July 1, 1957, he reported:

'The earth is seen racing to a hot, not a cold, end. Our world will end twice as quickly as science has expected. Our sun is not dying as formerly supposed, but is growing brighter and hotter. Oceans will eventually boil away. Our sun is absorbing material to put forth more energy.'

The conclusions reached at the International Science Symposium were incredible. *Our sun is absorbing material to put forth more energy.* Therefore, not only are the negative thoughts of mankind on Earth disturbing the solar body, but it is absorbing material from *somewhere* and is increasing its energy output. It is absorbing material from *where?*

TRAVELING THE PATH BACK TO THE ROAD IN THE SKY

In 1955-56 I was in correspondence with a well-known foreign scientist who said that after intensive research by government scientists they came to the terrifying conclusion that our planet is moving very rapidly on a collision course with a gigantic embryonic sun.

On February 23, 1956, an important letter was sent to me from a man who had formerly been in charge of his government's UFO investigation team. He said:

You are probably aware of the recent increase in sunspot activity and the abnormal behavior of radio wave propagation. Also, it is fairly obvious that the weather conditions are quite disturbed. We know that this is in line with the space people's predictions, but they gave us very little by way of explanation.

I have been keeping a running check on gravity variations, and by piecing together various apparently unrelated facts I have figured out what I think is the right answer.

I think that our solar system is drifting through space on a collision *course* with a large body of matter, mostly hydrogen, in a very rarified state. I estimate this mass to be about 330 times that of our sun, and about 150,000 times the diameter of our solar system. Within this embryonic star there is bound to be quite a collection of cosmic debris, and if we are due to pass through the middle of it, we will be in for a pretty rough time. The fact that the sun will be gaining hydrogen during its passage will result in increased solar activity, with an accompanying increase in temperature and surface disturbances which will reflect on our weather. I would expect that a small increase in sun temperature would cause a heavy evaporation of water from the earth and thick cloud formations, with the climate becoming most unpleasant. I would expect heavy precipitation, probably faster than natural drainage can cope with it. The resulting large accumulations of water will produce earthquakes and a general change in topography. I think we are just now entering the outer fringes of this cosmic mass.

This speculation seems to be in line with statements made by the space people from time to time; predictions contained in the Holy Bible; current scientific observations throughout the world, and my own observations. It seems like a reasonable thing which certainly could happen astronomically.

The same day the above letter was written, Paul Harvey reported on his newscast that the cosmic ray bombardment from the Sun at 3:30 a.m.

TRAVELING THE PATH BACK TO THE ROAD IN THE SKY

(E.S.T.), was the greatest ever recorded or known on Earth.

My letter from the government scientist said:

'... they (the space people) gave us very little by way of explanation ...' This definitely indicates that the Government investigation team had been in contact with the *visitants!* This man spoke of a 'collision course' and this was the official conclusion reached by the foreign researchers I was in correspondence with during 1955-56. In the above letter, the scientist spoke of the fact that our 'sun will be gaining hydrogen during its passage' through the embryonic star. This is exactly in line with the conclusions reached by the International Science Symposium and also with the statements made by Dr. Nassau when he said: 'Our sun is absorbing material to put forth more energy.' It is obvious that our sun is increasing its energy output due to its passage through the great star, and as the above letter states: '... we are just now *(1956)* entering the outer fringes of this cosmic mass.'

This, then, is the new area of the Universe that our entire Solar System is entering. This is what the space intelligences were referring to in 1952 during our radio contacts in Arizona. The new area isn't the real cause of the electron increase, but the embryonic sun is. Here also is the cause behind recent solar disturbances and explosions and the fact that the *visitants* are once again present in the skies of our generation. This is the reason why we are being rapidly pushed by our extra-terrestrial neighbors into the Interplanetary Brotherhood. This is the emergency reason for the presence of the UFOs today. But what of tomorrow?

Remember, Dr. Schein, at the University of Chicago, said: "... part, *if not all,* of the cosmic radiation continuously bombarding the Earth comes from *outside* of the Solar System."

And Dr. Deutsch, at Mount Wilson and Palomar Observatories, said: '...cosmic rays coming to Earth may be material thrown off from rotating stars with strong magnetic fields.'

The increase in cosmic ray activity is due to the embryonic star which is definitely 'outside of our Solar System.' And this new star is certainly 'rotating .., with a strong magnetic field'.

Cosmic rays travel to Earth from space with terrific speed and energy. No known star is able to propel atomic particles at such speeds with such energy. The particles bombard atmospheric particles (the latter splits, etc.)

TRAVELING THE PATH BACK TO THE ROAD IN THE SKY

and the reaction continues, explaining how we can measure this radiation. Cosmic rays penetrate everything known. Even after penetrating the atmosphere, such rays contain enough energy to penetrate a one thousand storey building upon reaching the ground.

If the cosmic radiation is directly proportional to our distance from the embryonic star-sun, this sun is like none so far observed. It would have to be gigantic (as my letter of February 23, 1956, stated) with a tremendous energy capacity. Such a giant star-sun might be invisible to our sight (spectrum). However, its high energy content might react with atomic particles within our spectrum and thereby we would be affected. In other words, cosmic rays might well be the atomic radiation of a gigantic super-super-sun that is invisible to us because of its high energy state.

What does our collision with an embryonic star mean for *tomorrow?*

Could such an occurrence or the resultant damage to our own sun be referred to in Holy Scripture when a 'flaming sword of the God of wrath' is mentioned?

"... for the *sword* of the Lord shall devour from the one end of the land even to the other end of the land: no flesh shall have peace." (Jeremiah xii:12).

The ancient prophecies of past civilizations say that the Earth will eventually be completely destroyed by fire. The *'flaming sword* of God' may refer to a time in the future when our Sun has absorbed too much material from the embryonic sun and the result will be a nova, an exploding star in a tiny section of Creation. But does this mean the end of mankind? Certainly not!

What does the embryonic sun and the collision mean to the people of Earth?

We have been experiencing changes in weather throughout the world, and this will continue. There will be more earthquakes and more disasters. Atomic bombs are only accentuating the already unstable condition caused by our entry into this new area of space. Atomic detonations are not the main cause of present changes on Earth even though they are experimented with directly over the world's major fault lines (like hitting a cracked egg with a hammer!). The real *cause* is the gigantic new star.

Now we know why the UFO intelligences would impose their superior culture over our inferior culture. There is an emergency in the heavens and

TRAVELING THE PATH BACK TO THE ROAD IN THE SKY

all the inhabited planets belonging to the Space Confederation have been alerted. The Earth will eventually be destroyed, for space intelligences have said: 'We will land upon your planet and we will aid in the development of a New Age and a new technology. This will continue for a time, and then the Earth will disintegrate in thought.'

The *visitants* are literally pushing us into a consciousness where we can accept the inhabitation of space, space ships and space people. The Earth planet must rejoin the Interplanetary Brotherhood, and quickly!

"...the night cometh, when no man can work." (St. John ix: 4).

We are now on the outer *fringes* of a great cosmic mass. The energy from the magnetic field of this mass is vibrating at an incredible speed and if we are to be part of the remnant that remains we must learn to live with it and to vibrate at its rate.

Recent findings by Dr. Seymour Kety and his associates at the National Institute of Mental and Nervous Diseases indicate that the physical human brain is not a 'thinking' machine, but at best can be compared to a radio set.

In *Other Tongues—Other Flesh,* I said:

Therefore, if man's brain is nothing but a receiving and transmitting instrument similar to a radio set, he must be able to receive and interpret the music of the spheres or the Great Cosmic Intelligence that forever is permeating all space; man merely must tune in to it. Those who refuse to receive the new vibrations mentally, will lose their physical equipment on Earth and thereby give up their radio sets that will not accept the new lessons. They will go elsewhere and acquire new sets that will allow them to learn and progress as they must.

Other parts of the human body are affected by the new vibrations also. The pineal gland and the solar plexus become radioactive under the influence of the cosmic *rays*. The body is in continual touch with the whole existence. The skin is no border of the body as we sometimes imagine; there is continuous mutual meeting and mingling of the single human body and the whole of the cosmos which also includes other human bodies. In the human body there are said to be six hundred million psychic centers. By psychic is meant the extensional apertures. Many more centers exist, of course, in the known cosmos. As the single human being comes in contact with the great influx of Cosmic Energy, he will realize that he possesses some very strange

TRAVELING THE PATH BACK TO THE ROAD IN THE SKY

abilities and powers. The rays will actually stimulate the pineal gland and the third eye of the human will be opened once again. Those individuals who refuse to accept the higher vibrations mentally, allowing for great spiritual growth and advancement, will experience a definite *physiological* reaction. In the study of the electro-chemistry of the blood, the answer to what will take place is found.

The blood stream is composed of the serum and the cellular constituents, plus colloids. The countless millions of cells in the circulating blood must maintain their ability to remain free of all other elements in the stream. Research is revealing the importance of electro-chemistry. All blood cells carry a charge, the charge is of the same denomination. Like charges repel, and so the cells as well as the colloids repel each other resulting in the existence of electrical cushions capable of preventing the cells from touching one another. When thrombosis (clotting) occurs, it is precipitated by the discharge of cell or colloid charges which allows for the agglutination or formation of the clots.

Each human blood cell is surrounded by a *Resonating Electro-Magnetic Field;* if a person refuses to accept the new Universal lessons presented to him for his use, he sets up an action within his body that causes the RMF (magnetic field) to collapse. Clotting occurs and he is said to have died of a heart attack. The only reason heart attacks are on the increase is because of the new vibrations (from the embryonic sun) and man's inability to cope with them, accept them, and understand them. Therefore, no god of wrath destroys man; man eliminates himself by his thoughts.

The Holy Bible contains many references that obviously are connected with the *cause and effect* of the increased vibratory rate.

'And so it is written, the first man Adam was made a living soul; the last Adam was made a quickening spirit.' (I Corinthians xv: 45).

'The first man is of the earth, earthy: the second man is the Lord from heaven.' (I Corinthians xv:47).

'And as we have borne the image of the earthy, we shall also bear the image of the heavenly. Now this I say, brethren, that flesh and blood cannot inherit the kingdom of God; neither doth corruption inherit incorruption. Behold, I shew you a mystery; We shall not all sleep, but we shall be changed, In a moment, in the twinkling of an eye, at the last trump: for the trumpet shall sound, and the dead shall be raised incorruptible, and we shall be

TRAVELING THE PATH BACK TO THE ROAD IN THE SKY

changed. For this corruptible must put on incorruption, and this mortal must put on immortality.' (I Corinthians xv: 49, 50, 51, 52, 53).

While great destruction will sweep over the Earth, space intelligences have definitely stated in many contacts that after this is over, a Golden Age will develop on this planet which will last for about 1,000 years. Then the Earth will come to an actual end. Because of the new vibrations we must learn to live with and vibrate with, we are to become quickening spirits, and we are to bear the image of the heavenly.

Shoghi Effendi, in *The Promised Day To Come,* gives us a view of the future:

A tempest, unprecedented in its violence, unpredictable in its course, catastrophic in its immediate effects, unimaginably glorious in its ultimate consequences, is at present over the face of the earth. Its driving power is gaining in range and momentum. Its cleansing force, however undetached, is increasing with every passing day. Humanity gripped within the clutches of its devastating power, is smitten by the evidences of its resistless fury. Humanity can neither perceive its origin, nor probe its significance, nor discern its outcome. Bewildered, agonized and helpless, it watches this great and mighty wind of God invading the remotest and fairest regions of the earth, rocking its foundations, deranging its equilibrium, sundering its nations, disrupting the homes of its peoples, wasting its cities, driving into exile its kings, pulling down its bulwarks, uprooting its institutions, dimming its lights, and harrowing up the souls of its inhabitants.

Shoghi Effendi tells us that a violent tempest will be 'unimaginably glorious in its ultimate consequence'. Its cleansing force is related to the day of Purification of the Hopi Indians. The 'tempest over the face of the earth' comes from the magnetic field of the new sun, and 'humanity can neither perceive its origin... probe its significance... nor discern its outcome'.

Every legend and prophecy of ancient people speaks of the Earth being destroyed by fire, and, as we mentioned before, the 'flaming sword' of a wrathful God may refer to such destruction. Before this takes place, however, hu-manity will work for several centuries with the men from other worlds to develop a new civilization on Earth that will take its place within the Interplanetary Brotherhood or the Space Confederation. Wonderful and fantastic advancement will be made.

Several years ago, Dr. Wilton Krogman, world-famous physical anthro-

TRAVELING THE PATH BACK TO THE ROAD IN THE SKY

pologist, spoke before the New York Academy of Science. He said that in 5,000,000 years the human race will have progressed to the stage where men will communicate with each other by thought-waves, in much the same way as short waves are now used for radio communication. He said that this far distant civilization would be one where everyone would know each other's thoughts completely. I think Dr. Krogman is absolutely correct about the thought transmission, but it's hardly five million years away! Thought transference is being practiced on Earth today, and has been practiced for centuries by highly developed beings on this planet. As the new vibrations become more intense, mind reading and mind readers will be as common as speech is now. Dr. Krogman is being somewhat conservative in his estimate of the age of this 'far distant' civilization.

After the planet Earth once again takes its rightful place at the Council Table of the Peaceful Planets, a period of harmony will be established that corresponds to the millennium of Christian prophecy found in *Revelation* Chapter 20. During this period, mankind will be prepared for the greatest adventure of all-a literal march across Time and the Stars!

Because the magnetic field of the embryonic sun will eventually become too intense for life on Earth, mankind (or the remnant that remains) will not only have to leave the Earth which has served as a home for several million years, but the complete *evacuation of the entire Solar System will be necessary.*

The new stellar giant will absorb and destroy our planet, our Solar System, and many other solar systems of the Milky Way Galaxy. The *visitants* are now attempting to prepare the remnant on Earth for the evacuation, a migration through interstellar space to a new home.

Remember, Jesus, the Christ, said: '... My kingdom is not of this world...' (St. John xviii: 36).

In the above quotation from St. John, we find that the word *world* comes from the Greek *kosmos,* and it can be translated: 'age'. or 'world system'. In other words, Jesus, the Christ, said: '... My kingdom is not of this *world system* (age) ...' He was saying that He did not belong to this Solar System... His home or kingdom was not of this *world system.*

'And I saw *a new heaven* and a *new earth:* for the first heaven and the first earth were passed away ...' (Revelation xxi: 1).

TRAVELING THE PATH BACK TO THE ROAD IN THE SKY

In our English versions of the Bible, there are *two* words that are translated as 'new'. One of these words refers to *time,* the other word refers to *quality.* In Revelation xxi: 1, the word 'new' means that the *quality* of the Earth will be changed but not the actual substance. Also, there is supposed to be some resemblance between the 'first earth' and the 'new earth'.

If the quality of the Earth is to be changed, this definitely refers to the high vibratory rate created by our entry into the magnetic field of the embryonic star-sun. The actual substance of the Earth is not to be changed until the end of the millennium.

'For I reckon that the sufferings of this present time are not worthy to be compared with the glory which shall be revealed in us. For the earnest expectation of the creature waiteth for the manifestation of the sons of God.' (Romans viii: 18, 19).

The sufferings of *today* mean nothing when we consider the glory of *tomorrow* 'which shall be revealed in us'.

The blessed meek and the *peaceful ones* on the Earth have expected the manifestation of the sons of God and these sons of the Creator are in our skies at the present time; the manifestation took place when the UFOs made their appearance in our generation.

'Because the creature itself also shall be delivered from the bondage of corruption into the glorious liberty of the children of God.' (Romans viii: 21).

The eager longing of creation has awaited the revelation of the sons of God and mankind will be delivered from his bondage of corruption and shall know the glorious liberty of the visitants, who are the children of God.

'Whereby the world that then was, being overflowed with water, perished: But the heavens and the earth, which are now, by the same word are kept in store, reserved unto fire against the day of judgement and perdition of ungodly men.' (2 Peter iii: 6, 7).

Here is an obvious reference to the time when the world was destroyed by water. Of course, the physical planet itself was not destroyed, only the life upon it. The Earth of *today* is to be destroyed by fire.

'... the heavens shall pass away with a great noise, and the elements shall melt with fervent heat, the earth also and the works that are therein shall be burned up.' (2 Peter iii: 10).

Many individuals have felt that the statement about the elements melting with fervent heat refers to the destruction caused by atomic detonation. However, such statements as this and the heavens passing away with a great noise and the heavens being on fire shall be dissolved can easily refer to the entry into the magnetic field of the new star-sun.

We must be very careful in our interpretations, for the Bible passages in some places refer to the new vibratory rate that will cleanse and purify the Earth. Such a purification could be called fire since it is directly connected with magnetism, vibration, frequency, cosmic rays, etc.

In other places in the Bible reference is made to the time when the millennium is over on the Earth and it is finally absorbed along with the entire Solar System into the centre of the embryonic starsun. This will also be destruction by fire, but fire of a different kind that will cause our sun to explode (nova) as the Earth disintegrates in thought.

'Nevertheless, we, according to his promise, look for new heavens and a new earth, wherein dwelleth righteousness.' (2 Peter iii: 13).

'For behold, I create new heavens and a new earth: and the former shall not be remembered, nor come into mind.' (Isaiah lxv: 17).

The promise for the remnant that remains is found in Isaiah lxvi: 22: 'For as the new heavens and the new earth, which I will make, shall remain before me, saith the Lord, so shall your seed and your name remain.'

'And there shall be signs in the sun, and in the moon, and in the stars; and upon the earth distress of nations, with perplexity; the sea and the waves roaring; Men's hearts failing them for fear, and for looking after those things which are coming on the earth: for the powers of heaven shall be shaken. And then shall they see the Son of man coming in a cloud with power and great glory. And when these things begin to come to pass, then look up, and lift up your heads; for your redemption draweth nigh.' (St. Luke xxi: 25, 26, 27, 28).

Although the events of the near future will be cataclysmic when the powers of heaven shall be shaken, we are not to be afraid. We are to look up, and lift up our heads, for our redemption draweth nigh.

We shall be shown a mystery; we shall all be changed. In a moment, in

TRAVELING THE PATH BACK TO THE ROAD IN THE SKY

the twinkling of an eye, this mortal must put on immortality.

The Hopi people are referring to this change that shall take place in the twinkling of an eye when they talk of the Purification Day and their true white brother who will return sounds like the Son of man coming in a cloud with power and great glory. The Hopi say that the cleansing of the land will make it possible for those saved to have *everlasting life.* This sounds like the Bible statement that 'this mortal must put on *immortality'*.

Let's not look to the material things of the Earth; let's not fear those things of the physical world when the very Stars are beckoning, and they are beckoning as they never have before in the history of hu-manity.

One day the remnant that remains will band together and establish heaven on earth, a colony that will know the meek of Earth and the peaceful of the Stars. The foundation will be laid for 'One City of the Universe'.

What is meant in the Holy Bible by such statements as those found in St. Matthew xxiv: 28, and St. Luke xvii: 37: '...there will the *eagles* be gathered together.'

The answer may be found in Isaiah xl: 31: 'But they that wait upon the Lord shall renew their strength; they shall mount up with wings as *eagles...*'

Is it possible that the eagles and the visitants in the UFOs are one and the same thing?

Our nearest neighbors in space knew that the Solar System would eventually be absorbed by the embryonic sun, and they have been trying to indoctrinate the people of Earth into a new way of life since the late 1800's. Space intelligences didn't obviously interfere until that day in 1947 over Mount Rainier, Washington. They tell us they are going to prepare us for a journey to what they call 'the void of eternal light'. We shall take a journey through space that defies description.

The statement: 'Know ye not that ye are gods!' thunders out of the past, but man on Earth still does not realize the truth of these words. Perhaps the greatest message that the *visitants* have brought us is the fact that man must learn that he is a potential god. In all of us abides a spark of God, and that spark is the *true* self, the revealed capacity of every man to manifest divinity.

Remember what we said when we discussed *The Time-Spanners?* We

TRAVELING THE PATH BACK TO THE ROAD IN THE SKY

will not become 'El's' simply because we do not belong to the Cyclopean (Elder) Race. However, in order to escape the cataclysmic effects of the embryonic sun we will eventually have to conquer Matter-Energy-Space and Time.

Remember the present plan of the Universal Hierarchy?

'The production of a subjective synthesis in hu-man-ity and of a telepathic interplay which will eventually *annihilate Time!*'

Even though man on Earth will develop space travel on an interplanetary and an interstellar basis shortly after his return to the Interplanetary Brotherhood, it will be impossible to escape the destruction caused by the embryonic sun about 1,000 years from now when the Earth disintegrates in *thought*. A space ship couldn't be designed and constructed that could travel such vast distances of the Universe! How then will the remnant escape?

Remember what we said before?

'We will not become "El's" but we will follow the "gods" through the "womb of Time" to be unfettered and free. For this we were created, for this we live, and for this we shall be ELevated to beyond the stars.'

The members of the Space Confederation know that the forbidden secret of the 'El's' can be found under the Earth in the amaranthine crystalline world of the great Time-Spanners. If the remnant will allow the *visitants* to search for this secret, they will give us their knowledge in return. They know that this secret is necessary if mankind is to escape the stellar giant whose effects are becoming greater every day. They know that they too must be ELevated to beyond the stars or be destroyed when the elements 'melt with fervent heat'.

Our journey and migration in space will be a journey in Time—or should we say Timelessness!

Could there be a more glorious promise? Hu-man will become simply MAN, at last free and knowing Truth. Since the day the first hu-man being stood erect and knew that he was a potential god has there ever been greater news of his godhood?

We are all only actors in life's drama with our entrances and our exits. The Earth planet is like the 'great play' and we have all had our parts whether large or small. But soon we shall move on to the 'greater play' and the ap-

TRAVELING THE PATH BACK TO THE ROAD IN THE SKY

plauding of the celestial host shall ring in our ears.

M. Pickthall described our passage in Time/Timelessless well, when he said:

'And fearfully we tread cold space, Naked of flesh and winged with flame . . . Until we find us face to face, Each calling on the other's name.'

Again the handwriting on the wall appears, and again it says: *Counted, Weighed, and Divided.* Again sounds are heard from a great *road,* sounds from the eternal *road in the sky* that leads to the very gates of modern Babylon.

In this book we have only had a glimpse of this road as it encountered the *yesterday* of the mighty 'El's', the Marcahuasi monoliths, the Beacons for the Gods, the Martian Miniatures, the 'strange beings', 'high places', fault lines and space ships, and the dense tropical rain forest known as the Silent World.

We caught a glimpse of this road as it encountered the *today* of *the blessed meek* and of its travelers known as the *visitants.*

The peaceful ones and their ancient legends of *the other side of the sky* gave us a glimpse of this road as they knew it in the dim past and what it means in the future of *tomorrow. The Unholy Six* showed us where this road developed a fork and divided into two branches going in opposite directions, but soon shall know neither branch nor division, but be one pathway to godhood. We caught a glimpse of *tomorrow* from the handwriting on the wall that heralds not the Persian host, but the Host of Heaven.

We have learned only a little about this road that existed before *The Time-Spanners* and shall exist long after the 'One far-off Divine Event to which the whole Creation moves.'

A long and glorious road still exists in the heavens, and visitors from outer space are traveling it once again even as they did in times past. This road is greater in magnitude and importance than all the roads of the Roman Empire and the roads of Lord Inca.

The roads of Rome and Peru were constructed to accommodate a conquering army, and the *road in the sky is* also a road of conquest, for space intelligences have definitely stated that they are here to invade and conquer us. However, there is one slight difference. They are here to conquer us with Love.

TRAVELING THE PATH BACK TO THE ROAD IN THE SKY

This road of the Stars has known many chariots of light, but it has never known the marching feet of doomed men; this road has known weapons of Truth but it has never known the machines of war. This road is full of activity, the trumpets are sounding, and a great Host approaches.

A Frenchman once wrote: 'A people is like a man. When he has disappeared, nothing is left of him unless he has taken the precaution to leave his imprint on the stones of the *road.*'

And space intelligences once said: 'Return home, Earth. Come to the emptiness of *our* beings. You have been so long absent from our hearts and souls.'

As we return home may we leave our imprint on the stones of the radiant *road in the sky.*

As you travel the highway of the stars, walk with God and keep in step with the Universe.

GEORGE HUNT WILLIAMSON came to realize that in America if you try to buck the status quo or change the system you can easily be slandered and identified as a dangerous dissident whether it be a communist, a fascist, or a neo Nazi. Many of the UFO contactees of the early days of the UFO/New Age movement were thusly labeled.

Williamson – aka Brother Philip – was at the forefront of those the government was keeping an eagle eye on for fear the Russians might be using him as a highly sophisticated mind managed and manipulated "Mind Soldier." *TRAVELING THE PATH BACK TO THE ROAD IN THE SKY* includes the entire text of Williamson's most accredited work linking ancient civilizations with the remote beginnings of humanity and visitations from outer space.

In addition, a vast update on Williamson's conflicted personality and his FBI papers has been added to this volume, as well as a fascinating commentary by Brad Steiger, who was to meet with Williamson to receive some important information when *"Brother Philip passed away unexpectedly."* —

TURN PAGE FOR MORE INFORMATION >>

J. EDGAR HOOVER'S G-MEN IDENTIFIED GEORGE HUNT WILLIAMSON AS A COMMUNIST OR AT PARAMOUNT A "MIND CONTROLLED SOLDIER" OF THE SOVIET UNION. . . OTHER UFO CONTACTS FROM THE EARLY UFO ERA WERE THUSLY LABELED!

THESE CLASSIC BOOKS BY GEORGE HUNT WILLIAMSON — AKA BROTHER PHILIP — HAVE BEEN GREATLY EXPANDED AND UPDATED WITH ADDED COMMENTARY BY TODAY'S LEADING RESEARCHERS

A member of Williamson's group received an interesting communications from an entity who identified itself as being a Time Spanner: . . . "WE are not of the world you are in. We are in a different type of place. We are in one of the many other streams of time."

"Tomb raider" Williamson poses with two friends from the past.

☐ **TRAVELING THE PATH BACK TO THE ROAD IN THE SKY**—by Brother Philip with Nick Redfern and a special commentary by Brad Steiger

A STRANGE SAGA OF SAUCERS, SPACE BROTHERS AND SECRET AGENTS—George Hunt Williamson – known as Brother Philip throughout the highlands of Peru – traveled the longest highway in this world leading him to discover a vast road into the sky that can be linked to the arrival of visitors from the universe throughout the ages. Here are the Hopi Sunclan legends of the "Giant Star." The secret of the Stone Tablets of Peru. The Time Spanners. The Beacon of the Gods. The Martian Miniatures. Fossils, Footprints and Fantasy. Evidence for the Silent World. The Unholy Six.

Also this is the book that gives Williamson's inside battle with the FBI and the Silence Group. His dealings with the mysterious disappearance of Hunrath and Wilkinson (were they murdered or abducted by UFOs?). The smuggling claims and his "association" with a sexy saucer pilot whom the FBI identified as a "ravishing woman commandant!" This is the title we recommend for those just getting into the *"Williamson Phenomenon."* — **$20.00**

☐ **SECRET OF THE ANDES AND THE GOLDEN SUN DISC OF MU**—by Brother Philip aka George Hunt Williamson with updates by Brent Raynes, Joshua Shapiro, Tim Swartz, John J. Robinson, Tim Beckley and Harold T. Wilkins

JOIN BROTHER PHILIP AS HE EXPLORES A HIDDEN MONASTERY HIGH IN THE ANDES WHICH HOSTS THE SUN DISC – A MAGICAL RELIC OF LOST CONTINENT SURVIVORS.—Here are the extraordinary spiritual adventures of Brother Philip in this lofty ashram high above the world, out of sight of prying eyes who would like to capture the Sun Disc for nefarious purposes. If is a fascinating story of good versus evil that is all the more relevant in these chaotic days around our planet.

The Disc eventually found its way to Lake Titicaca and was placed in a subterranean temple of the Monastery of the Brotherhood of the Seven Rays. Here it was used not only by the students of life daily, but also by the Masters and the Saints from the Mystery Schools throughout the world.

When the spiritually advanced Incas came to Peru they placed the Disc of the Sun in a specially constructed Garden of Gold where it will remain until the day "when man is spiritually ready" to receive it and use it once again. On that day the Golden Disc will be taken out of its subterranean chamber and placed high above the Monastery of the Brotherhood. — **$20.00**

☐ **OTHER TONGUES – OTHER FLESH REVISITED!**—by George Hunt Williamson, Added Comments by Joshua Shapiro

'IN MY HOUSE THERE ARE MANY MANSIONS," JESUS STATED. NOW HERE IS THE PROOF!—"Evidence has been accumulated that there are people on earth that don't really belong here!" George Hunt Williamson, stated as early as 1955, a popular belief among New Agers even today.

This doesn't mean they came here aboard a flying saucer, disembarked, put on a tweed suit, polished up their earthly languages and moved into the house next door. It does mean, however that there is a special class or order of beings in the Universe that are different from us because of the fact that they must wander from one world to another, and from place to another. They are the "chimney sweeps" of creation. It is their specific job to be the "trash cans" of the Universe and aid their fellow man on these backward worlds."

They come in many disguises. . . Most are friendly. A few are *NOT!* They include: **THE WANDERERS — THE MIGRANTS — THE PROPHETS — THE HARVESTERS — THE AGENTS — THE INTRUDERS — THE GUESSERS.**

Williamson also deciphers the strange symbols left from a depression of the bottom of the spaceman's shoes in the soil from which a plaster-of-paris cast was made on the spot. This is the famous George Adamski contact with Orthon in the desert which Williamson was the primary witness to. It is said to reveal our ancient origins. — **$20.00**

☐ **THE SAUCERS SPEAK: CALLING ALL OCCUPANTS OF INTERPLANETARY CRAFT**—By George Hunt Williamson and Alfred Bailey. With Nick Redfern and Sean Casteel

SETI HAS IT ALL WRONG! THERE IS INTELLIGENT LIFE IN THE COSMOS — AND WE HAVE ALREADY COMMUNICATED WITH BEINGS ON OTHER WORLDS AND IN OTHER DIMENSIONS!—It is not necessary to construct giant interstellar telecommunication dishes to send amateurish binary signals into the universe.

George Hunt Williamson was able to establish radio communications with the occupants of UFOs as far back as 1952, approximately the same time the Air Force set up a Top-Secret project known as MQ707, in an official attempt to establish telecommunications with space beings in order to get them to land at Edwards Air Force Base, where it is claimed that President Eisenhower had met with Ultra-Terrestrials face-to-face. Furthermore, the FCC, along with other government agencies, has been checking out reports of mysterious interference over various broadcast frequencies. Whether it's a powerful TV station in England, high frequency channels reserved strictly for astronaut communication, ham radio sets or CB equipment, some unknown source – on or off the planet – has the ability to "cut in" and take over the airwaves as they see fit. — **$15.00**

ALL BOOKS ARE LARGE FORMAT AND ARE FULLY ILLUSTRATED
Enjoy one or order all 4 Williamson books for just $62.00 + $6.00 S/H

**Timothy Beckley · Box 753
New Brunswick, NJ 08903**